D1285753

Architecture and **Modernity**

MIT Press | Cambridge, Massachusetts | London, England

Hilde **Heynen**

Architecture and **Modernity**

A Critique

This book was set in Univers by Graphic Composition, Inc. and was printed and bound in the United States of America.

Library of Congress Cataloging-in-Publication Data
Heynen, Hilde.
Architecture and modernity : a critique / Hilde Heynen.
   p. cm.
Includes bibliographical references and index.
ISBN 0-262-08264-0 (hc : alk. paper)

   1. Architecture, Modern—20th century.
   2. Architecture and society—History—20th century.
   3. Philosophy, Modern—20th century—Influence.
   I. Title.
NA680.H42 1999
724'.6—dc21   98-38512
                                                      CIP

for **Robbe, An,** and **Anskim**

Architecture Facing Modernity

1

Constructing the Modern Movement

2

Reflections in a Mirror

3

Architecture as Critique of Modernity

Acknowledgments

This book would never have materialized without the help and encouragement of many people. When it was still in the stage of a Ph.D. dissertation, one of my main interlocutors was Geert Bekaert, whose essay on imitation laid the foundation for my interest in mimesis. To my other advisor, André Loeckx, I owe special thanks, not only for his institutional support, but also for his continued presence as my most challenging and demanding intellectual sparring partner. Herman Neuckermans I thank for the opportunity he gave me to do research at the Katholieke Universiteit Leuven.

In an initial stage of my investigations, I enjoyed the hospitality of Michael Müller in Bremen, who was a very helpful guide for studying the work of Walter Benjamin. I have learned a lot from discussions with friends, among whom I should mention Christine Delhaye, Bart Verschaffel, Lieven de Cauter, and Rudi Laermans. My coeditors of the Dutch *Benjamin Journaal* contributed, through their comments and criticisms, to the chapters on Benjamin and Adorno: René Boomkens, Ineke van der Burg, Koen Geldof, Ton Groeneweg, Paul Koopman, Michel van Nieuwstadt, and the late Wil van Gerwen, who passed away much too early.

In 1991 and 1992 I had the opportunity to test some of the thoughts developed in this book by exposing myself to the scrutiny of the students in the MIT program on History, Theory, and Criticism. I wish to thank Stanford Anderson for his invitation, David Friedman for his coaching, and Sibel Bozdogan for her friendship and support. Together with the students they made my months at MIT a very worthwhile experience. The postdoctoral fellowship I received from the Getty Grant Program enabled me to transform a dissertation into a book. During that process much was added and many things changed; in particular the case study on New Babylon was elaborated, facilitated by the generous help of Constant.

For encouraging me all the while and pushing me to finalize the manuscript, I wish to thank Mark Wigley, Michael Hays, Beatriz Colomina, and Richard Plunz. Donald Gardner was invaluable as a translator. Whatever awkward formulations survived in the final text are completely my own responsibility.

I am grateful to Roger Conover for his confidence in my ability to write this book, to Julie Grimaldi for her continuous help with the whole process, to Mitch Evich and Matthew Abbate for their very careful and consistent editing, and to Jim McWethy for his design work.

I dedicate the book to my children Robbe, An, and Anskim Goris, who lived with me through all the difficulties and gratifications of its coming-into-being.

Beauty today can
have no other measur
except the depth to
which a work resolves
contradictions. A work
must cut through the
contradictions and
overcome them, not
by covering them up,
but by pursuing them

Theodor W. Adorno, 1965:

"Schönheit heute hat kein anderes Mass als die

Tiefe, in der die Gebilde die Widersprüche

austragen, die sie durchfuhren und die sie

bewältigen einzig, indem sie ihnen folgen,

nicht indem sie sie verdecken."

Architecture and **Modernity**

Introduction

This book grew out of a puzzlement I felt when studying the ideas embodied in modern architecture. My perplexity had to do with the inadequacy of the concept of modernity that was operative in the modern movement. To my eyes—trained as they were by the study of critical theories such as those of Walter Benjamin or Theodor Adorno—the concept of modernity I found in the work of Sigfried Giedion or in the periodical *Das Neue Frankfurt* seemed rather naive and unbalanced. I was puzzled by the gap between the discourse of the modern movement on the one hand and cultural theories of modernity such as those of the Frankfurt School on the other. If one realizes for instance that Ernst May (the architect behind *Das Neue Frankfurt*) and Theodor Adorno were both working in the same city during the same period (Frankfurt in the late 1920s), it seems rather strange that there are no traces of any intellectual exchange between them.

Researching this topic gradually resolved my puzzlement as to the factual circumstances of this absence of exchange. My fascination for the related theoretical
questions nevertheless remained, as may be judged from the material presented in
this book. I still consider it exceptionally intriguing to see how many divergent positions have been developed with respect to the question of what architecture is supposed to be and how it should relate to societal conditions brought about by
modernity. It was my aim in writing this book to clarify several of these positions and
to highlight in what respect precisely they differ from one another.

The book thus discusses the relationship between modernity, dwelling, and
architecture. Modernity is used here in reference to a condition of living imposed
upon individuals by the socioeconomic process of modernization. The experience of
modernity involves a rupture with tradition and has a profound impact on ways of life
and daily habits. The effects of this rupture are manifold. They are reflected in modernism, the body of artistic and intellectual ideas and movements that deal with the
process of modernization and with the experience of modernity.[1]

Modernity is understood in different ways by a wide range of authors and critics. One can see it as determined by the opposition between a capitalist civilization
and its cultural, modernist counterpart. The relation between these poles, however,
is conceived of in divergent ways: some perceive them as not related at all; for others there is a dialectical relationship at stake in which modernism consciously or unconsciously, directly or indirectly, positively or negatively reflects the effects of
capitalist development. Further distinctions and specifications can be made: one can
discern an avant-garde attitude that aims at the reintegration of art and life; one can
moreover distinguish between programmatic and transitory conceptions of modernity, as well as between "pastoral" and "counterpastoral" modernisms.

Within the fields of philosophy, sociology, and cultural theory, such issues are
indeed extensively discussed. Critical theories such as those of the Frankfurt School
gave birth to a complex and sophisticated discourse concerning modernity and modernism. The history and theory of twentieth-century architecture on the other hand
developed rather independently from this rich tradition; even many of the more recent developments in architecture went along without taking into consideration critical positions such as those of the Frankfurt School. This book aims at facing this rift.
It tries to interrelate both strings of intellectual discourse. On the one hand it discusses architecture from the perspective of critical theory, and on the other hand it
modifies positions within critical theory by linking them with architecture.[2]

The book should operate on two levels. First, it contains a theoretical discussion of the relation between architecture, modernity, and dwelling. There is a line of
argumentation spanning the whole book, which is basically structured according to
a dialectical triad. Chapter 1, "Architecture Facing Modernity," formulates the problem: how does architecture relate to modernity? Chapter 2, "Constructing the Modern Movement," gives the thesis: the first answer to this question as it was given by
major representatives of the modern movement. The antithesis is found in chapter

3, "Reflections in a Mirror," which discusses positions developed outside of and in opposition to the modern movement. Chapter 4, "Architecture as Critique of Modernity," can be considered the synthesis, in which reconsiderations of thesis and antithesis, combined with other material, lead to a more balanced answer on the problem stated in the beginning. The synthesis aimed at, however, is by no means a completely integrated or definitive outlook on the relationship between architecture and modernity, but rather a provisional formulation of a complex and multilayered understanding of that intricate relationship.

Second, the book is also meant to be read as an introduction for architectural students to the discourse of critical theory. The subchapters on Benjamin, Bloch, and Adorno can be studied independently from the rest. It is my hope that the subchapter on the Venice School will fill a similar role and facilitate access to texts that are renowned for their difficulty.

I chose an approach that links a broadly conceived theme—the relation between architecture, modernity, and dwelling—to a detailed discussion of specific case studies. This approach implies that the book's coverage may be neither representative nor complete. Nevertheless for me the decisive consideration was that only an in-depth treatment of specific cases can really provide a thorough understanding of the issues at hand. The book therefore is not exhaustive in its discussions of relevant authors and architects. Major personalities such as Le Corbusier and Mies van der Rohe will only appear in a casual way. There are nevertheless good reasons for the choices that were made.

Apart from the first chapter, which refers to a whole range of authors, the other chapters are mostly built around some key figures. The second chapter focuses on Sigfried Giedion and Ernst May. Giedion is chosen first of all because the author of *Space, Time and Architecture* (1941) can be considered the ghostwriter of the modern movement. As secretary to CIAM (Congrès Internationaux d'Architecture Moderne) he was involved with modern architecture on a personal level, knowing all the protagonists and interacting with them on a regular basis. It was partly due to his work that the movement was seen as a whole, because in his writings he brought its different tendencies together under the banner of the new space-time concept. Dealing with Ernst May and *Das Neue Frankfurt* brings complementary issues into the discussion: modern architecture's social aims, its involvement with housing, and its quest for a new lifestyle.[3] Frankfurt, where May and his team built some 15,000 housing units between 1925 and 1930, was the scene of one of the most successful achievements that the still youthful modern movement could claim to its credit. It was because of this that the second CIAM congress, focusing on the theme of the *Existenzminimum*, was organized in Frankfurt in 1929.

Together these two cases give a good picture of the notions and approaches that were typical of the discourse of modern architecture in its initial phase. They show the ambiguities of a position that wants to face the challenge of modernity by lining up with the avant-garde in art and literature while at the same time clinging to traditional architectural values such as harmony and permanence. It thus becomes clear that the modernism of the modern movement was not always critical of modernity, but rather adopted a "pastoral" attitude that aimed at smoothing out differences and conflicts.

Chapter 3 explores ideas and attitudes that take a critical distance from this "pastoralism." It focuses on personalities who disagree with the notion that it is possible to develop a harmonious culture within the bounds of a modernizing society. The chapter opens with a short discussion of Adolf Loos's opinions on dwelling and architecture. Loos chronologically precedes the modern movement, but his ideas contain the seeds of what will be worked out later as a complex critique of the movement's notions about architecture and modernity. Loos holds the view that modernity provokes an inevitable rupture with tradition that has as a consequence the disintegration of one's experience of life. This evolution, he thinks, obliges architecture to deploy a number of languages corresponding to a multitude of different experiences—private versus public, interior versus exterior, intimate versus public.

Walter Benjamin, the second key figure in this chapter, takes up some of Loos's ideas but reworks them in an interpretation of modern architecture that goes beyond anything written by his contemporaries. He too understands modernity in the first instance as a condition that differs fundamentally from tradition. According to him the difference lies in the fact that modernity generates a poverty of genuine experiences. In Benjamin's view modern architecture takes this crisis of experience into account, because it creates spaces with no fixed character, where light, air, and permeability are the dominant elements. In modern architecture therefore the impetus is found for the creation of a desperately needed "new barbarism" that responds to the requirements of a new society, one that would no longer be based on mechanisms of exploitation and exclusion.

Like Benjamin, Ernst Bloch is a philosopher of the left who, between the wars, moved in the orbit of the Frankfurt School and happened to be more than superficially interested in architecture. Bloch's philosophy is entirely dedicated to utopian hope. In his opinion the disintegration of life is essentially connected with the social order of capitalism—with its drive to a superficial rationalization and efficiency, its dislike of fantasy and ornament, and its tendency to limit oneself to what is immediate and obvious. Bloch sees the "poverty" of modern architecture as an extension of bourgeois capitalism. For this reason, he argues, this architecture is incapable of offering any utopian prospect of a future form of society. With this viewpoint, Bloch represents a very critical voice that, unlike Benjamin's, denies modern architecture its claim to embody any hope for emancipation and liberation.

The concluding section of chapter 3 is devoted to the authors of the school of Venice (Tafuri, Cacciari, Dal Co). They are well known for their radicalization of earlier critical theories, which they integrate in a comprehensive analysis of the relation between capitalist civilization and the culture of architecture. The Venetians have an outlook on modernity that is rather pessimistic, not to say cynical. Their analyses of modern architecture and its discourse provide a highly charged criticism that holds that every attempt at synthesis, every attempt to create a unified culture, is ideological and therefore false. They thus disclaim that architecture would be capable in one way or another of actually contributing to a project of emancipation and social progress. In the process they often seem to go so far as to deny any possibility of architecture adopting a critical stance vis-à-vis societal developments.

Chapter 4 then aims at developing a position that avoids the traps of being either simply complicit with modernity or so cynical as to foreclose any possibility for critique. It sets out to discuss the difficulties of such an ambition by an assessment of Constant's New Babylon project. Connected with the last avant-garde movement, which was the Situationist International, and thus linked with the critical theory of Henri Lefebvre, this project elucidates the antinomies that are evoked by the striving for a critical architecture: although it was meant in the beginning as a quasi-realistic but critical alternative to contemporary urbanistic practices, it soon turned out to be just an illusory image of a postrevolutionary society, relevant in a purely artistic realm rather than in that of contemporary urban praxis.

Adorno is the subject of the second section in this chapter, because his *Aesthetic Theory* provides excellent tools to discuss such antinomies. Adorno's work contains a profound reflection on the relation between art and modernity, which relies upon a specific philosophical conception of modernity as well as upon an explicit sensibility for aesthetic problems of modernism. His assessment of art's critical potential is based on the conviction that art's dual nature—its being socially fabricated as well as autonomous—generates a capacity for resistance and criticism. Turning toward Adorno provides the possibility of conceiving of a similar critical relationship between architecture and modernity in a way that accounts for its dilemmas and antinomies.

The concept of *mimesis* plays a crucial role in Adorno's thought, as well as in contemporary French theory, as for instance in the work of Lacoue-Labarthe or Derrida. Mimesis refers to certain patterns of similarity or resemblance. It has to do with copying, but a specific form of copying that implies a critical moment. The complex figure of thought contained in this concept offers an illuminating frame of reference for reflecting on the potentially critical character of works of architecture. In the last section of chapter 4 I explore how mimesis can provide a meaningful key to understanding architecture's critical potential. I illustrate this by discussing two recent projects: Daniel Libeskind's Jewish Museum in Berlin and Rem Koolhaas's design for a Sea Terminal in Zeebrugge.

The basic premise of this book, which is more theoretical than historical, is that the issue of modernity is of fundamental importance for architecture. This importance goes beyond an assessment of the modern movement. It extends to considerations about themes that recently have been found crucial in architectural discourse. A broadly set-up reflection on modernity is in my opinion capable of offering a productive key for the interpretation of issues such as the condition of post-modernity, architecture's relation to the city and the territory, its awareness of history and tradition, its involvement with the media and the public realm. These issues are not covered as such in this volume, but I hope to have at least indicated how a serious involvement with critical theory can provide valuable clues for intensifying and enriching the theoretical debate about architecture's role in society. For if architecture is not able to design a brave new world in which all our problems are solved, neither is it doomed to just give in to impulses stemming from societal developments in which it has no say whatsoever. It is my belief that architecture *has* the capacity to articulate in a very specific way the contradictions and ambiguities that modern life confronts us with. In this articulation it can generate a sense of involvement with as well as critique of modernity.

Man must
constantly
destroy himself
in order
to construct
himself
all over again.

Theo van Doesburg, 1918

Architecture Facing Modernity

1

Concepts of Modernity

What is modernity? What does this word that plays such a crucial role in theoretical discourse actually mean? Etymologically speaking, one can identify three basic levels of meaning accorded to the word *modern*.[1] In the first and oldest sense it means *present*, or current, implying as its opposite the notion of earlier, of what is past. It is in this sense, for instance, that the term is used in the expression *modernus pontifex*, referring to the man who at present occupies the throne of St. Peter. The term *modern* was employed in this sense as long ago as the Middle Ages. A second meaning of the word is the *new*, as opposed to the old. Here the term *modern* is used to describe a present time that is experienced as a period, and which possesses certain specific features that distinguish it from previous periods. It was this sense of the term that began to prevail in the seventeenth century. During the course of the nineteenth century yet a third level of meaning became important. The notion of modern then acquired the connotation of what is *momentary*, of the transient, with its opposite notion no longer being a clearly defined past but rather an indeterminate eternity.

The current, the new, and the transient: all three of these levels of meaning refer to the peculiar importance that is ascribed to the present in the concept of modernity. Modernity is what gives the present the specific quality that makes it different from the past and points the way toward the future. Modernity is also described as being a break with tradition, and as typifying everything that rejects the inheritance of the past.

Modernity, Octavio Paz says, is an exclusively Western concept that has no equivalent in other civilizations.[2] The reason for this lies in the view of time that is peculiar to the West, by which time is regarded as being linear, irreversible, and progressive. Other civilizations base time on a static concept—the timeless time of primitive civilizations, for whom the past was the archetype of time, the model for the present and the future—or a cyclical one—such as that of classical antiquity by which the distant past represented an ideal that would return at some time in the future. For medieval humanity earthly time was no more than a preparation for the time of eternity, so that the concrete course of history was only of secondary importance. It was during the Renaissance that the idea began to gain currency that history contained a course of development that could be influenced in a certain direction. The humanists wanted to revive the ideal of classical antiquity and to approximate it ever more closely. This endeavor, however, was not devoid of paradoxes. In the famous seventeenth-century *Querelle des Anciens et des Modernes*[3] the question was raised whether the "Moderns" could not rival or even surpass the "Ancients" in their attempts to achieve the highest ideal of art. The main result of this discussion was that the cyclical model was definitively replaced by a progressive model that viewed every age as unique and unrepeatable and as an advance on the achievements of preceding periods.

During the Enlightenment the idea of modernity became bound up with the notion of critical reason. A typical feature of critical reason is that it does not have any inalienable essence, any foundation that cannot be questioned, any revelation. It does not believe in any principle except the principle that all principles should be submitted to critical investigation. Octavio Paz:

> Critical reason, by its very rigor, accentuates temporality. Nothing is permanent; reason becomes identified with change and otherness. We are ruled not by identity, with its enormous and monotonous tautologies, but by otherness and contradiction, the dizzying manifestations of criticism. In the past the goal of criticism was truth; in the modern age truth is criticism. Not an eternal truth, but the truth of change.[4]

Modernity is constantly in conflict with tradition, elevating the struggle for change to the status of purveyor of meaning par excellence. Already in the eighteenth century modernity is thus a condition that cannot be pinned down to a fixed set of attributes. It was in the nineteenth century that modernization also gained ground in the economic and political fields. With industrialization, political upheavals, and increasing urbanization, modernity became far more than just an intellectual concept. In the urban environment, in changing living conditions, and in everyday reality, the break with the established values and certainties of the tradition could be both seen and felt. The modern became visible on very many different levels. In this respect distinctions should be drawn among modernization, modernity, and modernism.[5] The term *modernization* is used to describe the process of social development, the main features of which are technological advances and industrialization, urbanization and population explosions, the rise of bureaucracy and increasingly powerful national states, an enormous expansion of mass communication systems, democratization, and an expanding (capitalist) world market. *Modernity* refers to the typical features of modern times and to the way that these features are experienced by the individual: modernity stands for the attitude toward life that is associated with a continuous process of evolution and transformation, with an orientation toward a future that will be different from the past and from the present. The experience of modernity provokes responses in the form of cultural tendencies and artistic movements. Some of these that proclaim themselves as being in sympathy with the orientation toward the future and the desire for progress are specifically given the name *modernism*. In its broadest sense, the word can be understood as the generic term for those theoretical and artistic ideas about modernity that aim to enable men and women to assume control over the changes that are taking place in a world by which they too are changed.[6]

Modernity, then, constitutes the element that mediates between a process of socioeconomic development known as modernization and subjective responses to it in the form of modernist discourses and movements. In other words, modernity is a phenomenon with at least two different aspects: an objective aspect that is linked to socioeconomic processes, and a subjective one that is connected with personal experiences, artistic activities, or theoretical reflections.

Exactly what the relation is between modernization and modernism—between the objective social given of modernity and the way it is subjectively experienced and dealt with—remains an open question. Some people tend to separate the two domains completely, creating a division between objective conditions and subjective experiences. Matei Calinescu, for instance, separates them without any hesitation and talks in terms of two contrasting modes of the modern:

> At some point during the first half of the nineteenth century an irreversible split occurred between modernity as a stage in the history of Western civilization—a product of scientific and technological progress, of the industrial revolution, of the sweeping economic and social changes brought about by capitalism—and modernity as an aes-

thetic concept. Since then, the relations between the two modernities have been irreducibly hostile, but not without allowing and even stimulating a variety of mutual influences in their rage for each other's destruction.[7]

The discussion of modernity is inseparably bound up with this problem of the relation between capitalist civilization and modernist culture. The different positions that have been adopted in this debate have to do with how this relationship is understood: is it a matter of totally independent entities or is there a critical relation between them? Or is it rather a determinist relation, implying that culture cannot but obediently respond to the requirements of capitalist development? In the case of architecture this question is a very loaded one because architecture operates in both realms: it is unquestionably a cultural activity, but it is one that can be realized only within the world of power and money. In the case of architecture, aesthetic modernity cannot avoid entering into a relationship with the bourgeois modernity of capitalist civilization. It is the nature of this relationship that is discussed in this book.

In order to be more specific in my analysis, I distinguish between different concepts of modernity. A first distinction can be made between programmatic and transitory concepts of modernity. The advocates of the former interpret modernity as being first and foremost a *project*, a project of progress and emancipation. They emphasize the liberating potential that is inherent in modernity. A programmatic concept views modernity primarily from the perspective of the new, of that which distinguishes the present age from the one that preceded it. A typical advocate of this concept is Jürgen Habermas, who formulates what he calls the "incomplete project" of modernity as follows:

> The project of modernity formulated in the eighteenth century by the philosophers of the Enlightenment consisted in their efforts to develop objective science, universal morality and law, and autonomous art according to their inner logic. At the same time, this project intended to release the objective potentials of each of these domains from their esoteric forms. The Enlightenment philosophers wanted to utilize this accumulation of specialized culture for the enrichment of everyday life—that is to say, for the rational organization of everyday social life.[8]

In this programmatic approach two elements can be distinguished. On the one hand, according to Habermas—with specific reference to Max Weber—modernity is characterized by an irreversible emergence of autonomy in the fields of science, art, and morality, which must then be developed "according to their inner logic." On the other hand, however, modernity is also seen as a *project*: the final goal of the development of these various autonomous domains lies in their relevance for practice, their potential use "for the rational organization of everyday social life." Habermas's view places great emphasis on the idea of the present giving form to the future, that is, on the programmatic side of modernity.

In contrast, the transitory view stresses the third level of meaning implied in the modern: the transient or momentary. A first formulation of this sensitivity can be found in the celebrated definition of Charles Baudelaire: "Modernity is the transitory, the fugitive, the contingent, the half of art of which the other half is the eternal and the immutable."[9] Throughout the development of modern art, this moment of transitoriness has been emphasized. From the field of art it has been transferred toward a more global conception of modernity, as is made clear by Jean Baudrillard. In an article for the *Encyclopedia Universalis* he defines *la modernité* as a characteristic mode of civilization that is in opposition to tradition.[10] The desire for innovation and the rebellion against the pressure of tradition are part of the generally accepted ingredients of the modern. Baudrillard, however, radicalizes these elements. In his view, the desire for innovation and the revolt against tradition are not, as with Habermas, subsumed in a general drive toward progress, but gradually become autonomous mechanisms. In his account, the transitory aspect therefore has primacy. He sees the cycle of modernity, in which crisis succeeds crisis, as running away with itself:

> Modernity provokes on all levels an aesthetics of rupture, of individual creativity and of innovation that is everywhere marked by the sociological phenomenon of the avant-garde . . . and by the increasingly more outspoken destruction of traditional forms. . . . Modernity is radicalized into momentaneous change, into a continuous traveling, and thus its meaning changes. It gradually loses each substantial value, each ethical and philosophical ideology of progress that sustained it at the outset, and it becomes an aesthetics of change for the sake of change. . . . In the end, modernity purely and simply coincides with fashion, which at the same time means the end of modernity.[11]

Modernity, according to Baudrillard, establishes change and crisis as values, but these values increasingly lose their immediate relation with any progressive perspective. The result is that modernity sets the scene for its own downfall. Thinking through the transitory concept of modernity to its conclusions can lead to the proclamation of the end of modernity and to the postulation of a postmodern condition. Thus the discussion between modernism and postmodernism that has caused such a furor should not be regarded as a totally new element, but rather as the creation of a radical opposition between insights and ideas that had already played a role in the earlier debate about modernity.

Since the appearance of the term *postmodernism*, it has become clear that the first meaning of the modern—the modern as being what is current—can no longer be applied without qualification. The postmodern actually comes after the modern, and is therefore more current than current. Logically speaking, the modern is therefore relegated to the past. Things are not so clear-cut, however, because one should not assume that the postmodern condition simply replaces modernity. It rather seems to open up a new and complex layer of meaning of the modern by highlighting its paradoxical aspects.[12]

A second distinction regarding concepts of modernity involves pastoral and counterpastoral views.[13] A pastoral view denies the contradictions, dissonances, and tensions that are specific to the modern and sees modernity as a concerted struggle for progress, uniting workers, industrialists, and artists around a common goal. In a view of this sort, the bourgeois modernity of capitalist civilization and the aesthetic modernity of modernist culture are given a common denominator while the underlying conflicts and discrepancies are ignored. Politics, economics, and culture are all united under the banner of progress. Progress is seen as harmonious and continuous, as though it developed to the advantage of everyone and without any significant interruptions. Typical of this view is Le Corbusier's: "A great epoch has begun. There exists a new spirit. There exists a mass of work conceived in the new spirit; it is to be met with particularly in industrial production. . . . Our own epoch is determining, day by day, its own style."[14] The counterpastoral view is exactly the opposite; it is based on the idea that there is a fundamental discrepancy between economic and cultural modernity, and that neither can be achieved without conflicts and moments of fissure. A counterpastoral view regards modernity as characterized by irreconcilable fissures and insoluble contradictions, by divisions and fragmentation, by the collapse of an integrated experience of life, and by the irreversible emergence of autonomy in various domains that are incapable of regaining their common foundation. Typical, for instance, is the conviction that art is by definition anti-establishment and that enmity between established social interests and avant-garde artists is unavoidable. The "International Situationist Manifesto" illustrates this well:

> The Church used to burn those whom it called sorcerers in order to repress the primitive tendencies to play preserved in popular festivals. In the society that is at present dominant, which mass-produces wretched pseudo-games devoid of participation, any true artistic activity is necessarily classified as criminal. It remains semi-clandestine and comes to light as scandal.[15]

What makes modernity so fascinating is the relationship between all these divergent aspects, programmatic and transitory, pastoral and counterpastoral. Marshall Berman argues that for the individual the experience of modernity is characterized by a combination of programmatic and transitory elements, by an oscillation between the struggle for personal development and the nostalgia for what is irretrievably lost: "To be modern is to find ourselves in an environment that promises us adventure, power, joy, growth, transformation of ourselves and the world—and at the same time, that threatens to destroy everything we have, everything we know, everything we are."[16] When it comes to formulating answers to the challenges of modernization, he discerns an abundance of insights coupled with a sharpness of tone in nineteenth-century writers such as Baudelaire, Marx, and Nietzsche that originates in their constant struggle with the ambiguities and contradictions of modern life. There is a tension in these writers between pastoral and counterpastoral views: they were at the same time enthusiastic supporters and deadly enemies of modernity, and it was precisely this that gave them their creative power.

It seems to me that this tension between criticism and commitment remains essential if one is to relate in a meaningful way to the modern. One cannot simply get rid of modernity. It has become so deeply rooted in contemporary societies that it is no longer possible to find a place where its influence does not prevail. This also means that to repudiate modernity as a monolithic whole that deserves to be censured is a conservative and reactionary attitude; not only does it ignore the fact that we are "modern" whether we want to be or not; it also reneges on the promises of emancipation and liberation that are inherent in the modern. At the same time one cannot afford to be blind to the reality that these promises have not been fulfilled. The process of modernization has certainly not brought welfare and political emancipation everywhere and to everyone. A critical attitude has therefore become more necessary than ever, although it must be admitted that it is not immediately clear what this criticism should be based on or what form it should take. This is a question that—in architecture, at any rate—is by no means easily answered.

Dwelling Fades into the Distance . . .

Modernity has often been described as a condition of "homelessness." Peter Berger, Brigitte Berger, and Hansfried Kellner, for instance, gave their book about "modernization and consciousness" the title *The Homeless Mind*.[17] From the perspective of a sociology of knowledge they describe the typical features of the consciousness of modern individuals. The technological development of production and the bureaucratic organization of social life, which are the two most important carriers of the process of modernization, depend on principles such as rationality, anonymity, and an increasing abstraction in social relations. This leads to a pluralization of social life: people live at their work, at home, in clubs and societies, each time in different situations where other norms and rules may apply and that may even be mutually contradictory. Moreover, these contexts themselves are liable to change over time:

> The pluralistic structures of modern society have made the lives of more and more individuals migratory, ever-changing, mobile. In everyday life the modern individual continuously alternates between highly discrepant and often contradictory social contexts. Not only are an in-

creasing number of individuals in a modern society uprooted from their original social milieu, but, in addition, no succeeding milieu succeeds in becoming truly "home" either.[18]

Modernity frees people from the limitations imposed on them by their family or clan or by their village community, offering them unheard-of options and often material improvements as well; there is, however, a price to pay. The renunciation of the traditional framework of reference for their lives means a loss of certainties and of meaning. For many people it is far from easy to learn to live with this.

In the context of philosophy, too, modernity is often described as a condition that is diametrically opposed to dwelling. It is worth taking a look at Martin Heidegger, the leading representative of this kind of criticism.

"Building, Dwelling, Thinking" is the title of a lecture that Heidegger gave at the 1951 *Darmstädter Gespräch,* which had as its theme *Mensch und Raum* (Man and Space).[19] At first sight the text is very accessible and can be read as an introduction to Heidegger's thought. Heidegger begins with an etymological explanation: the Old English and High German word for building, he says, *buan,* means to dwell. Moreover, *buan* is related to "I am": it refers, then, not only to building and dwelling but also to being. Heidegger then develops the idea that dwelling is the principal term of the three. Dwelling refers to a way of being that has to do with a cautious and guarded attitude. The main feature of dwelling is to preserve and care for, to allow things to exist in their essence. What has to be nurtured and preserved is the dweller's relationship with *das Geviert:* the fourfold of heaven and earth, divinities and mortals. Heaven stands for the cosmos, the course of the seasons, the cycle of day and night; the earth is there to serve and to support, as life-giver; the divinities are the beckoning messengers of the godhead; and the people are called mortals because they can die, because they are capable of death *as* death. This leads to the fourfold definition that mortals dwell insofar as they save the earth, receive heaven as heaven, await the divinities as divinities, and are capable of death as death. In other words, the person who "dwells" is someone who is open to these fundamental dimensions of "being."

It may be useful here to look a little more closely at Heidegger's concept of *Seinsvergessenheit* (forgetfulness of Being). Although he does not use the term explicitly in this text, the idea does play a substantial role. For Heidegger, true "being" means to be open to the fourfold, to tend the fourfold in its essence. But that is just what is lacking in our present condition. Modernity is characterized by forgetfulness of Being: people no longer grasp "Being"; they are not open to the fourfold. What prevails is an instrumentalist attitude based on considerations of usefulness and efficiency, from which cautiousness and cherishing are far removed.

Heidegger's concept of truth is inseparable from his ideas about Being. He rejects the classical theory of *adequatio:* in his view, truth does not lie in statements and facts being identical. His concept of truth refers to the Greek notion of *alētheia.*

Truth here is not a state of affairs but an occurring: the disclosure, the bringing into the open. This disclosure is never final or definitive. There is a continual play between the concealed and the unconcealed that can be observed by anyone who is sufficiently open and receptive.[20]

In "Building, Dwelling, Thinking," it is said that only the person who takes up a position of cherishing and sparing knows how to dwell and hence how to build. Dwelling, according to Heidegger, does not stem from building, but the other way round: true building is grounded in the experience of true dwelling. "Building," after all, means that a place is brought into being where the four dimensions that surround dwelling are made tangible, a place where the fourfold is gathered. "Building" means to make a place out of undifferentiated space, where the earth appears as earth, the heaven as heaven, the divinities as divine and mortals as mortal. The nature of building is letting dwell. It follows that "only if we are capable of dwelling, only then can we build."[21] As an example, Heidegger refers to a two-hundred-year-old farmhouse in the Black Forest. Such a farmhouse is placed on the wind-sheltered mountain slope looking south. An overhanging roof bears the snow and offers protection from storms. Indoors the altar corner is not forgotten, and there are appropriate places for the childbed and the laying out of the dead. The farmhouse thus assembles the fourfold and bears witness to an earlier, authentic mode of dwelling.

But this does not yet resolve the question as to dwelling at present. Heidegger continues:

> What is the state of dwelling in our precarious age? On all sides we hear talk about the housing shortage, and with good reason. . . . However hard and bitter, however hampering and threatening the lack of houses remains, the *real plight of dwelling* does not lie merely in the lack of houses. . . . The real plight lies in this, that mortals ever search anew for the nature of dwelling, that they *must ever learn to dwell.*[22]

In another essay from the same year, "Poetically Man Dwells," Heidegger refines the theme of dwelling by linking it with the poetic. He makes an analogy between authentic dwelling, preserving the fourfold, and poetry. Poetry he characterizes as taking measure. This measuring has nothing to do with a scientific activity, for it relates to a very specific dimension. The poet, after all, takes measure of the "between" that brings together heaven and earth, divinities and mortals. It is a question of measuring in the strict sense of the word: the measuring that indicates a measure for the scope of "being," the measuring that extends to the unveiling of the fourfold.

The essay ends on a similar note to the first: "Do *we* dwell poetically? Presumably we dwell altogether unpoetically."[23] Heidegger suggests that this unpoetic dwelling results from our inability to take measure, from our being cursed with a calculating measuring that does not suffice for a genuine meting out. Authentic dwelling is nonetheless inseparably linked with the poetic: "The poetic is the basic capacity for human dwelling. . . . When the poetic appropriately comes to light, then man dwells humanly on this earth, and then—as Hölderlin says in his last poem— 'the life of man' is a 'dwelling life.'"[24] If we take these texts of Heidegger seriously, we will conclude that there is a virtually unbridgeable gulf between modernity and dwelling. That at least is the conclusion that Massimo Cacciari comes to in "Eupalinos or Architecture."

Cacciari concentrates on what he calls the *Fragwürdiges* of the essay: what is worth questioning is in particular the condition of homelessness perceived by Heidegger, and the possible consequences of this situation for architecture. Heidegger, according to Cacciari, poses the question of whether poetical dwelling is still possible in our times, and it is this question above all that needs answering. Cacciari's answer is negative. The development of modern civilization has made the world uninhabitable; "Non-dwelling is the essential characteristic of life in the metropolis." Modern life no longer has anything to do with the dwelling referred to by Heidegger: there is an unbridgeable distance separating the metropolis from dwelling as proportionate to *das Geviert*, the fourfold of earth, heaven, divinities and mortals. For Cacciari, then, it is clear that "the home is past, it no longer is."[25]

This is not the first time that opinions of this sort have been uttered. Theodor Adorno said something very similar in almost identical terms: "Dwelling, in the proper sense, is now impossible. . . . The house is past."[26] Adorno's discourse, however, does not entirely coincide with that of Heidegger or Cacciari. For him the impossibility of dwelling originates in the first place in an ethical sensibility: "it is part of morality not to be at home in one's home. . . . Wrong life cannot be lived rightly."[27] The fundamental injustice of the social system, which we all participate in whether we want to or not, produces so profound a sense of discomfort that it is impossible for us to feel at home in a world of this sort. Adorno perceives this underlying reality in the actual forms that dwellings take. The traditional homes of the bourgeoisie are no longer able to conceal their hypocrisy: the security that they offer the privileged cannot be thought of separately from the oppression that is necessary to maintain these privileges. Functional "modern" homes, bungalows, and apartments are empty and meaningless shells for their occupants. No amount of "design" can do anything to change that. Worst of all, however, is the situation of those who do not have any choice—homeless people, foreigners, and refugees. For them even the illusion of dwelling is impossible to maintain.

Dwelling fades into the distance . . . The metaphors used to describe the experience of modernity very often refer to dwelling as the "other face" of modernity, as that which under modern conditions is made impossible. Different approaches— the existential with Heidegger, the ethical with Adorno, and the sociological with Berger, Berger, and Kellner—all conclude that modernity and dwelling are diametrically opposed to each other. Under modern conditions the world has become impossible to live in; modern consciousness is that of "the homeless mind," and foreigners and migrants provide a model for the experience of every individual in a

House in the Norwegian forest: architecture as the embodiment of belonging and rootedness.

(From Christian Norberg-Schulz, *The Concept of Dwelling*.)

1

modern, mobile, and unstable society. Dwelling is in the first instance associated with tradition, security, and harmony, with a life situation that guarantees connectedness and meaningfulness. Considerations such as these underlie the dilemmas that architecture is faced with.

The Dilemmas of Architecture

Architecture inevitably has to deal with the tension that exists between modernity and dwelling. Architecture designs dwelling, giving it form; its task is the materialization of the world in which we dwell. It would seem to go without saying that this principle must constitute the vanishing point of architectural discourse. But what is one supposed to do if modern conditions mean that dwelling itself has become impossible? What if the diagnosis of "homelessness" is correct? What approach can architecture possibly adopt? The answers that have been given to these questions are far from unequivocal, and opinions about what exactly is (or ought to be) the role of architecture and what position it takes (or ought to take) vis-à-vis modernity are extremely disparate.

Two different lines of thought, for instance, have been followed in interpreting the texts of Martin Heidegger that I just discussed. The utopian and nostalgic concept of Christian Norberg-Schulz and the radical and critical approach of Massimo Cacciari referred to above represent the two poles of this debate.

Norberg-Schulz takes as his starting point Heidegger's notion of the *thing* as that in which the fourfold is assembled. From this he infers that a thing has to possess three qualities: it has to evoke an image, be concrete, and have significance. By means of this operation he translates Heidegger's metaphors into a plea for a figurative architecture, an architecture in which one can recognize these three qualities. He argues that, from a Heideggerean point of view, man "dwells" if he experiences his existence as meaningful. This experience of meaning is made possible when the architectonic design of a place offers the opportunity for orientation and identification. This means that the built space must be organized in such a way that concrete places are created, places that are characterized by a specific *genius loci*. The task of architecture consists in making this *genius loci* visible (figure 1). Norberg-Schulz distinguishes four modes of dwelling: natural dwelling (the way in which the settlement embeds itself in the landscape), collective dwelling (embodied in urban space), public dwelling (as seen in public buildings and institutions), and finally private dwelling (living in a house). These different ways of dwelling are connected to each other through a play of spatial relationships (center, path, domain). What is remarkable is that this line of thought answers fully to the humanist conception of dwelling as being surrounded by ever-widening concentric circles (the house, the street, the village, the region, the nation). This idea refers to life in the warm seclusion of a traditional community, but is much less applicable to the functional networks and relationships that determine life in a modern society.

The illustrations that Norberg-Schulz uses to make this train of thought clear are certainly eloquent, however. He has a preference for images from Mediterranean and classical tradition, and he emphatically contrasts these images of "figurative" architecture with the "non-figurative" quality of functionalism that is based on an abstract idea of space instead of concrete places. It is in this concrete, place-bound dwelling that Norberg-Schulz sees man returning home: "When dwelling is accomplished, our wish for belonging and participation is fulfilled."[28]

The categories that confer meaning on dwelling here refer to fullness, belonging, rootedness, organic solidarity between man and place and between man and man. A figurative architecture can embody all of this. Norberg-Schulz apparently is convinced that the homelessness that Heidegger talks about is only of temporary nature, and that functionalist architecture bears part of the responsibility for this. If architects would only turn their backs on this pernicious abstraction, then the possibility of authentic dwelling would again be realized: "A work of architecture . . . helps man to dwell poetically. Man dwells poetically when he is able to 'listen' to the saying of things, and when he is capable of setting what he apprehends into work by means of the language of architecture."[29] For Norberg-Schulz, then, "homelessness" is not so much a fundamental condition of contemporary man but rather an incidental loss that can be redressed by a better understanding of the relation between architecture and dwelling.

Massimo Cacciari understands this issue totally differently. For him, it is inconceivable that one would be able to put "Building, Dwelling, Thinking" into practice in such an instrumental way so as to construct a new language of architecture. While Norberg-Schulz thinks that Heidegger's "aim was not to offer any explanation, but to help man to get back to authentic dwelling,"[30] Cacciari argues that the essay "confirms the non-existent logic of the dwelling-building-dwelling cycle and thereby dismantles *a priori* any claim that assumes such logic to be purposeful or denotative."[31] Each writer thus ascribes a completely different status to this essay.

Cacciari's argument runs as follows: As a result of the reduction of the relationship between man and world, as a result of the forgetfulness of being, poetical dwelling has become impossible, and therefore poetic architecture has also become impossible. Real dwelling no longer exists, and authentic building has also disappeared. The only thing left over for architecture is to reveal the impossibility of poetical dwelling through an architecture of empty signs. Only an architecture that reflects the impossibility of dwelling can still lay claim to any form of authenticity. Sublime uselessness is the highest that architecture can attain in these circumstances.

Cacciari discerns this silent, reflective architecture in the work of Mies: "Glass is the concrete negation of dwelling. . . . From the 1920–1921 project for a glass skyscraper in Berlin . . . up to the Seagram Building in New York, one can trace this constant in all of Mies's work: a supreme indifference to dwelling, expressed in neutral signs. . . . The language of absence here testifies to the absence of dwelling."[32] The upshot of Cacciari's reasoning points in particular to the gulf that separates him from Norberg-Schulz. It is difficult to conceive of a greater contrast than that between Mies's silent towers of glass (figure 2) and Norberg-Schulz's figurative architecture. The difference between the two authors has to do with the fact that their assessments of modernity are in conflict at every point—the former sees the characteristics of modernity as incidental and reversible, while in the view of the latter they are fundamental and ineluctable.

Similar conflicting assessments of modernity can also be found elsewhere. A good example is the debate conducted in the pages of *Lotus International* between Christopher Alexander and Peter Eisenman.[33] Alexander defends the thesis that architecture must primarily appeal to human feelings, and that its essential purpose must be to bring about an experience of harmony. Eisenman, on the other hand, emphasizes the importance of reason. He considers that there is a fundamental disharmony in the modern world that architecture is obliged to confront: an architecture concerned only with making people feel good is one that has its head in the sand. In Alexander's view, modernity is a sort of temporary aberration, as though humanity had gone off course and had to be persuaded to cast aside this heresy and base itself once more on a holistic world view. In most cultures up to about 1600, he argues, a world view prevailed by which man and the universe were seen as more or less in-

terrelated and inseparable. Modernity, perhaps unwisely, departed from that idea. Alexander suggests that "the constitution of the universe may be such that the human self and the substance that things are made out of, the spatial matter or whatever you call it, are much more inextricably related than we realized."[34] In Alexander's view, it is the task of architecture to offer human beings experiences of harmony that are rooted in the "hidden order" that he postulates.

Eisenman's objections to this notion are sweeping. He argues that it is not really perfection that appeals to our deepest feelings and that perfection can only exist through that which is imperfect. The imperfect—the fragment, the incomplete, that which is too large or too small—might in fact more easily relate to our feelings of fragility and vulnerability and thus form a more effective expression of the modern condition. Modernity has to do with the alienation of the self from the collective, and with our resulting sense of unease. Architecture cannot afford to ignore experiences of this sort; on the contrary, its task is to acknowledge them, confronting them on their own terms.

These divergent viewpoints—the nostalgic and utopian one of Norberg-Schulz and Alexander, and the radical and critical one of Cacciari and Eisenman—give an adequate picture of the dilemmas that architecture has to face. Cacciari and Eisenman base themselves on the experience of anxiety that is inherent in modernity, and they give a logically consistent description of its implications for architecture. There is, however, a certain rigidity in their stance that makes it hard to accept their conclusions without question. An architecture that complied with their drastic requirements of negativity and silence would inevitably make an abstraction of the concrete needs and desires of the actual people that would have to use it and dwell in it. One might well ask whether that is appropriate. What both Cacciari and Eisenman are in fact doing is transposing notions from the realm of arts and literature to architecture. One cannot, however, do this without making certain adjustments. Adolf Loos warned that a house is not a work of art. A painting hangs in a museum, a book is something that you can close when you have read it, but a building is an omnipresent environment for one's everyday life: it is intolerable for it to be critical and negative in the same way as modern art and literature.

The views of Alexander and Norberg-Schulz are even more vulnerable to criticism. Alexander's holistic metaphysics is untenable if one bears in mind the philosophical developments of the last century. If these have any single characteristic in common, it is the notion that we live in a "post-metaphysical" epoch, that metaphysics, in other words, has lost all credibility. Alexander's "theory" tends toward mysticism and has unmistakably totalitarian tendencies. In his world view there is no room for heterogeneity or difference. According to him everybody is familiar with the same "universal" feelings[35] and everyone's experiences are basically similar. These are extremely questionable assumptions on which to base a theory.

Similar objections can be made to Norberg-Schulz's theory. Norberg-Schulz interprets Heidegger in a fairly simplistic and instrumental way, by which the Spirit of

Place and the organic relationship between man and house takes on a mythical character. Rootedness and authenticity are presented as being superior to mobility and the experience of rootlessness. What is more, he seems to be completely unaware of the violence that is implicit in concepts like this: it is no coincidence these words are part of the basic vocabulary of Nazi ideology. Levinas pointed out that the eulogizing of place, of the village and the landscape, in Heidegger's work, and the scorn he expresses for the metropolis and technology, provided a fertile soil for racism and anti-Semitism.[36] The same tendency can be found in every theory of architecture that postulates the ideals of rootedness and connectedness.

Both Alexander and Norberg-Schulz appear to adopt a position outside of modernity. In this respect they resemble Heidegger, whose work contains a radical critique of modernity, but from a perspective outside of the process and without any commitment to the modern. Heidegger did not develop his criticism of modernity from the standpoint of a modern sensibility, from a sense of criticism as being integral to the modern. When he condemns modernity he does not do so on the basis of its own standards; rather, he attempts to find an Archimedean point of leverage for his critique outside of modernity. He bases this critique on the past (the concept of Being of the pre-Socratic philosophers) and on a quest for an "originality" and "truth" that repudiate in uncompromising fashion the inauthenticity of modern existence. Norberg-Schulz and Alexander also follow this sort of strategy; with them it becomes an occasion for a discourse that at first sight is highly democratic and acceptable, but which on closer inspection verges on abandoning the whole project of modernity, and with it all prospect of emancipation and liberation.

But perhaps the most important objection to be made both to Cacciari and Eisenman and to Alexander and Norberg-Schulz is that none of them has anything that resembles a theory of the ambivalence of modernity. This is obviously the case with Alexander and Norberg-Schulz because they situate themselves outside modernity and cannot feel any empathy with the promises inherent in it. Cacciari and Eisenman, on the other hand, do base their arguments on an experience of the modern, but they only deal with the theme of the necessity of negation. They talk about silence, empty signs, fragmentation and necessary incompleteness, dissonances and fragility. It is as though all joy is absent from their discourse, as though they are unaware that modernity is not only an occasion for loss and bereavement but also creates opportunities for progress and development. For this reason they end up appearing to share the negative assessment of modernity of Alexander and Norberg-Schulz. The relation of fragility and vulnerability with the utopian moment, with the promise of liberation and emancipation, is not acknowledged in their work.

The dilemmas that architecture is faced with have to do then with the fundamental issue of its attitude to modernity and to dwelling. If architecture opts for harmony and the organic commitment to a place, then it runs the risk of creating a manner of "dwelling" that is purely illusory. Modernity has made such deep inroads into the lives of individuals and communities that it is questionable whether authentic "dwelling"—a mode of dwelling that would express the cherishing of the four-fold—exists any longer. Perhaps we are dealing with a concept of dwelling that has become superseded because it depends on an unqualified experience of a tradition. In the absence of any tradition, it can only function on an imaginary level; it is no more than an image. Therefore, a discourse that appeals to this idea of dwelling in order to create a theory of architecture chooses to ignore the moments of fissure that are inherent in modernity. If, on the other hand, architecture opts for revealing the void, for silence and fragmentation, it is bound to repudiate the deep-rooted needs and desires that are basic to dwelling and that have to do with the need for security and shelter.

These dilemmas are fundamental and cannot be ignored. They oblige one to adopt a mode of thought that deals with the tensions that are peculiar to modernity so that they become an integral part of any discourse about architecture and dwelling. I see it as absolutely essential that this discourse be explored. This is also crucial within the context of recent debates such as those on postmodernism or on deconstructivist architecture. What I have in mind is a mode of thought that moves dialectically without denying the dilemmas and which acknowledges the conflicts and ambiguities that are peculiar to modernity without watering down their implications with noncommittal answers.

I have attempted
to establish,
both by argument
and by objective evidence,
that in spite of the
seeming confusion
there is nevertheless
a true, if hidden, unity,
a secret synthesis,
in our present civilization.

Sigfried Giedion, 1941

Constructing the Modern Movement

An Architectural Avant-Garde?

At one moment at least in recent architectural history an attempt was made to come up with a consistent but comprehensive response to the challenge of modernity. The modern movement saw itself embodying a concept of architecture that constituted a legitimate answer to the experience of modernity and to the problems and possibilities resulting from the process of modernization. In its initial phase it had strong ties to avant-garde movements such as futurism and constructivism. It shared their opposition to tradition and to the false claims of nineteenth-century bourgeois culture. One should wonder, however, how far this alliance goes and whether the basic conceptions about the new architecture do line up with the position of the avant-garde in art and literature.

The phenomenon of the artistic avant-garde is historically linked to the rise of kitsch.[1] Both avant-garde and kitsch can be seen as reactions to the experience of fissure that is typical of modernity. The accelerated changes in traditional values and living conditions that are brought about by modernity lead individuals to experience a split between their inner world and the behavior patterns required of them by society. Modern individuals experience themselves as "rootless": they are not in harmony with themselves and they lack the self-evident frame of reference of norms and forms that one has in a society where tradition prevails. That at least is the diagnosis shared by a whole range of intellectuals writing on modernity.

At the beginning of the twentieth century it was clearly stated, by Adolf Loos among others, that it was the task of intellectuals and artists to face this fissure and to look for a new basis of culture, because culture could no longer be established on a self-evident continuation of tradition.[2] The space left vacant by the decline of tradition was laid claim to by the avant-garde that regarded itself as "the only living culture we now have."[3] As against the pseudo-values of kitsch, the avant-garde posited the ideals of purity and authenticity. Kitsch, they argued, is pleasant; it focuses on easy entertainment; it is mechanical, academic, and cliché-ridden. Because of this it glosses over the effects of the split character of modern life: kitsch maintains an illusion of wholeness by which individuals can painlessly forget their inner conflicts. The avant-garde, on the other hand, refuses to deny these conflicts by ignoring the fissures and ruptures that do exist—rather it combats them openly. The strategy of the avant-garde thus consisted of a direct attack: perceiving that outer forms no longer correspond to inner feelings, the avant-garde chooses to destroy these forms in order to expose their hollowness. Therefore, it is constantly engaged in an iconoclastic struggle. Marinetti's appeal, "Let us kill the moonlight!" can serve as a model for the logic of negation that the avant-garde advocates: all norms, forms, and conventions have to be broken; everything that is stable must be rejected, every value negated.

In doing so the avant-garde radicalizes the basic principle of modernity—the urge toward continual change and development, the rejection of the old and the longing for what is new. In its historical manifestations—futurism, constructivism, dadaism, surrealism, and kindred movements—it represents a "spearhead" of aesthetic modernism, which in itself can be said to have a broader basis (not every modernist writer or artist belongs unquestionably to the avant-garde).[4] Renato Poggioli characterized the avant-garde by four moments: activism, antagonism, nihilism, and agonism.[5] The activist moment meant adventure and dynamism, an urge to action not necessarily linked to a positive goal. The antagonistic character of the avant-garde refers to its combativeness; the avant-garde is always complaining, it wages a continuous struggle—against tradition, against the public, and against the establishment. This antagonism goes hand in hand with an anarchistic aversion to all rules and norms, a revulsion against every institutionalized system. Activism and antagonism are pursued in a way that is so absolute that an avant-garde movement finally overtakes itself in a nihilistic quest, in an uninterrupted search for purity, ending up by dissolving into nothing. The avant-garde is indeed inclined to sacrifice itself on the altar of cultural advance—if the price of obtaining mastery over the future is one's own destruction, it is fully prepared to pay it. It is in this masochism that what Poggioli calls the agonistic phase lies: it wallows pathetically in morbid pleasure at the prospect of its own downfall, in the conviction that it is there that it will find its supreme fulfillment. In so doing it also complies with the military metaphor implicit in its name: it is the fate of the avant-garde to be slaughtered so that others will have the opportunity to build after them.

From this description the avant-garde emerges as the embodiment par excellence of a transitory concept of modernity. It comprises the most radical expression of a "culture of crisis." In Calinescu's words, "Aesthetically the avant-garde attitude implies the bluntest rejection of such traditional ideas as those of order, intelligibility, and even success . . . art is supposed to become an experience—deliberately conducted—of failure and crisis. If crisis is not there, it must be created."[6] According to Peter Bürger, however, the intense energies of the avant-garde did have a programmatic intention. Bürger, whose interpretation is based mainly on an analysis of dadaism and surrealism, argues that the avant-garde was concerned to abolish the autonomy of art as an institution.[7] The negative logic of the avant-garde has in his view a clearly defined aim: to put an end to art as something separate from everyday life, as an autonomous domain that has no real impact on the social system. The avant-gardists aimed to achieve the "sublation" of art in practical life: "The avant-gardists proposed the sublation of art—sublation in the Hegelian sense of the term: art was not to be simply destroyed, but transferred to the praxis of life where it would be preserved, albeit in a changed form. . . . What distinguishes them . . . is the attempt to organize a new life praxis from a basis in art."[8] The avant-garde, then, does not so much have in mind the integration of art with the *current* praxis of life, with bourgeois society and its rational plans. It aims rather for a *new* life praxis, a praxis that is based on art and that constitutes an alternative for the existing order.

The issues and themes around which the modern movement in architecture crystallized are related to the avant-garde logic of destruction and construction. Here too what was involved first of all was a rejection of the bourgeois culture of philistinism that used pretentious ornament and kitsch and which took the form of eclecticism. In its stead the desire for purity and authenticity was given precedence. All ornamentation was regarded as unacceptable; instead, authenticity was required in the use of materials, and it was thought that a constructional logic should be clearly visible in the formal idiom.[9] In the twenties these themes also acquired a distinct political dimension: the New Building[10] became associated with the desire for a more socially balanced and egalitarian form of society in which the ideals of equal rights and emancipation would be realized.

The architectural vanguard nevertheless did not become as uncompromising and as radical as its counterparts in art and literature. Most architects never renounced the principle of rationality, even if it stood for a bourgeois value. As Michael Müller has pointed out, the protagonists of the new architecture were not in principle opposed to every rational ordering of things. On the contrary, they argued for a more thoroughgoing rationalization that combated the irrational remnants of the tradition.[11]

It would be a conceptual misunderstanding, therefore, to identify the modern movement as *the* architectural avant-garde of the twenties and thirties. Although the movement's most heroic phase nearly coincided with constructivism and dadaism, and notwithstanding the fact that there existed historically well-documented relations between artists and architects, modern architecture showed in most of its manifestations a face which was clearly distinct from the radicality and destructiveness of the artistic avant-garde. It is nevertheless productive to confront the concept of the avant-garde with the ideas that were structuring the discourse of the modern movement. For the movement was hardly a unified whole, but rather consisted of widely differing trends and tendencies.[12] Some of these were clearly much closer to genuine avant-garde sensibilities than others. That was, for instance, the case for the left-wing tendency of which Hannes Meyer was an exponent.[13] Avant-gardistic impulses which aimed at the "sublation" of architecture can also be said to have played a decisive role in the movement's initial phase. In later developments, however, this moment of "sublation" was gradually neutralized and emasculated. The avant-garde aspirations from the beginnings, which were influenced by a transitory concept of modernity, became reforged into a fairly univocal program in which the need for a permanent redefinition of one's own aims no longer played a crucial role. A symptomatic manifestation of this evolution can be detected in the work of Sigfried Giedion.

Sigfried Giedion: A Programmatic View of Modernity

Sigfried Giedion (1888–1968) was first confronted with contemporary architecture at the age of thirty-five, after an initial training as an engineer followed by a doctorate in art history.[14] He himself said that his fascination was aroused by a visit to the *Bauhauswoche* in 1923 and by his encounter with Le Corbusier in 1925.[15] From that moment on he devoted all his energies to the defense and propagation of these new ideas. In his articles and books he committed himself uncompromisingly to the cause of modern architecture. He often did this explicitly in his capacity as a historian: his line of argument took the form of a historical writing that covered developments up to and including his own time. Criticism of Giedion's work has mainly been leveled at this "operative" aspect of his work as a historian.[16] His outlook is based on the assumption that a single vast evolutionary pattern underlies the history of architecture and that this evolution develops more or less in a linear fashion, culminating in twentieth-century modern architecture, which is presented by Giedion as "a new tradition."

This linear view of history and the programmatic and pastoral concept of modernity that goes with it is particularly conspicuous in his major work, *Space, Time and Architecture*. The two books on modern architecture that he wrote prior to this— *Bauen in Frankreich, Bauen in Eisen, Bauen in Eisenbeton* and *Befreites Wohnen*—

are less univocal and betray ideas and notions that were clearly colored by transitory experiences of modernity.

New Experiences and a New Outlook

Bauen in Frankreich draws a picture of the development of French architecture in the nineteenth and twentieth centuries with particular reference to the influence of new materials and construction technology. Giedion defends the thesis that the most important contributions of the nineteenth century lay in the domain of iron and glass structures and in working with concrete. These technologies formed as it were the "subconscious" of architecture, which first became manifest in the twentieth century due to the New Building:

> What remains unfaded of the architecture [of the last century] is those rare instances when construction breaks through. Construction based entirely on provisional purposes, service and change is the only part of building that shows an unerringly consistent development. Construction in the nineteenth century plays the role of the subconscious. Outwardly, construction still boasts the old pathos; underneath, concealed behind facades, the basis of our present existence is taking shape.[17]

The key expression that Giedion used to describe the qualities of the new architecture is *Durchdringung* (interpenetration). The almost archetypal spatial experience that gave rise to this expression was the result of the sensations aroused by nineteenth-century girder constructions such as the Eiffel Tower[18] and the Pont Transbordeur in Marseilles, a very specific kind of bridge where a moving platform is making the connection between the two landings (figures 3 and 4).[19] Giedion's fascination with these structures arose from the sensation of motion and from the experience of an intermingling of spaces. The description of the Eiffel Tower, for instance, emphasizes the unique effect of a "rotating" space that is produced by climbing the spiral flights of steps (figure 5). Exterior and interior spaces are as a result constantly related to each other, to such an extent that in the end one cannot make any clear distinction between the two. This new kind of spatial experience is fundamental in the New Building:

> In the air-flooded stairs of the Eiffel Tower, better yet, in the steel limbs of a *pont transbordeur*, we confront the basic aesthetic experience of today's building: through the delicate iron net suspended in midair stream things, ships, sea, houses, masts, landscape and harbor. They loose their delimited form: as one descends, they circle into each other and intermingle simultaneously.[20]

Pont Transbordeur (1905) and
harbor of Marseilles.

(From Sigfried Giedion,
Bauen in Frankreich, fig. 1.)

Giedion comments:
"A mobile ferry suspended by
cables from the footbridge high
above the water connects traffic
on the two sides of the harbor.
This structure is not to be taken
as a 'machine.' It cannot be
excluded from the urban image,
whose fantastic crowning it
denotes. But its interplay with
the city is neither 'spatial' nor
'plastic.' It engenders *floating*
relations and interpenetrations.
The boundaries of architecture
are blurred."

Pont Transbordeur, Marseilles.
(From Sigfried Giedion,
Bauen in Frankreich, fig. 61.)

Eiffel Tower (1889),
interior of pier.
(From Sigfried Giedion,
Bauen in Frankreich, fig. 2.)
Giedion comments:
"Instead of a massive tower, an
open framework condensed into
minimal dimensions. The
landscape enters through
continuously changing snippets."

4

5

Giedion's fascination was nothing new or even out of the ordinary. The glass and iron structures of the nineteenth century—exhibition halls, railway stations, arcades, conservatories—provoked strong reactions right from the start. They were favorite subjects for modernist painters, from Manet to Delaunay (figure 6), and they aroused fierce polemical debate, the Crystal Palace in London being a good example.[21] Neither was it the first time that the importance of these constructions designed by engineers had been acknowledged in an architectural discourse where they were seen as the prelude to a future architecture. In the work of Scheerbart and in Sant'Elia's and Marinetti's futurist manifesto, however, these statements sounded like echoes of distant unattainable visionary dreams, while Giedion succeeded in combining the lyrical character of his homage with an extremely convincing, sober analysis of very real and realizable buildings and spaces.

Giedion treated these fascinating spatial experiences in a very specific way, transforming them into a description of the new architecture that at the same time served as a guideline for future developments. In fact, he uses his descriptions of the new experiences of space to constitute the foundation of the new architecture, which he recognizes in the idea of *Durchdringung* (figure 7). The term is used in different constellations. First and foremost it is used as a description of various spatial configurations: the penetrating of a fairly well-defined volume by an element of much smaller proportions, as for instance with Mart Stam's design for the Rokin in Amsterdam in 1926;[22] the intermingling of spaces on various levels through the partial absence of floors, or of interior and exterior space through the use of transparent walls, as in a number of Le Corbusier's houses (figures 8 and 9);[23] the interpenetration of equivalent volumes so that the building is composed of various juxtaposed volumes that are interlocked in such a way that the borders between one and the other are no longer clearly defined, as in Gropius's Bauhaus.

For Giedion, *Durchdringung* thus refers to an essential characteristic of the new architecture: its capacity to interrelate different aspects of space with one another.[24] Giedion was not the only one to attach such an importance to the idea of *Durchdringung*. László Moholy-Nagy, who was the book designer of *Bauen in Frankreich*, also took the idea of spatial interpenetration to be the hallmark of the future architecture. In his own book from 1929, *Von Material bis Architektur*, which is

Robert Delaunay, *Tour Eiffel*, 1909–1910.
(Emanuel Hoffmann-Stiftung, Basel;
photo: Oeffentliche Kunstsammlung
Basel, Martin Bühler.)

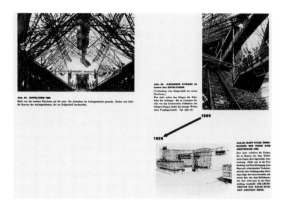

Two pages from *Bauen in Frankreich* showing how Giedion links the new experiences of space, which he designates with the term *Durchdringung*, with the characteristics of the New Building, here illustrated by Mart Stam's project for the Amsterdam Rokin from 1926.

7

Le Corbusier, Villa on the Sea, 1921.
(From Sigfried Giedion, *Bauen in Frankreich*, fig. 105.)

Giedion comments:
"Without having found an architectural form, these designs already contain the vertical fusing of space, broad openings, and the greatest possible avoidance of partition walls made possible by the ferroconcrete skeleton."

8

Le Corbusier, Cook House, 1926–1927.
(From Sigfried Giedion, *Bauen in Frankreich*, fig. 109.)

Giedion comments:
"View from the study to large room, stairs, and roof terrace. Exterior space (roof terrace) and the various interpenetrating levels of the interior space are blended together."

9

organized around a sequence of some two hundred figures, Moholy-Nagy inserts a telling image entitled "architecture" as the culminating one (figure 10). His caption reads: "From two overlapping photographs (negatives) the illusion comes forth of a spatial interpenetration, which only the next generation might be able to experience in reality—as glass architecture."[25]

The most striking feature in Giedion's discourse on this topic is that this spatial *Durchdringung* leads to a symbiosis with all kinds of metaphorical meanings associated with the word.[26] The result is that a mutual relation is created between the new concept of space and a social reality that is also characterized by interpenetration in many areas. Due to Giedion's rhetorical strategy, it becomes clear that *Durchdringung* stands for a weakening of hierarchical models on all levels—social as well as architectural. Here is a key passage in which the multilayered character of the concept of *Durchdringung* can clearly be recognized:

> It seems doubtful whether the limited concept of "architecture" will indeed endure.
>
> We can hardly answer the question: What belongs to architecture? Where does it begin, where does it end?
>
> Fields overlap [*Die Gebiete durchdringen sich*]: walls no longer rigidly define streets. The street has been transformed into a stream of movement. Rail lines and trains, together with the railroad station, form a single whole.[27]

Here Giedion links the question of the autonomy of architecture as a discipline with the observation that spatial realities such as streets and stations no longer represent sharply defined entities; our experience of them is essentially defined by patterns of movement and interpenetrating elements. He suggests implicitly that architecture no longer has anything to do with objects: if it is to survive at all it must become part of a broader domain in which it is not so much objects as spatial relations and ratios that are of central importance. The title of this paragraph consequentially should have been "Architecture?" but the question mark was left out by the publisher of the book—much to Giedion's annoyance.[28]

A similar train of thought underlies the slogan "Konstruktion wird Gestaltung" (construction becomes design) that Giedion originally had in mind as the title for his book.[29] This expression perfectly sums up his basic idea: architecture is no longer concerned with representative facades and monumental volumes; instead, its aim is to design new relationships based on a structural logic.

The sensitivity to the transitory aspect of modernity that we can see in *Bauen in Frankreich* is still more pronounced in Giedion's next publication. *Befreites Wohnen* (1929) is a small book that gives a picture of the aims and achievements of the New Building with the aid of photos accompanied by a commentary. Whereas the first book is at some points hesitant to embrace full-heartedly the new spatial

"Architecture" according to
László Moholy-Nagy.
(Concluding illustration in
Moholy-Nagy's *Von Material
zu Architektur*; photo:
Jan Kamman/Schiedam.)

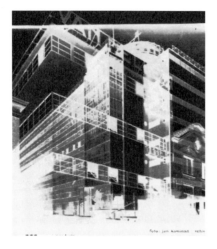

10

sensibility,[30] the second takes it up in a more radical fashion. Here Giedion opposes in an explicit manner traditional ideas such as attributing to the house an eternal value. Instead he argues, "The house is a value of use. It is to be written off and amortized within a measurable time."[31] This is feasible, according to Giedion, when building production is organized on an industrial basis, so that building costs and rents are reduced. Houses should not look like fortresses; rather, they should allow for a life that requires plenty of light and wants everything to be spacious and flexible. Houses should be open; they should reflect the contemporary mentality that perceives all aspects of life as interpenetrating: "Today we need a house, that corresponds in its entire structure to our bodily feeling as it is influenced and liberated through sports, gymnastics, and a sensuous way of life: light, transparent, movable. Consequentially, this open house also signifies a reflection of the contemporary mental condition: there are no longer separate affairs, all domains interpenetrate."[32] Giedion explicitly refers in this text to Sant'Elia, whose idea it was that a house should only last one generation. In the manifesto that Sant'Elia wrote with Marinetti in 1914 it is indeed stated:

> We have lost the sense of the monumental, of the heavy, of the static; we have enriched our sensibility by a taste of the light, the practical, the ephemeral and the swift. . . . An architecture so conceived cannot give birth to any three-dimensional or linear habit, because the fundamental characteristics of Futurist architecture will be obsolescence and transience. Houses will last less long than we. Each generation will have to build its own city.[33]

Nowhere else in Giedion's work is this concept of deliberate transitoriness so emphatically stated as in *Befreites Wohnen*, a book that in terms of its rhetorical structure also has the character of a manifesto. Openness, lightness, and flexibility are associated here with the other slogan words of the New Building: rationality, functionality, industry, experiment, *Existenzminimum*. All this, states Giedion, leads to liberation, not only from the weight of the tradition, but also from too high rents. He even adds that women too will take advantage of the new outlook on dwelling, since their household chores will be reduced to a minimum. Thus they will be capable of freeing themselves from their narrow focus on house and family.

Together these two early books to a certain extent take up the challenge of an avant-garde position in architecture. Based on an antagonism against traditional notions and institutions in architecture, they display an attitude which celebrates the new and is fascinated by the idea of transitoriness. Giedion even lives up here to the radicality which such ideas call for, in that he explicitly questions the nature of architecture. Most interesting in this respect is the thought that architecture might no longer limit itself to the design of representative buildings but should develop instead into to a more comprehensive discipline that is focusing upon the whole environment. Herewith Giedion formulates as a goal for architecture its breaking out of the limits imposed upon it by tradition and by its functioning as an institution. What could be the result of such a strategy is hinted at in a caption for some illustrations of an industrial landscape in *Bauen in Frankreich* (figures 11 and 12). The landscape consists

Industrial landscape.
(From Sigfried Giedion,
Bauen in Frankreich, fig. 4.)
For Giedion this landscape
with its different levels of
transportation prefigures the
future development of cities,
where the interpenetration of
different domains will be evident.

11

Petroleum tank, concrete bridge,
street, trestle (Marseilles).
A detail from the same industrial
landscape.
(From Sigfried Giedion,
Bauen in Frankreich, fig. 3.)

12

of a montage-like superposition of heterogeneous elements (a petrol tank, a railway bridge, a factory with smoking chimneys, a shed, electricity cables). "The various traffic levels, the juxtaposition of objects determined only by necessity offer—so to speak unconsciously and as raw material—possibilities for how our cities may later be designed openly without the constraints of preestablished levels."[34] These illustrations along with Giedion's commentary contain for me the most telling moment in the book: the point at which there is a clear indication that architecture may well have to merge with vulgar reality and accept juxtaposition and montage as design principles which allow for this merging. In this passage one can clearly see that the idea of "montage"—a key concept for the avant-garde, according to Bürger[35]—is at work, even if the term as such is not used explicitly.

Space, Time and Architecture: The Canon of Modern Architecture

The foreword to the first edition of *Space, Time and Architecture* (1941) states that this book is intended "for those who are alarmed by the present state of our culture and anxious to find a way out of the apparent chaos of its contradictory tendencies." These contradictory tendencies are a product of the gap between thought and feeling, which in turn is the result of the enormous technological and industrial developments of the nineteenth century. Here Giedion is giving the familiar diagnosis pointing out a discrepancy between the advance of humanity in the realm of thought and in the realm of feeling. In his view, however, this split can be overcome: "In spite of the seeming confusion there is nevertheless a true, if hidden, unity, a secret synthesis, in our present civilization."[36] Giedion sees the possibility of a synthesis in the development of a new awareness of time and space. According to him, a new sense of space and time prevails in contemporary architecture and painting just as much as in science. The new approach no longer treats them as separate dimensions but as related phenomena.[37] Giedion quotes the mathematician Hermann Minkowski, who began the introduction of his book *Space and Time* by stating: "Henceforth space by itself and time by itself, are doomed to fade away into mere shadows, and only a kind of union of the two will preserve an independent reality." According to Giedion, one can talk here of a remarkable parallel with the development of painting: it was around the same time that cubism and futurism in their quest for new means of expression created what he calls "the artistic equivalent of space-time."[38]

Giedion defends the hypothesis that one can identify parallel developments in different disciplines by appealing to the *Zeitgeist:* "It seems unnatural for a theory in mathematical physics to meet with an equivalent in the arts. But this is to forget that the two are formulated by men living in the same period, exposed to the same general influences, and moved by similar impulses."[39] In the key chapter on "Space-Time in Art, Architecture and Construction," the supposed affinity between these different developments is demonstrated by a strategic use of illustrations. For instance, the Bauhaus in Dessau by Walter Gropius (figure 14) is illustrated next to *L'Arlé-*

Picasso, *L'Arlésienne*,
1911–1912.
(From Sigfried Giedion, *Space,
Time and Architecture*, fig. 298.)

Walter Gropius, Bauhaus Dessau,
1926.
(From Sigfried Giedion, *Space,
Time and Architecture*, fig. 299;
photo: Bauhaus-Archiv, Berlin, by
Lucia Moholy.)

13

14

sienne by Picasso (figure 13),[40] while in the commentary constant reference is made to the qualities of transparency and simultaneity that are peculiar to both these works. (In the case of the Bauhaus, what is involved is the creation of a simultaneity between interior and exterior spaces and the transparency of the walls; with the painting *L'Arlésienne* it is a matter of the transparency of overlapping surfaces and the simultaneous depicting of different facets of the same object.)

The central thesis about the importance of the space-time concept in the new architecture is developed and tested against the work of five masters of modern architecture: Walter Gropius, Le Corbusier, Mies van der Rohe, Alvar Aalto, and Jørn Utzon.[41] Giedion regards the new concept of space as the most typical feature of the new architecture. It was the product of a combination of an advance in the use of materials and construction technologies on the one hand and the artistic discoveries of cubism, futurism, and similar movements on the other. These artistic developments led to a new vision of space that was not based on perspective, that emphasized simultaneity (the depiction of an object from different viewpoints at the same time), and that also stressed dynamics, focusing on the movement of objects and attempting to depict it in painting.

The interplay between these factors—the constructional and the artistic—opened the way for a new awareness of space in modern architecture. Buildings were no longer visually rooted in the ground but seemed to float above it while their different volumes interpenetrate each other instead of simply being juxtaposed. These features together with a plentiful use of glass—a material that according to the author was primarily used because of its dematerializing qualities and which had the effect of making interior and exterior space appear to interpenetrate—led to an "unprecedented many-sidedness," creating the sense of a movement in space that seems, if but for an instant, to be frozen.[42] Giedion had identified this frozen movement earlier in the stairwell of Gropius's factory building at the Werkbund exhibition in Cologne in 1914, but it was the Bauhaus in Dessau, also by Gropius and dating from 1926, that he discussed as the example par excellence of this new concept of space.

The new concept of space in modern architecture therefore proclaims and affirms time as a fourth dimension in a way that was quite unprecedented. The experience suggested by this architecture has a space-time character: it is not determined by the static qualities of a fixed space but by an uninterrupted play of simultaneous experiences of varying (spatial) character—experiences that, traditionally speaking, could only be perceived one after the other. The typical features of modern architecture, then, are simultaneity, dynamism, transparency, and many-sidedness; it is a play of interpenetration and a suggestive flexibility.

In his conclusion Giedion emphasizes the importance of organic and irrational elements in architecture, which in his view run the risk of being suppressed as a result of too great an emphasis on rationality. Architecture is faced with the task of achieving a balance between the rational and geometric on the one hand and the organic and irrational on the other—between the domain of thought and that of feeling. "The outstanding task of our period [is] to humanize—that is to reabsorb emotionally—what has been created by the spirit. All talk about organizing and planning is in vain unless we first create again the whole man, unfractured in his methods of thinking and feeling."[43] In *Space, Time and Architecture* Giedion thus built up a case for the thesis that modern architecture, as a legitimate heir to the most relevant architectural trends of the past, is capable of contributing to bridging the gap between thought and feeling because it relies upon the concept of space-time, just as the sciences and the arts do. The whole aim of *Space, Time and Architecture* was thus to canonize modern architecture as a "new tradition."

Space, Time and Architecture is not a pioneering text in the strict sense of the word: the book does not break new ground or announce a completely new paradigm. A number of elements of this paradigm had been around for some time already: the moral appeal (Morris, Loos); the concept of space-time and its application in architecture (van Doesburg, Lissitzky); the relating of new materials and construction technologies on the one hand with architectural design on the other (Le Corbusier); the fact that architecture and city planning influence each other and are mutually dependent (CIAM texts); the concern with the organic and the functional (Moholy-Nagy, the Bauhaus). It was Giedion, however, who forged these various elements of the modern movement into a closely-knit whole and who gave it a historical legitimization, tracing its roots back to the tradition of baroque architecture and to nineteenth-century technological developments.

But it is not only on this intrinsic level that *Space, Time and Architecture* shows all the signs of a canonization; extrinsically too, it undertook a similar role in stimulating the process of the social acceptance of modern architecture. Written in America between 1938 and 1940, it has undergone countless reprints and revised editions and has functioned as obligatory reading for generations of students in architecture. It thus marked the end of a period of searching and questioning, a period of heated debates and experiments often in conflicting directions, and the beginning of a new period in which the direction to take was supposed to be clearly mapped out.

From Avant-Garde to Canonization

This development from avant-garde to established order can also be detected in the internal evolution of Giedion's writings. At first sight there would appear to be little more than a shift in terminology (space-time instead of *Durchdringung*). Closer analysis, however, shows that there is more at stake here. The development takes place on two levels. First, there is a shift in Giedion's notions about the social role of architecture. Secondly, a difference in tone can be discerned between *Bauen in Frankreich* on the one hand and *Space, Time and Architecture* on the other. These texts belong to different genres.

The first difference concerns the way that the relation between architecture and society is understood. Before 1930 the new architecture was deliberately presented as being closely bound up with social developments or even as anticipating them. This is implied among other things in the metaphorical use of the term *Durchdringung*, with its connotations such as social mobility, emancipation, and liberation. In *Bauen in Frankreich* Giedion states explicitly that it is no longer the upper classes that advocate and make possible the building of progressive architecture but other, less privileged layers of the population.[44] *Befreites Wohnen* contains a detailed plea for the *Existenzminimum*, calling it the most important task for the New Building; it treats it as the point of departure for the development of a new culture of everyday life. In both publications, therefore, the new architecture is bound up with processes of social emancipation. In *Space, Time and Architecture*, on the other hand, this connotation is no longer crucial: the social implications that are inherent in *Durchdringung* are not transferred to the concept of space-time. Social and political connotations have been purged along with all references to social experiments and to the revolutionizing aims of the new architecture. The question "whether 'architecture' can have any future" is no longer raised. Nor are the liberatory character of modern architecture and its social dimension in any way highlighted. Explicit references to a sociopolitical purpose are no longer present. Instead of *Durchdringung*, an expression with a range of connotations, the notion of space-time appears. This concept does not have any obvious social connotations; instead it suggests that developments within architecture correspond to those on a "deeper" level of reality—the "secret synthesis" that lies hidden behind chaotic appearances. Behind the two apparently parallel terms, *Durchdringung* and space-time, two different notions about the scope of architecture and its social role lie concealed.

The second shift has to do with the whole tenor of the text, its tone. In contrast with his earlier books that represented a genuine inquiry, accompanied by doubts and a sense of wonder, *Space, Time and Architecture* sounds like the incantatory discourse of a prophet who does not doubt that he knows the truth. Due to this self-assurance, a programmatic concept of modernity ends up pervading the whole book. This programmatic concept has less to do with a specific political idea than with the conviction that modern architecture contains the potential for building a new world, one in which the evils of the present time will be vanquished and where the challenge of the future will be taken up. In *Bauen in Frankreich* and in *Befreites Wohnen* an attempt was made to formulate a transitory vision that saw the new architecture as a constant quest to give expression to change and evanescence. This endeavor is much less important in *Space, Time and Architecture*. Giedion still refers here to a transitory experience of dynamics and movement, but it is no longer decisive as a concept for his view of architecture. His description of the rise of the new architecture as "the growth of a new tradition" puts the emphasis on the programmatic aspect: he conceives of modern architecture here not so much as a paradoxical "tradition of the new" but much rather as the unqualified inauguration of a "new tradition."[45] This "new tradition" constitutes the most authentic expression of the underlying unity that he discerned in the apparent chaos of the time, and he therefore also combated every tendency toward superficiality and all attempts to reduce modern architecture to a fashionable trend.[46] Instead he stressed the rootedness of architecture in the past and its intimate involvement with the deepest essence of his own time. These elements form the crux of his argument that space-time architecture is the only viable contemporary form of architecture.

This double shift maps out a path by which the architecture of the modern movement gradually becomes disconnected from the logic of the avant-garde, which was first of all one of negation and destruction. In *Space, Time and Architecture* and in Giedion's later work, one can still see minor traces of an avant-garde concept. The diagnosis of the "fissure between thinking and feeling" and the rejection of the kitsch culture of the "prevailing taste" are arguments that Giedion had in common with the pioneers of the avant-garde.[47] He has, however, abandoned one of the more fundamental concept of the artistic avant-garde—that of transitoriness.[48]

Giedion's arguments in *Space, Time and Architecture* are not only based on a more programmatic intent, they show pastoral tendencies as well. He specifically bases his case on the notion that the strength of the new architecture lay in its potential for combating the worst evil of the age—the fissure that had come about between thought and feeling; it would succeed in doing so because it displays a sensitivity to both artistic and scientific aspects, giving form to a new concept of space that developed in parallel fashion in both domains.[49] In so doing it would contribute to a process of reconciliation and synthesis.

In his early work Giedion already advocated the endeavor to bring art and life together to form a new reality. In *Bauen in Frankreich* he stated:

> We are being driven into an indivisible life process. We see life more and more as a moving yet indivisible whole. The boundaries of individual fields blur. . . . Fields permeate and fertilize each other as they overlap. . . . We value these fields not as hierarchically but as equally justified emanations of the highest impulse: LIFE! To grasp life as a totality, to allow no divisions, is among the most important concerns of the age.[50]

In *Space, Time and Architecture* this rhetoric about bringing art and life together is less explicit. But here too he argues that "the outstanding task of our period [is] to humanize—that is to reabsorb emotionally—what has been created by the spirit."[51] The aim is integration—to make life complete once again and to rely on art and architecture to achieve this. Once again, however, a certain shift in position can be detected. In the quotation from 1928 Giedion comes very close to the avant-garde idea that social life should be organized on the basis of art. In 1941, on the other hand, the role of art and architecture is limited to healing the wounds inflicted upon the individual by social developments. He no longer claims that developments in architecture have any impact on society as a whole. If one calls "avant-garde" a position that is characterized by a logic of negation and a critical attitude vis-à-vis social conditions, it is clear that the architecture Giedion is advocating in *Space, Time and Architecture* cannot be labeled as such any more.

Das Neue Frankfurt: The Search for a Unified Culture

In 1925 Ernst May was appointed *Stadtbaurat* in his native city of Frankfurt. In practice this meant that he was head of the department of housing and city planning with very broad powers to combat the increasingly desperate housing need in Frankfurt. May and his associates succeeded in building an impressive number of housing units in the space of only a few years.[52] Every eleventh resident in the conurbation of Frankfurt obtained a new dwelling through this program, in most cases in one of the large modern-looking *Siedlungen* (settlements) that May built in a circle around the city (figure 15). This vast construction program was promoted by the publication of a monthly magazine called *Das Neue Frankfurt* that was aimed at an international readership. Not only was architecture in Frankfurt extensively discussed and documented in its columns; the magazine also covered an extremely wide range of topics whose common denominator was "modern design."[53] Theater, photography, films, art and industrial design, and other subjects were all discussed. Particular attention was paid to the subject of "education," in keeping with the view that upbringing and education formed the key to the creation of the new man who would be capable of understanding and appreciating the new culture that was being developed with so much enthusiasm.

Like Giedion, Ernst May was one of the most important figures of the early years of the CIAM. He was one of the founding members who met in La Sarraz in 1928, and he was responsible for the proposal to hold the second congress in Frankfurt in 1929. On this occasion he prepared a report on the subject of the congress, "Die Wohnung für das Existenzminimum." The success achieved in Frankfurt was one of the most important that the still youthful modern movement could claim to its credit. Making use of the possibilities created by the social policies of the Weimar Republic, a housing program was realized that was unrivaled elsewhere in Germany (with the possible exception of Berlin). The impact of the sheer number of dwellings

Map of present-day Frankfurt indicating the *Siedlungen* built by May and his group. Those discussed or mentioned in this chapter are: (1) Westhausen, (2) Praunheim, (3) Römerstadt, (18) Riedhof, (22) Hellerhof.

(From Volker Fischer and Rosemarie Höpfner, eds., *Ernst May und Das Neue Frankfurt 1925–1930,* p. 105.)

15

First issue of *Das Neue Frankfurt*, October 1926.

16

was very considerable; when one bears in mind that Loos built only a few villas and that Le Corbusier's greatest achievement in the 1920s was a tiny estate in Pessac consisting of some thirty homes, May's fifteen thousand is an impressive total in every respect.

Ideas and Intentions

May stated his vision of modernity and the goals he had in mind in a programmatic article in the first issue of *Das Neue Frankfurt* (figure 16).[54] In it he recalled some major metropolises of the past that he regarded as examples of "unified complexes of culture": Babylon, Thebes, Byzantium, and others. In his own epoch, however, this notion of a "unified cul-ture" was nowhere to be found. In the nineteenth century, culture had evolved into a chaos of tendencies with the result that humanity ran the risk of becoming a slave to its own creations in technology and industry. There was, however, some reason for hope. Paradoxically, the world war produced a change of direction. People had begun to see through the superficiality of the "worship of the golden calf," and this change paved the way for a "deeper attitude toward life." In this way the foundations were laid for a new homogeneous and unified culture, that would compare favorably with any that had come before.

> See how all the evidence of present-day design tends toward a single conclusion! ... already streams from a hundred and a thousand springs, brooks and rivulets are coming together which will go to make up a new culture, a closed culture that will flow forward in a wide bed like a confident river. Everywhere we come across the endeavor to root out everything that is feeble, imitative, hypocritical and false. Everywhere we notice the purposeful struggle for a bold new design, for honesty in the use of materials, and for truth.[55]

To bring about a breakthrough in this new culture, deliberate steps had to be taken. That was the task May set himself in Frankfurt, and it is in this context that the magazine *Das Neue Frankfurt* should be seen:

Human willpower alone will never bring about a new development. Deliberate measures, however, can smooth the way and accelerate the tempo. This is the aim of the monthly magazine *Das Neue Frankfurt*. The point of departure is the design of the organism of the metropolis, with particular reference to its economic foundations. But the magazine will widen its coverage to include every domain that is relevant to the designing of a new unified metropolitan culture.[56]

"Modernity" for May thus meant the creation of a new unified metropolitan culture. A notion like this clearly implies the dominance of a programmatic concept of modernity. Rationality and functionality were the qualities that were given first priority. "Rationality" in this context should be interpreted in a broad sense: what May and his associates had in mind was a culture that anticipated a future society, rationally organized and conflict-free, made up of people with equal rights and common interests.[57] This distant ideal and the concrete housing needs of Frankfurt combined to form the basic tenets of housing policy in this city.

In this endeavor the architects of *Das Neue Frankfurt* gave priority to the industrialization of the construction process and the principles of Taylorism in the use of space:[58] they were apparently convinced that the "rational" character of these technologies developed in the context of the capitalist system did not conflict with the "rationality" of the society they had in mind—a society based on equal rights and homogeneity. The purpose of the Frankfurt experiment fitted perfectly in the scheme of the optimistic, pastoral ideology of Enlightenment that took the view that "progress" was the result of an increasing rationality at all levels of life and of society. In this scheme of things, the social aspect occupied a prominent place: it was the deliberate aim of May and his team to ensure that the housing needs of the poor and the underprivileged were alleviated, as one aspect of the increasing emancipation of all individuals. For this reason it fits perfectly into what Habermas describes as "the modern project." In any case, the aim was to harness the achievements of avant-garde artists and developments in the field of technology for the actual (architectural) design of the daily lives of a large portion of the population.

The emancipation May and his associates had in mind was not purely a material one; it also implied the enhancement of the culture of everyday life. The aim was to increase people's awareness of the positive aspects and new possibilities of an epoch in which the results of the industrial revolution affected every part of daily life. The new architecture would have to be consistent with the new conditions of that life:

The achievements of the twentieth century that surround our everyday existence have given a completely new form to our lives and have had a fundamental influence on our way of thinking. For reasons such as this it is becoming increasingly clear that in its design and construction, housing too will have to undergo changes similar to those that led from

the stage coach to the railways, from cars to airships, from the tele-
graph to the radio, or from the old craftsman's workshops to factories—
a change that goes hand in hand with the transformation of the entire
productive and economic life of former times into that of our own
century.[59]

An openness to everything that is mobile and transitory is another feature of the new
form of everyday life:

Because the outside world of today affects us in the most intense and
disparate ways, our way of life is changing more rapidly than in previous times. It goes without saying that our surroundings will undergo
corresponding changes. This leads us to layouts, spaces, and buildings
of which every part can be altered, which are flexible, and which can be
combined in different fashions.[60]

The new culture thus should match the character of the new epoch, which
was seen as a source of new possibilities. The experiences of the First World War—
so it was thought—had convinced everyone of the urgency of bringing technological
and scientific developments under control. The postwar period was seen as an opportunity for a new start, offering the chance of establishing a culture that would
guide the process of modernization in a positive direction. Furthermore, it was precisely those facets of modernity that were viewed negatively in conservative circles—"lack of style" and lack of *Gemütlichkeit* (coziness), the rapid pace of life and
the increasing bombardment of impressions and experiences, and the break with traditional values—that were seen as stimuli for the design of this new culture. Everything new was greeted with enthusiasm—speed and movement (the increasing
impact of trains, cars and airplanes), the beginnings of the democratizing of sport and
leisure activities, the relaxing of social codes coupled with increasing social mobility.[61] All this was seen as the beginning of a process that would lead to a genuinely
humane society of emancipated men and women in which equal rights would go
hand in hand with a high degree of personal freedom.

A certain tendency toward asceticism was unquestionably present in the
"struggle for a bold new design, for honesty in the use of materials, and for truth"
that May announced in the first issue of his magazine. This tendency had to do with
the idea that one could get to the essence of things only by stripping away all excess
and by rejecting everything that was superfluous. A pure and sober architecture of
the utmost simplicity was the correct foundation for a contemporary culture of everyday life. Truth should be the criterion rather than representation (figure 17). Mart
Stam states this conviction eloquently:

Correct measures are those that conform to our requirements, that fulfill these needs without any pretensions, that do not claim to be more

than they are. Correct measures are those that result in a minimum of ostentation. Everything else is ballast. . . .

The struggle for modern architecture then is a struggle against pretentiousness, against every excess and for a human scale.[62]

Behind this approach is the notion that every object should be understood in terms of its inmost essence. This essence conforms to its function, to what it can be used for. Beauty exists when people succeed in giving this essence as accurate a form as possible, without any "excess" or anything that is extraneous or superfluous. It was this conviction that made the project of housing for the *Existenzminimum* more than a purely instrumental answer to the housing situation.[63] The architects of the New Building were not only interested in the program of housing for the underprivileged classes for extrinsic, social reasons. They also saw it as an opportunity to realize an ascetic ideal—housing reduced to its essence, pure, minimal, and authentic.

In the course of time, however, a slight shift of emphasis in the issues of *Das Neue Frankfurt* became apparent. During the early years virtually no attempt was made to analyze the economic and social aspects of housing policy in Frankfurt: they were apparently regarded as self-evident aspects of the struggle to create a new culture. Gradually, however, these themes began to be treated independently of the cultural context, as autonomous problems. In 1928, for instance, in the special issue about housing, the necessity of rationality and functionality in housing design was still defended on the grounds of a general concept of dwelling culture, while in 1929 in the issue on *billige Wohnungen* (cheap housing), published on the occasion of the CIAM congress in Frankfurt, much more stress was laid on hygiene and on social and economic arguments.[64] Unquestionably, the economic crisis had forced architecture to concentrate more on economic necessities, and this led to a more pronounced consideration of building costs.[65] After 1929, when the consequences of the economic crisis clearly began to make themselves felt, public housing was treated primarily as an economic and financial problem, and rationality and functionality in design was mainly thought of in terms of cost-effectiveness.

Even so, functionalism in *Das Neue Frankfurt* continued to be seen as part of a project for emancipation. It was the aim of May and his associates to provide the mass of people on the housing lists with decent accommodation that would free them from intolerable living conditions. These new homes would allow them to en-

Cover of *Das Neue Frankfurt*, January 1928.

17

joy a minimum of modern comforts (figure 18) together with direct contact with nature—all at a rent they could afford. The rationalization of the construction process
and the development of housing for the *Existenzminimum* was subordinate to the
purpose of being of service to as many people as possible with the (inevitably limited) means that were available. Ernst May:

> Let us suppose we put this question to the army of the underprivileged,
> who eagerly and impatiently demand decent accommodation. Should
> they have to put up with a situation where a small number of them en-
> joy sizable dwellings while the great majority are condemned to go on
> suffering deprivation for many more years? Shouldn't they rather be
> content with a small home that, despite its limited space, would still
> meet the requirements one has the right to expect of a contemporary
> dwelling, if this will ensure that the evil of the housing shortage can be
> abolished in a short period of time?[66]

May's arguments make it clear that a shift had occurred in the policy of *Das
Neue Frankfurt*. The term *Existenzminimum* no longer implied dwellings that re-

The famous Frankfurt kitchen,
designed by Grethe Schütte-
Lihotzky in 1926. This kitchen
was built in in most of the
dwelling units built by May and
his group.

(Photo: Institut für
Stadtgeschichte der Stadt
Frankfurt am Main.)

duced housing to its essentials; instead what was discussed was a choice between two evils. It was better to have too-small homes for many people than "good" homes for the few. This argument is yet another token of the degree to which the *Das Neue Frankfurt* project was committed to a genuinely dynamic movement for emancipation that often tended to violate the purity of ideological positions.

The Dialectics between an Avant-Garde and a City

May and his associates explicitly saw themselves as belonging to the modern movement. This also can be seen in their production: in Frankfurt traditional principles were broken with, and a whole new course was followed both in terms of architectural design and of the tissue characteristics and morphology of the *Siedlungen* and of the city as a whole.

A comparison between two parts of one *Siedlung*, Hellerhof, may serve to highlight the contrast between the traditions in public housing that were current at the beginning of the century and May's innovative approach (figures 19 and 20). In the first part we see large detached houses put down in the middle of a plot of ground. From the outside they look like the homes of well-to-do citizens, with their pitched roofs and stepped gables, the symmetrically placed windows and doors, and meander strips in the masonry. On each story are four flats that get their light in part from the very small courtyard. Two of these dwellings are north-facing.

The dwellings that Mart Stam built next to them hardly a generation later differ radically from these buildings. Not only are they completely different in their exterior layout—long, whitewashed blocks without any ornament and with large window openings and balconies—the relation with the street is conceived of quite differently: with Stam there is a clear separation between the front and the back of the dwellings, and practically all the dwellings have an east-west orientation. The most striking difference, however, is in their floor plans. In the earlier dwellings the various rooms are more or less the same size and are placed in a random order (figure 21). With Stam, on the other hand, we see a distinct contrast in size (every room is designed as much as possible to fit its intended function) and the spatial organization is based on considerations of functionality and orientation (figure 22). With Stam, moreover, the standard of amenities—built-in kitchens and bathrooms and central heating—is much higher, while an attempt is also made to give each flat a private outdoors space in the form of a tiny garden or a terrace.

This contrast is indicative of the new direction taken by the housing department in Frankfurt after May was appointed in 1925. May and his associates succeeded in making extensive use of a number of the achievements of the experiments of the avant-garde, both in the arts and in architecture, and deploying them to carry out an ambitious socially based construction program. The constant guiding principle in this process was the concrete link with the actual city of Frank-

Aerial photograph of the *Siedlung* of Hellerhof. The houses on the left were built around 1901; the long white blocks, designed by Mart Stam, date from 1929–1932.

19

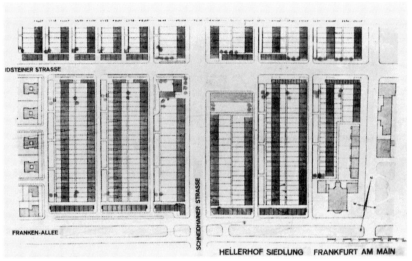

IDSTEINER STRASSE

SCHNEIDHAINER STRASSE

FRANKEN-ALLEE

HELLERHOF SIEDLUNG   FRANKFURT AM MAIN

20

Layout of Hellerhof.

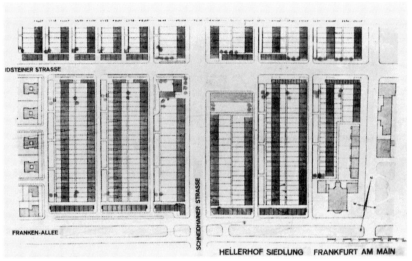

furt. As a result a sort of dialectics developed between the modern design principles that served as guidelines and the concrete context in which the work was carried out. This dialectic explains the profusion of May's achievement in Frankfurt.[67]

May's planning was based on the concept of the *Trabantenstadt*.[68] The *Trabantenstadt* consists of a core city surrounded by a number of satellites (*Trabanten*), at a certain distance from the center but with very good transport connections. To a certain extent this concept shows the hallmarks of fragmentation and decentralization, but it is built according to a distinct organic pattern. The city admittedly is split into separate parts: the urban tissue does not extend in a continuum but is broken by green areas, being fragmented as a result (figure 23). The hierarchy between the nucleus of the city and the satellites is preserved, however, and the general structure of the city is characterized by the fact that the city center also has a central function, serving as the "nucleus" or "heart" of the city. It contains all the important civic amenities and the main commercial, administrative, political, and economic activities

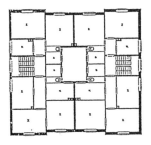

Hellerhof, plan of the houses
from 1901.

21

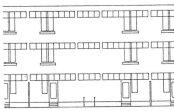

Ansicht vom Gartenhof.

Ansicht von der Straße.

22

Plan and facades of the blocks
designed by Mart Stam.

all take place here. This hierarchical structure with its centralizing tendency is combined with distinct zoning. Without it being explicitly stated in principle at that time (the Charter of Athens was only drawn up in 1933), the construction of the *Siedlungen* created a de facto functional segregation. The *Siedlungen*, after all, consisted primarily of housing.[69] Consequently, a clear trend emerged of creating a geographical separation between housing (in the *Siedlungen*), work (in the industrial terrains on the banks of the Main), trade, culture, and education (in the city center), and an infrastructure of roads and railways that forms an essential connecting element.[70]

On the level of the morphology of the city we come across the symbiosis of an organic design model and an approach that is based on financial and functional considerations. The aim of the latter was to see that the four functions of housing, work, trade, and traffic, which were intertwined in the traditional city, would be separated. The different activities would in this way be prized loose from their original context and reassembled in a different relation to each other. Montage and organic design converge in a concept that preserves the hallmarks of hierarchy and centralism, while giving them a different filling-in, so that the different parts of the city become independent.

The master plan for development (*Flächenverteilungsplan,* figure 23) certainly attests to an attempt to plan Frankfurt as a single whole. It is going too far, then, to interpret the *Siedlungen* as Tafuri does as "islands" in an "anti-urban utopia," floating isolated in space and linked with the city only in a haphazard fashion.[71] Analysis of these plans clearly shows that May's Frankfurt was planned as a coherent spatial unity consisting of urban areas with different characteristics.

23

Ernst May and collaborators, master plan for the development of the city, 1930.

Axonometric scheme of the
Siedlung of Römerstadt, 1927.

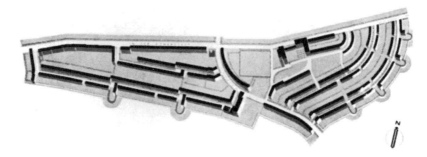

24

The center of the city has the highest density of development and it is surrounded by a belt of nineteenth-century developments that are supplemented and, where necessary, completed with new *Siedlungen*. The *Siedlung* of Bornheimer Hang, for instance, completes the eastern side of this belt. Architecturally the "outskirts" of this *Siedlung* were given details that are reminiscent of a medieval rampart: on the ridge of the hill, the east side of which remained undeveloped otherwise, a continuous development was built with alternately three and four stories. These first "outskirts," however, do not constitute the outer boundary of the city; instead they mark the beginning of the greenbelt that is an integral part of the urban area. Where an initial development already existed around the radial exit routes, an additional development was provided, punctuating the greenbelt with built-up areas. Numerous smaller projects of *Das Neue Frankfurt*, including, for instance, the *Siedlung* of Lindenbaum (where Walter Gropius was responsible for the architecture), form part of this addition to a radial development. Finally, the larger *Siedlungen* in Westhausen, Praunheim, and Römerstadt to the west and Riederwald to the east belong to the outer "ring" of the city, constituting so-called *Vorortstrabanten*—suburbs which are related to the city but which also exist as entities in their own right. In the spots where this ring verges on the Main we find the industrial terrains—that of Fechenheim in the east and Höchst in the west. To the south of the Main the ring is broken, making way for the *Stadtswald*.

All this means that the city has to be read as a whole and that the greenbelt should be regarded as a complex of "city parks" rather than as a nonurban area situated between the nucleus of the city and the *Trabanten*.[72] This reading goes against the interpretation of the *Siedlungen* as "islands" that have nothing in common with the existing city. From the interplay of morphology and architectural formal idiom at every level, one can clearly see that the aim was to treat the city as a whole and to inaugurate the new era by developing a dialectic between a new formal idiom and the existing traditions of an existing city.

As to the tissue characteristics and morphology of the *Siedlungen* themselves, an evolution can be clearly discerned. The layout of the estates that were conceived of before 1929 show plenty of evidence of the influence of garden city principles. The later developments, however, were based on a strict pattern of open row housing (*Zeilenbau*) that is much more rationalist.

The *Siedlung* of Römerstadt (1927–1929) is the most famous and convincing example of May's city planning (figure 24). The basic idea behind Römerstadt was to make good use of the qualities of the landscape: the development follows the contours of the hillside in the form of terraces while it is related to the valley of the Nidda by viewpoints on the bastions that punctuate the retaining wall between the *Siedlung* and the valley (figure 25). There is an obvious hierarchy with a main street (the Hadrianstrasse), residential streets, and paths inside the blocks, a hierarchy that the architecture accentuates. The difference between the public front and the private back of the dwellings is strikingly emphasized by the neat design of the entrance section on the front (with a canopy over the front door and a design that prevents passersby from peering in). The blocks, however, are no longer closed like the nineteenth-century type. By staggering the long straight streets at the height of the bastions, long monotonous sightlines are avoided (figure 26). All of these elements bear the clear imprint of Unwin's design principles.[73]

25   Aerial photograph of Römerstadt.
(From Christoph Mohr and Michael Müller, *Funktionalität und Moderne*, p. 135.)

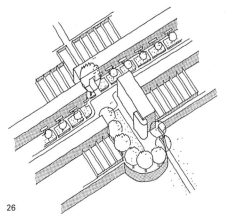

Axonometry of a bastion in Römerstadt.

(From D. W. Dreysse, *May-Siedlungen*, p. 13.)

26

There are, however, a number of important new features: the brilliant interplay of curved and rectangular shapes, both in the layout of the streets and in the relating architectural elements: rounded ends for the buildings at the height of the bastions in the western part—the part with the straight streets (figure 27); right-angled ends for the buildings in the corresponding eastern part; rounded ends, rounded windows, and quarter-circle transitions to overcome the differences in height in the northern block of the Hadrianstrasse, the block that lies opposite the exits of the straight streets; right angles and rectangular windows for the southern block that overlooks the junctions of the curved streets and the Hadrianstrasse; the taut architectural design; the irregular street profile (no front gardens on the southern row of houses, while the northern ones do have them). The undulating course of the Hadrianstrasse, which is highlighted by the curved shapes of the blocks on the inside of the curves, makes plain its function as a traffic artery,[74] suggesting an image of dynamic movement.

All told, Römerstadt is a very successful combination of a number of earlier, organic design principles with the sensation of simultaneity and movement created by the dynamism of a new architectural idiom.

Another successful example of the interplay between old and new morphological principles is Riedhof (1927 and the following years). The principle of *Zeilenbau*, the open row layout, was exploited here for the first time (figure 28). The open row provided a radical alternative to the closed block of nineteenth-century architecture with its rectangular construction. The closed block differentiates sharply between front and back, but in the view of the avant-garde architects the disadvantages of this layout are striking: an unattractive orientation for part of the buildings, poor lighting and ventilation, and awkward treatment of the corners. The idea was to overcome the drawbacks of the closed block by opening it up and by having the rows of houses no longer built face to face, but giving them all an identical orientation, so that front and back facades look out on each other. The main argument for this *Zeilenbau* is its attractive orientation and the possibility of creating identical dwellings every-where, this implying not only that money was saved but also that each individual was treated equally.

Open row design is nonhierarchical; it is not centralized but based on seriality, with identical rows of identical housing units, reminding one of the factory line. In Riedhof an extremely interesting modification of this principle was applied. The *Zeilenbau*, which theoretically can be extended to infinity, is locked into highly artic-ulated boundaries. At the eastern end of every row there is a hook-shaped enclosure, which in an initial movement increases the space between the rows, forming a court-

27

Public space on a bastion in
Römerstadt, looking into the
underpass leading to a footpath.

Axonometric scheme of the
Siedlung of Riedhof.

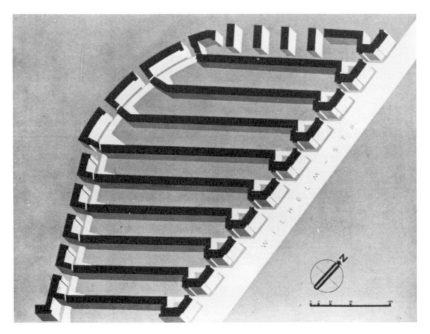

28

yard, while with a second movement it creates an abrupt reduction of the space, resulting in a narrowing that coincides with the junction of all the residential streets with the Stresemannallee (the former Wilhelmstrasse) that constitutes the eastern boundary of the housing complex. Alongside the Stresemannallee, the final wings of the hooks form a long, high, unbroken, and straight urban elevation that gives access at regular intervals to the residential streets.

On the west side each of the residential streets leads to the Heimatring (figure 29). These junctions also are given an architectural accent—every row is prolonged over the Heimatring and ends with a wing at right angles to the residential street, forming the urban elevation of the Heimatring. These striking ends mean that a clearly defined boundary is set up in this *Siedlung* between what is "inside" the *Siedlung* and what is "outside." In the *Siedlung* itself, however, there is no hierarchy, and, unlike Römerstadt, it has no definite center. This is partly due to the nonhierarchical character of the *Zeilenbau* principle and partly to the lack of community facilities such as those that contribute to the centralizing character of the Hadrianstrasse in Römerstadt (shops, catering facilities, and the school).

The *Zeilenbau* principle was modified not only by these very definite boundaries but also by the subtle way that every street is given its own character. It is true that the architecture of all the rows is very regular, but every street is given a specific character by the planting of a particular sort of tree—also the source of the street names, such as Unter den Kastanien and Unter den Akazien. In addition to this, the street areas are differentiated in length, reinforcing their individual character still more.

In the last *Siedlung* that May was responsible for, Westhausen (1929–1931), the *Zeilenbau* principle is applied in a completely orthodox fashion: all the rows of dwellings have exactly the same orientation—the low-rise rows are laid out in a north-south direction, their facades facing east and west, while the taller blocks of the gallery flats run east-west (figure 30). The low-rise buildings are built at right angles to the street and access to the dwellings is via a pedestrian path. A row of seven dwellings is bounded on the one hand by the street and on the other by a strip of grass that runs parallel to the street and which the path also leads to (figures 31 and 32). On one side of the path, one has access to the row of dwellings and on the other side to the gardens that belong to the upper flats. In Westhausen, too, some of the outskirts of the *Siedlung* are given special treatment, though this is less spectacular than in Riedhof. A special feature of the northern edge of the estate is the slight staggering in the row, while on the western edge where the high blocks designed by Kramer (figure 33) are situated, the orientation of the rows is given a quarter-turn.

On the whole the morphology of Westhausen, unlike that of Römerstadt, does not take advantage of the landscape. There is no visual relation with the valley of the Nidda, which is in the immediate vicinity of the estate. The head elevations of Kramer's blocks that look out on it are almost blind. In the Niddatal there is a large swath of allotments and footpaths that forms a buffer between the *Siedlung* and the

Riedhof, Heimatring.

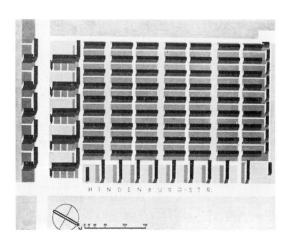

Axonometric scheme of the
Siedlung of Westhausen.

30

Scheme of the organization of
open spaces in Westhausen:
streets, pedestrian paths, grass
strips, and private gardens.
(From D. W. Dreysse,
May-Siedlungen, p. 20.)

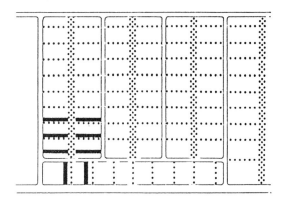

31

core of the city. However, one can get to it from Westhausen only by crossing the busy Ludwig Landmannstrasse. The structure of Westhausen is definitely nonhierarchical. It has no definite center and there is only one place with a striking individual design—the communal laundry with its tall chimney, situated in the southwest corner of the *Siedlung*.[75]

The evolution from a garden city concept to open row development occurred largely because of growing problems with financing these housing schemes; at the same time it also fitted in with an increasingly radical tendency toward rationalization.[76] The earlier *Siedlungen*, including Römerstadt and Riedhof, were distinguished by the highly differentiated design of the urban spaces that was the result of using divergent types of dwelling and by applying architectural accents in appropriate places. After 1929 there is an unmistakable tendency toward great simplicity: there

Westhausen, pedestrian path
giving access to dwellings
and gardens.

32

are very few different types of dwelling in Westhausen (figures 34 and 35) and the differentiation of the urban spaces is carried out with a much more limited range of devices (there are no more architectural accents in the form of special corners, gate-houses, underpasses, and so on).

Even so, many of the most distinctive features of the achievements of *Das Neue Frankfurt* continue to be present in Westhausen: the neat, imaginative layout of the public spaces (the communal strips of grass and the sequence formed by foot-path, grass strips, and private gardens); the feeling for architectural detail (the protection against curious passersby that is provided by raising the ground-floor story, the provision of tiny front gardens, the entrances with canopies over them); the high standard of amenities and—considering the spatial limitations—the outstanding organization of the floor plans of the dwellings.[77] The systematic seriality punctuated by the variety in the character of public areas creates a neutrality and homogeneity that forms the basis for the equality, freedom, and mobility of the residents. Life here is anonymous, but space is provided for the individual needs of every resident. The morphology of the *Siedlung* is based on the extreme rationalism of the *Zeilenbau* principle, but this is coupled with the great care that is given to the design of the open

Blocks in Westhausen designed
by Ferdinand Kramer. View of the
north facade.

33

spaces. With simple means a differentiation is accomplished between the different
parts of the public areas. The urban spaces, such as streets, paths, public lawns, are
given quality by the interplay of rhythm and proportion; the sizes of these spaces (the
distance between the rows, the length of rows and blocks, the width of the paths,
streets, and strips of grass) are neither random nor minimal. Rather, their effect is
one of well-proportioned spaces with a high level of functionality. The transition between private, semiprivate, and public areas is skillfully achieved with the tiny front
gardens, low hedges, and light metal constructions that serve as stakes for fasten-
ing washing lines. This attention to detail ensures that the criterion of cost-
effectiveness does not mean that all nonessential features are given short shrift.

The result is a *Siedlung* in which all the elements are present that will later lead to a trivializing and instrumentalizing of the functionalist principles, but still one where the freshness of the ideas and the enthusiasm of the designers strikes one immediately. The repetition of the same units over and over leads to a monotony here that is not cheerless, but makes for an atmosphere of solidarity.[78] The extreme simplicity and asceticism of the design were less a result of the need to keep costs down than of a desire to invite the residents to participate in a new and contemporary style of living.

To sum up, the architecture of *Das Neue Frankfurt* is calm and not at all extreme. The contrast with tradition is striking but not totally pervasive. The rejection

Plans of the low-rise buildings
in Westhausen: one apartment
on the first floor and one on
the second.

Zweifamilienhaus.

Keller.

Erdgeschoß, 40 qm.

Obergeschoß, 42 qm.

34

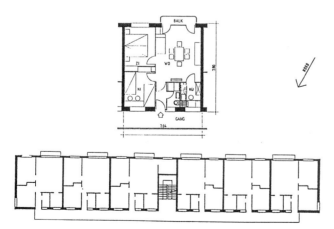

35

Plan of a typical apartment
in the four-story blocks
designed by Ferdinand Kramer.

of all forms of ornament and the use of flat roofs and large balconies point to a deliberate tendency toward innovation, as do the employment of techniques of industrial construction, the functional floor plans, the high quality of the fittings, and even the choice of colors.

Even so, tradition continues to make itself felt under the surface. This can be seen in the endeavor to create a calm and orderly urban image,[79] in the stressing of symmetry and harmony, and in the frequently organic layout of the *Siedlungen*. The volumes of the dwellings are closed and are clearly demarcated, while the window openings in general are somewhat on the small side and are distributed in a balanced fashion along the facade. The design of the urban image is based on an alternation of seriality and symmetry. The housing units are often asymmetrical in their construction, but the fact that they alternately mirror each other means that a general picture is created in which symmetry and axiality are dominant.

Generally speaking, the architecture of *Das Neue Frankfurt* is not really radical in terms of its design. It lacks a number of salient features that are fundamental to the work of other avant-garde architects. Flexibility, mobility, and dynamism, for instance—essential elements in Giedion's concept of modern architecture—do not predominate there. As for Le Corbusier's five points (*pilotis, fenêtres en longueur, plan libre, façade libre*, and *toit-jardin*),[80] only the last element was realized in Frankfurt at all extensively. *Pilotis*—an anti-organic feature par excellence because they reduce the relation between the building and the ground to a minimum—were seldom if ever used; the *fenêtres en longueur* hardly ever occur in dwellings in the *Siedlungen*, Riedhof being an exception in this respect. (They occur a little more frequently in the larger projects such as the school in Römerstadt.) Nor were the floor plans of May's houses based on a *plan libre*: the articulation of the space was functional and supporting walls were used; and the facade designs were not "free" but were decided on the basis of internal requirements and the principles of calm and symmetry.

A comparison between a space-time construction by van Doesburg (figure 36)—which is a perfect example of Giedion's notion of *Durchdringung*—and a colored-in isometric projection by Hans Leistikow, which presented the color scheme for the *Siedlung* of Praunheim (figure 37), leads to similar conclusions. Already in the coloring one can identify a number of striking differences.[81] With van Doesburg, the color is applied to distinguish the different planes as much as possible from each other in order to "dissolve" the cube; it is the "planes floating in space" that are stressed, not the volume that they combine to create. In the isometric projection for Praunheim, on the other hand, the effect of the color, generally speaking, is not used to "dissolve" the volumes: the colors continue round the corner, and the differences are decided on the basis of the direction from which the plane is usually observed (in other words, white is used for the surfaces that face "outward" and red and blue for those that face "toward the inside": from a distance, therefore, it is the white that is dominant in the *Siedlung*). With van Doesburg, "inside" and "outside"

Theo van Doesburg, *Space-Time Construction III*, 1923.

36

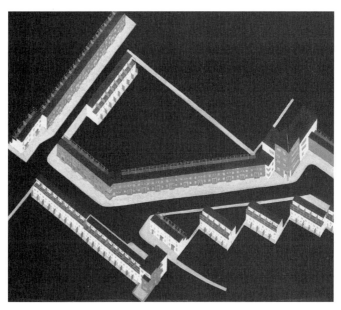

37

Hans Leistikow, color scheme for Praunheim.

(Photo: Institut für Stadtgeschichte der Stadt Frankfurt am Main.)

interpenetrate and the boundary is not clearly drawn. In Praunheim, on the other hand, "inside" and "outside" are very clearly defined.

The formal idiom of the architecture of *Das Neue Frankfurt*, then, cannot be described as one of the most radical examples of avant-garde design principles.[82] Perhaps this is also the reason why Giedion displayed relatively little interest in Frankfurt.[83] What is built here does not reach the same level of innovation that Giedion detected, for instance, in Le Corbusier's work in Pessac.[84] Even so, taken as a whole, *Das Neue Frankfurt* displays a passionate commitment in its treatment of the city and of urban space. It is not for any unique, dazzling architectural feats that we remember it. Its qualities lie rather in the fact that it is an example of how to design a correct and attractive architecture on a larger scale—that of the urban space, the public domain. The *Siedlungen* of Frankfurt form a residential environment in which variety is combined with neutrality, where there is room for both anonymity and involvement, where one can find a whole range of types of both homes and public spaces, and where good connections with the city center are combined with the availability of parks and sports facilities. As far as these qualities are concerned, the achievements of *Das Neue Frankfurt* can still be described as exemplary.

Das Neue Frankfurt as Avant-Garde

The magazine *Das Neue Frankfurt* clearly regarded itself as participating in the international avant-garde. One can deduce this not just from its rhetoric but also from the list of its (occasional) contributors that included famous names such as El Lissitzky, Willi Baumeister, Sigfried Giedion, Adolf Behne, Hans Schmidt, Marcel Breuer, Johannes Itten, Oskar Schlemmer, and others. Typical is the fact that the dadaist Kurt Schwitters was invited to give a performance in Frankfurt during the second CIAM congress in 1929.[85]

The international character of the magazine was stressed right from the start. As May put it:

> Design in the city of Frankfurt am Main will be the main object of our study. That does not mean, however, that we will limit our circle of contributors to this city. On the contrary, our aim is to make our pages available to important figures from all parts of our country and from abroad who have similar aims in both theory and practice. They will serve as a stimulus, supplementing what we create here.[86]

This explicitly stated affinity with the international avant-garde does not alter the fact that what was at stake in *Das Neue Frankfurt* was quite specific. Unlike visual artists or theater directors, this group had to deal with a sociopolitical and physical context that limited their freedom of movement. Both the requirements and expectations of their client—the city government—and the physical presence of the existing city of

Frankfurt were factors that could not be ignored. The parameters within which they had to operate were fairly narrow.

It goes without saying that *Das Neue Frankfurt* cannot be regarded as an avant-garde group that advocated destruction. The rejection of tradition and the cult of the new were definitely elements in the Frankfurt experience, but their position lacked the radicalism of a genuinely extremist movement. May explains the group's relation to tradition:

> We wish to be proud of the traditions of our beautiful city on the River Main, of the way that it has succeeded in flourishing through times both hard and prosperous. We refuse, however, to pay homage to those traditions by imitating their achievements. On the contrary, we want to reveal these traditions in the manner they deserve, by giving a decisive form to the new, standing with both feet in the contemporary world and basing our conclusions on the actual conditions of contemporary life.[87]

If one juxtaposes this passage with the Futurist Manifesto of 1909, for instance, with its appeal to destroy museums, libraries, and academies, it is clear that May's attitude was much more ambivalent than that of Marinetti. In retrospect, it is this ambivalence that makes the achievements of Frankfurt so exceptional. It contains a promise of emancipation and equality transformed into an architectural language that is light, open, and neutral. At the same time, the memory of the city was not erased—the existing city with its historical strata is not denied or encroached on, but serves rather as a basis for the new additions. This results in the old and new complementing each other—something that would have been impossible with an avant-garde logic adhered to at all cost.

Another feature that is lacking in Frankfurt is the radicalization of modernity as a "culture of crisis." The emphasis was clearly on the task of building as much as possible within the shortest time possible. The operational concept of modernity for May and his collaborators thus was programmatic rather than transitory. It is hard to find any trace in *Das Neue Frankfurt* of what Calinescu describes as "an inbuilt tendency for the avant-garde eventually to destroy itself"—unless, of course, one would judge their somewhat naive assessment of the political conditions as such, which I think would be rather unfair. One could state that the Frankfurt avant-garde did in fact include a notion of "the sublation of art into the praxis of life" in its program, in the sense that it was their deliberate intention that their experiments in the arts and architecture would bear fruit in designing the surroundings of everyday life and in enhancing the dwelling culture of the population. In their eyes, however, the "transformation of art in the practice of life" did not imply any undermining of the rational organization of society—as was the intention of dadaism or surrealism. In *Das Neue Frankfurt* there was no opposition toward the instrumental rationality of the social order. On the contrary, their advocating industrialization, standardization, and rationalization was entirely in keeping with a societal modernization implemented according to the norms of an instrumental rationality.

The efforts of May and his associates were nevertheless not meant to support a development along capitalist lines. It is clear that it was their intention to take the rationality and functionality of the social order a stage further with the eventual aim of transcending the existing bourgeois social order.[88] Like Giedion, they were convinced that architecture could play a vital role in this social renewal, because it has the capacity to restore the broken relationship between subjective culture and objective culture.[89] In their view the daily presence of an efficient and functional architecture would stimulate individuals to respond in a less alienated fashion to the efficiency and functionality that are the hallmarks of objective culture.[90]

The group of *Das Neue Frankfurt* saw it as its task to create a new culture in the broadest sense of the word, one that would cover all aspects of social and personal life. They never actually succeeded in fulfilling what they set out to do, because the decisive societal changes they were preparing never did occur. This was partly due to political and social developments which took a regressive turn and made an end to opportunities that for a short period were actually there.

These opportunities were the result of a particular phase of development in German capitalism. After the troubled and turbulent years immediately after the First World War, a period of stability was inaugurated in 1923 with the Weimar Republic pursuing social democratic policies. One aspect of this policy of stabilizing the economic and social situation was the introduction of the *Hauszinsteuer*, a tax on rents that was imposed on owners of prewar real estate; due to rising inflation this tax yielded a sum many times the original rental. A considerable part of the revenues from this tax was spent on public housing. Nevertheless, the unprecedented rise in construction costs in combination with soaring interest rates meant that even before the economic crisis of 1929, the housing program in Frankfurt had to come under review. The rents on new housing that were calculated on the basis of their cost price and on the level of interest rates had simply risen beyond the means of the working classes to afford.[91] After 1929 the flow of funds from the state for public housing was increasingly blocked. Not surprisingly, May's departure for the Soviet Union in the autumn of 1930 coincided with the end of large-scale building operations in Frankfurt.

These circumstances have led a number of authors to interpret *Das Neue Frankfurt* as a step toward imposing increasing restraints and norms on social life rather than as an authentic contribution to the liberation of dwelling.[92] Juan Rodríguez-Lores and G. Uhlig go into some detail on this question. They make particular reference to the paradoxical relation between an originally leftist program of reforms and the technological battery of instruments that largely originated in, and responded to, the logic of capitalism. The result of a reformist strategy such as May's, they argue, was for the working class to become better integrated in bourgeois capitalist society, even though its original intention had been to combat this form of social organization and to reform it fundamentally. To the extent that the un-

"A homogeneous
metropolitan public."

(From Christoph Mohr and
Michael Müller, *Funktionalität
und Moderne*, p. 189.)

38

derlying aim of realizing a classless society was not achieved, the implicit promises
of modern architecture also turned out to be empty ones. The expectations aroused
were only fulfilled in the realm of aesthetics; at the level of praxis they remained
frustrated.[93]

Viewed in retrospect, this criticism is to a certain extent correct. The activists
of *Das Neue Frankfurt* assumed somewhat naively that transformations in the realm
of architecture would be sufficient in themselves to spark the process of a more general reform of society. As we know now, that hope was in vain. That the project failed
to be completed, however, was not only due to the unfavorable turn of political and
economic events, but also to misjudgments and false expectations of it initiators. It
is doubtful, for instance, whether the radical ambition to design the city according to
the needs of the collective could have any real meaning in a context where the capitalist system of ownership was left basically untouched. Uhlig and Rodriguez concur
with Tafuri in arguing that the construction of the *Siedlungen* attested to a strategy
of evasion: they certainly did not solve the real problems of the city that resulted from
the increasing commercialization of the center.

Other contradictions are also inherent in the discourse of *Das Neue Frankfurt*. It was assumed, for instance, that there was such a thing as a homogeneous metropolitan public (or that an entity like this would emerge in the future) and that this entity would be capable of responding in an appropriate fashion to the new architecture (figure 38). This assumption in fact is not compatible with the importance attached to qualities such as freedom, mobility, and transitoriness. When one aims to promote the freedom of every individual and to create as great a potential for change as possible, it is hardly logical to assume that all these individuals will make the same choices and will change in the same fashion. This, however, was the expectation that lay behind the supposedly homogeneous character of the metropolitan public.

May's treatment of the whole culture as an entity that, as it were, ceaselessly gives form to social reality should therefore be questioned. May's concept does not take into account contradictory tendencies and conflicts in interest that are inevitable in a modern society. His pastoral ideas cannot cope with contradictions that are inherent to capitalist development. He was therefore not capable of formulating an adequate reaction when economic imperatives became an obstacle for the realization of his cultural program.

But in the end these critical comments do not alter the fact that something of great importance was achieved in Frankfurt. Starting out from a pastoral and programmatic concept of modernity, a large number of interventions were actually completed that have enriched the city permanently. The unidimensionality and simplicity that were operative at a theoretical level did not extend to the built realizations. In fact, the confrontation between the new architecture and the existing city gave rise to an ambivalence which contained a critical utopian moment—the promise of emancipation and liberation—as well as a subtle respect for the existing city as a sediment for people's memories and as an indispensable substratum for the future. It is precisely for this reason that estates such as Westhausen, Römerstadt, and Riedhof form significant contributions not only to the history of Frankfurt but to that of architecture and urbanism as a whole.

Total
disillusionment
about the age
and nevertheless
an unreserved
profession of
loyalty to it . . .

Walter Benjamin, 1933

3

Reflections in a Mirror

The Experience of Rupture

In 1890 Hermann Bahr published a short essay in which he formulated the younger generation's frustration with the culture that surrounded them. He expressed their sense of disorientation, their feeling of having no genuine ties with the world around them. The feeling that is dominant, he states, is one of agony and despair: "Fierce pain permeates our time, and the agony has become intolerable. There is general clamor for the Savior; everywhere we find the crucified. Has the plague descended on this earth?" In the face of this catastrophe, however, one should not give up. Out of the agony of those who seek the truth, a new age would be born, the age of the modern: "That redemption will come from grief, and mercy from despair, that day will break after this horrible night and art will dwell among people—this glorious and rapturous resurrection is the faith of modernity."[1]

The modern was present already, he argued. It could be seen everywhere in the world outside. It was, however, not yet present in the spirit, nor did it yet fill people's hearts. The conditions of life had changed fundamentally and they would continue to change; people's minds, however, had not yet followed suit. This was why there was so much falsehood in cultural life, a falsehood that had to be done away with. The desire for truth would eventually bring people's outward circumstances and inner longings into harmony once more, creating a new identity between men and the environment they live in. The barriers between inside and outside had to be pulled down. Bahr called for a purge: everything that was old had to be got rid of, the dusty corners where the old spirit had made its home had to be swept clean. Emptiness was needed, an emptiness that would come from erasing all the teachings, all beliefs, and all knowledge of the past. All the falsehood of the spirit—everything that could not be brought into harmony with steam and electricity—had to be exorcised. Then and then only would the new art be born: "The entrance of outward life into the inner spirit: this is the new art. . . . We have no other law than the truth, as is experienced by everybody. . . . This will be the new art that we are creating, and it will be the new religion, for art, science and religion are one and the same."[2]

Bahr cherished the hope that the death throes of the old culture would herald in the birth pangs of a new culture, a culture that would erase the difference between outward appearance and inner spirit and thus would be based on truth, beauty, and harmony. This longing for a unified culture can also be recognized in Bahr's expectations regarding the house that he had Josef Hoffmann build for him. The architect, according to Bahr, should strive to express the personality of his client both in the house as a whole and in all its details. The ideal house should be a *Gesamtkunstwerk* that would reveal the inner truth of its inhabitant: "Above the door a line of a poem should be inscribed: the verse that expresses my whole being and what this verse expresses in words, should equally be said by all the colors and lines, and every chair, every wallpaper design and every lamp should repeat this same verse over again. In a house like this I would see my own soul everywhere as in a mirror."[3] In many ways Bahr's rhetoric seems like a forerunner of the avant-garde's call for purity and authenticity. Out of a diagnosis of the rupture provoked by modernity, he advocates a new beginning, based upon the rejection of the old. What distinguishes him from the later avant-garde, however, is his definitely pastoral conception of a unity that is to be established between art, science, and religion.

In a famous essay of 1903, "The Metropolis and Mental Life," Georg Simmel adopts a more distant approach in discussing the same phenomenon of the discrepancy between the outward conditions of life and one's inner sensibility. In Simmel's view the metropolitan condition is characterized by a profusion of constantly changing stimuli with which every individual is bombarded. In order to protect his life against this deluge of stimuli, the individual responds in a rational manner. Human beings, after all, are more capable of adapting to change at a rational level than at the level of feelings and emotional relations: "Thus the metropolitan type of man—which of course exists in a thousand individual variants—develops an organ protecting him against the threatening currents and discrepancies of his external environment which would uproot him. He reacts with his head instead of his heart."[4]

Simmel discerns a link between the dominance of rationality in the social sphere and the money economy;[5] both systems rely upon purely functional relations among people and things. In the money economy, exchange value takes precedence over use value. This means that the particular character of separate objects is reduced to something that is purely quantitative: objects derive their value not from their inherent quality, but from their quantitative market value. For Simmel it is clear that an analogy can be drawn with the field of interpersonal relations: here too, he argues, emotional relationships used to depend on the individuality of the people concerned, while in the rational relations that are typical of the metropolis, people are treated like numbers. In relations of this sort, individuals are interchangeable entities:

> Money is concerned only with what is common to all: it asks for the exchange value, it reduces all quality and individuality to the question: How much? All intimate emotional relations between persons are founded in their individuality, whereas in rational relations man is reckoned with like a number, like an element which is in itself indifferent.[6]

Simmel nevertheless maintains that the anonymity and indifference of the metropolis do not imply an impoverishment compared with the seclusion and security of the small town or village. For the reserve of city dwellers toward each other and toward their environment provides a context which allows for a much higher degree of personal freedom than is known elsewhere.

According to Simmel, there is yet another feature that is characteristic of life in the metropolis: the increasing fissure between "objective" and "subjective" spirit. Objective culture—the ensemble of achievements in the fields of science, technology, scholarship, and art—accumulates at such a speed that it is impossible for the individual, concerned with the development of his own subjective culture, to keep pace with it. The division of labor means that individuals develop in a way that is increasingly specialized and one-track. This discrepancy is particularly apparent in the metropolis, where objective culture is embodied in institutional buildings and educational organizations, in infrastructures and administrative bodies, and where it is clear that the personality of the individual is no match for this overwhelming presence.

Implicit in the picture that Simmel draws is a fundamental criticism of Hermann Bahr's expectations. Bahr assumed that art and culture would be joined in a new synthesis with science and technology. Simmel's analysis suggests that this hope of a new harmony has little basis. Bahr, one might argue, represents the programmatic and pastoral concept of modernity that was also at a premium in the modern movement. Simmel, on the other hand, demonstrates that social reality might well form an obstacle in the way of achieving this synthetic ideal. The latter opinion is shared by the authors that are discussed in this chapter.

Adolf Loos: The Broken Continuation of Tradition

Adolf Loos (1870–1933) occupies a truly exceptional place in the history of architecture. The articles that he wrote for the Viennese press around the turn of the century won him fame as a critic of culture and essayist. In biting words he mocked everything he regarded as outdated and artificial. His main targets were the architects of the Sezession group, such as Hoffmann and Olbrich, and the practitioners of the applied arts.[7] In language that was remarkable for its ferocity, he attacked the Werkbund, the union of German industrialists and artists that had been set up to improve the quality of industrial products.[8] The backward habits and hypocrisy of the Viennese bourgeoisie were also a frequent target. He crusaded, for instance, for the universal use of bathrooms ("An increase in the use of water is one of our most critical tasks")[9] and argued for the adoption of Anglo-Saxon culture in Austria as an urgent priority.[10]

His architecture did not immediately win him the same recognition as his writings. This was largely because it was fundamentally at variance with the ideals of the modern movement and was therefore incompatible with the historiography of Giedion and Pevsner. The attitude adopted toward him was often ambivalent. He was respected and celebrated as a "pioneer of modern architecture"[11] with repeated reference to "Ornament und Verbrechen"—the only article he wrote that became really famous.[12] His other articles and the buildings that he actually built remained largely unnoticed and undiscussed for a long time. In particular, his invention of the *Raumplan*, the three-dimensional design, met with little response from his contemporaries.

Dwelling, Culture, and Modernity

Loos told a story about a poor rich man. The poor rich man had worked his way up from the lowest rung of the social ladder and now that he had finally become rich he was able to furnish his own house and to choose a famous designer to advise him. He was delighted with the result and moved into his new interior with a sense of perfect well-being. When the architect came to inspect his creation, however, he immediately spotted a number of eyesores and had them banished to the attic. No, those little cushions clashed horribly with the color of the sofa. And what on earth made him think that he could hang those hideous family portraits above the bookcase? Faced with such a torrent of criticism the poor rich man had to yield; every time the architect paid a call, more of his precious possessions disappeared. The man became increasingly wretched. True, his home was perfect now that there was no longer even a detail that needed changing or adding. The only problem was that he could no longer live in it: "He thought, this is what it means to learn to go about life with one's own corpse. Yes indeed. He is finished. He is complete!"[13]

Loos told this story in order to expose the architects of the Sezession. Hermann Bahr's ideal home was a sarcophagus in his eyes, condemning its occupant to passivity and making it impossible for him to alter anything. He would end up like a living corpse, as he could no longer permit himself to have any desires or wishes of his own. Loos argued for a strict separation between architecture and dwelling: architecture was not meant to be a reflection of the personality of its occupant; on the contrary it should be kept separate from dwelling. Its task was to make dwelling possible, not to define it. Dwelling has to do with one's personal history, with memories, and with the proximity of loved ones. Furnishing a house is the expression of this and should also offer its occupants the possibility of putting their personal stamp on it, changing it whenever they choose.

Loos remembered with nostalgia the house that he lived in as a child—a house that had not suffered the encroachments of "stylish" interior furnishings:

> I did not grow up, thank God, in a stylish home. At that time no one knew what it was yet. Now unfortunately, everything is different in my family too. But in those days! Here was the table, a totally crazy and intricate piece of furniture, an extension table with a shocking bit of work as a lock. But it was our table, ours! Can you understand what that means? Do you know what wonderful times we had there? . . . Every piece of furniture, every thing, every object had a story to tell, a family history. The house was never finished; it grew along with us and we grew within it.[14]

Living in a house is a personal matter and has to do with the development of individuals in the context of family life. It cannot be dictated by some interior designer.

To live properly in one's own home, however, one has to separate the interior from the world outside. The difference between public and private, between interior and exterior, must be given a distinct form. This is the work of the architect: "The house should be discreet on the outside; its entire richness should be disclosed on the inside."[15] This duality of inside and outside is achieved by providing a good design for the boundary—that is, for the walls. It is here, according to Loos, in the distinction between inside and outside, that architecture comes into its own. Architects should not impose any uniform "style" on a house; they should not try to impose a single formal idiom on the volumes, facades, layout, and garden design, as, for instance, was done by Josef Hoffmann in the Palais Stoclet (figure 39), which owes its precious quality to its consistent unity of design and to the subtle harmony between the details and the whole. In Loos's view, the important thing was to draw clear distinctions between different areas in the house, and to set up definite boundaries between them. The architectural quality of a building lay in the way that this interplay

Josef Hoffmann, Palais Stoclet,
Brussels, 1905–1911.

(Photo from *Moderne
Bauformen* 13, 1914.)

39

of demarcation and transitions was handled, in the structuring of the different areas,
and in defining their relationship. The filling-in of the different areas was something
to be decided by the occupants of the house and not by the architect.

Loos regarded cladding as the foundation of architecture. One's experience of
a space is primarily determined by the way that ceiling, floor, and walls are clad—in
other words, by the sensuous impact of the materials. An architect begins designing
a space by visualizing it. Only in the second instance is any attention paid to the frame
that will support the cladding. The architectural construction of the whole is therefore of secondary importance. For Loos the crucial requirement of authenticity had
nothing to do with the structure being visible in the architectural design (as the dominant tendency in the modern movement would argue), but rather with the cladding
being clearly visible as cladding. A material should not leave one in doubt as to its
character or function—cladding cannot be substituted for the material that it clads;
plastering should not be disguised as marble, nor should brickwork be treated with
the pretensions of stone. "The law goes like this: we must work in such a way that
a confusion of the material clad with its cladding is impossible."[16] Seen in this light,
authenticity does not mean a strict correspondence between inner and outer; on the
contrary, it consists of the deliberate construction of a mask that is recognizable as a
mask.

Loos went on to apply the principle of cladding at another level. He stated repeatedly that modern human beings need masks: their public images do not coincide

with their actual personalities.[17] This idea was essential to his assessment of modernity. Modernity, in his view, was synonymous with the actuality of tradition. This actuality, however, is very specific, because one can no longer talk of an uninterrupted continuity in the tradition. Economic developments and progress have led to a rupture in the organic relationship that existed between individuals and their culture. The natural development of tradition can therefore no longer continue perfectly smoothly.

For Loos culture meant "that balance of man's inner and outer being which alone guarantees rational thought and action."[18] Modern people, or rather, city dwellers, are rootless—they no longer have any culture. Tradition can no longer be taken for granted. The balance between inner experience and outward forms has been lost. This is why it makes no sense to attempt to create a contemporary "style" as the artists of the Sezession and the Werkbund did. A deliberate creation of this sort does not derive from any existing culture, and it is therefore doomed to remaining superficial and artificial. If there is such a thing as a modern style at all, it will be one that is not deliberately created.[19] The real style of the time, the style that is in harmony with the actual character of the culture of one's own age, does exist, but not where one would expect to find it: "We have the style of our time. We have it in those fields in which the artist, as a member of that association [the Werkbund], has not yet poked his nose."[20]

The distinguishing feature of this style is its lack of ornament. There is a tendency inherent in the evolution of culture toward excluding ornament from everyday household objects. Loos argues that "the evolution of culture is synonymous with the removal of ornament from objects of daily use."[21] Quality and good taste in contemporary household objects by definition means absence of ornament. People who have genuinely assimilated contemporary culture will no longer regard any ornament as acceptable.[22] The continuing production of decorative designs, as in the Sezession and the Werkbund, is a sign of degeneration and pretentiousness.

Since the organic unity that distinguished former cultures has been interrupted by modernity, the only way modern culture can advance, according to Loos, is by acknowledging this state of affairs and accepting that the relation between inner experience and outward forms cannot be perfect; there is a fissure between them. The most cultured person is the one who can adapt to every circumstance and who is capable of responding in an appropriate fashion on all occasions and in every sort of company.[23] This quality is achieved by imposing a deliberate partition or mask between inner and outer. The mask must be designed in such a way that the conventions are respected. Loos summed these requirements up with the word *Anstand* (propriety or decency): "I only require one thing of an architect: that he displays propriety in everything he builds."[24]

A house displays propriety if its appearance is unobtrusive.[25] Theoretically, this means that it must fit in with its surroundings and continue the traditions of the city where it is built. Architects who take their profession seriously will be sensitive to the historical background provided by the old masters, while adapting their manner of building to contemporary requirements. There are enough grounds for change—old crafts have vanished, technological advances make their demands, and functional requirements evolve over time. Tradition is not a sacred cow but a vital principle of development that should be able to adapt naturally to the demands of the industrial epoch.

Tradition, argues Loos, is the essence of architecture, but it should not be confused with superficial aspects of form. Tradition does not mean clinging to the old just because it is old, any more than it means copying themes from folklore or applying a pastoral style in the city. Loos was uncompromising in his condemnation of the practitioners of *Heimatkunst*.[26] Tradition for him had to do with ensuring that culture advances on the road to an increasing distinction and perfection. This was the proper notion of tradition for an architect.

None of this, however, should be applied to the realm of art. Art belongs to another order of things. Art is superior to culture, or rather, artists are ahead of their time. Architecture, therefore, is not an art, for it is concerned above all with decorum, with homeliness and with dwelling:

> The house has to please everyone, contrary to the work of art, which does not. The work of art is a private matter for the artist. The house is not. The work of art is brought into the world without there being a need for it. The house satisfies a requirement. The work of art is responsible to none; the house is responsible to everyone. The work of art wants to draw people out of their state of comfort. The house has to serve comfort. The work of art is revolutionary, the house conservative. The work of art shows people directions and thinks of the future. The house thinks of the present. Man loves everything that satisfies his comfort. He hates everything that wants to draw him out of his acquired and secured position and that disturbs him. Thus he loves the house and hates art. *Does it follow that the house has nothing in common with art and is architecture not to be included among the arts? That is so.* Only a very small part of architecture belongs to art: the tomb and the monument. Everything else that fulfills a function is to be excluded from the domain of art.[27]

Architecture belongs to the domain of culture; art transcends it. It is by this criterion that every form of "applied art" should be judged: applying art to the domain of practical everyday life means both prostituting art and failing to appreciate the practical. To give culture the space it requires, one must first be capable of distinguishing between an urn and a chamber pot, as Karl Kraus argued.[28]

An Architecture of Differences

Adolf Loos's architectural work is further evidence of the need he felt to make distinctions.[29] Separating the different aspects of life, designing contrasts and boundaries—these are the aims of his architecture. It attempts to give a form to the transitions between public and private, between interior and exterior. It regulates the relations between men and women, between hosts and guests, between members of the family and domestic staff. It is an architecture that deploys a very wide range of expression: it is severely geometrical in its treatment of exteriors; sensuous in its use of materials (marble, wood, carpeting); theatrical in the layout of the rooms; classical in some of its detail and references. It is an architecture that cannot be summed up under a single heading, but which always draws on a number of themes simultaneously.

Dal Co states that the work of Loos "never attempts to mediate between the difference of separate parts and situations. It does not hide its multiplicity; at most it will undertake the task of revealing it completely: it traces partitions and boundaries because it sees them as synonymous with the principal characteristic of architectural practice."[30] This range of idioms is indeed a typical feature of Loos's architecture. No matter what the circumstances or the context, the function or the materials, he never hesitates to draw on another repertoire of forms, and to juxtapose different idioms in the same design. The precision with which he does this is something that strikes one in all his buildings. His houses get their very specific character due to the alternation of different atmospheres and to the contrast between light and dark, high and low, small and large, intimate and formal.

And yet this plurality of spatial experiences is unified in a certain sense, since the experiences are brought together by the *Raumplan*, a technique of designing in three dimensions that Loos regarded as his most important contribution to architecture.[31] Designing for Loos involves a complex three-dimensional activity: it is like a jigsaw puzzle with spatial units of different heights that have to be defined first and fitted into a single volume afterward. The best description of it is given by Arnold Schoenberg:

> Whenever I am faced with a building by Loos . . . I see . . . a concept that is immediately three-dimensional, something that maybe only someone else who had the same qualities could grasp. Everything here is worked out, imagined, ordered and designed in space . . . as though all the shapes were transparent; or as though one's mental eye were confronted both with the space in all its details and as a whole at the same time.[32]

The *Raumplan* gives a form here to a theatricality that, as Beatriz Colomina argues, is typical of the architecture of Loos's dwellings: "The house is the stage for the theater of the family, a place where people are born and live and die."[33] This theatrical-

40   Adolf Loos, Moller House,
                                        Vienna, 1928, front facade.
                                        (Photo: Albertina, ALA 2445.)

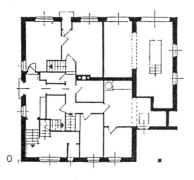

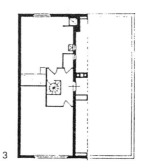

0

1

2

3

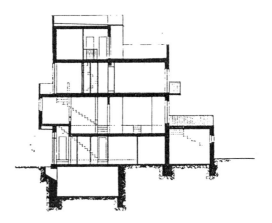

41

Adolf Loos, Moller House,
plans and section.

Adolf Loos, Moller House,
axonometry of the layout of
the interior.

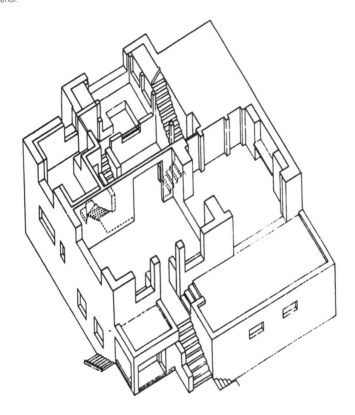

42

ity can be seen in the way Loos creates a choreography of arrivals and departures:
through the frequent shifts in direction that oblige one to pause for a moment, and
through the transition between the dark entrance and the light living area, one gets
a sense of deliberately entering a stage set—the stage of everyday life. In the Moller
house (Vienna, 1928), for instance, the sequence of living areas is built around a central hall (figures 40 and 41). After going through the small entrance, the visitor has to
turn left and mount a flight of six steps to the cloakroom. After the somewhat suffocating feeling of the entrance, this feels like a first breathing space. The route continues: once again one climbs a flight of stairs—this time with a bend in it; only then
does one arrive in the huge hall that comprises the heart of the house. The rooms
with a specific function are grouped around the periphery of this high-ceilinged salon: a "ladies' lounge" (*Damenzimmer*) abutting on the front facade and built a few

steps higher than the level of the hall; the music room, which is at the same level as the hall and which abuts on the rear facade; immediately adjoining it, and four steps higher, the dining room, which also abuts on the rear facade (figure 42).

Each room is characterized by different materials and proportions. The ladies' lounge, which is situated in the bay window above the front door, has light wood paneling, and the fixed benches there are covered with a checked material (figure 43). It is like an alcove and has a wide opening onto the hall. In the music room darker colors prevail and the furnishings are largely peripheral: okumé paneling, a polished ebony floor, and blue material for the fixed benches just inside the garden facade (figure 44). Despite its visual relation with the dining room and the hall, and despite the fact that it can be entered from the garden, the dominant darker colors give this room an introspective character; this impression is reinforced by the slightly protruding ceiling surround that is also clad with okumé, and which contains the indirect lighting. The dining room is a light, open room that leads directly to the terrace (figure 45). The ceiling of this room is bounded by a plastered surround. It is supported by four projecting corner columns; these, like the skirting boards, are clad with travertine. The fitted cupboards and the rest of the walls also are clad with the same okumé plyboard material as in the music room; above the sideboards there are mirrors. The din-

Adolf Loos, Moller House,
ladies' lounge.
(Photo: Albertina, ALA 2455.)

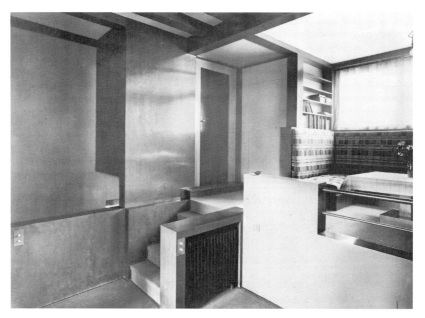

43

ing room is dominated by the dining table and the Thonet chairs in the middle. Both the dining room and the music room are linked to the garden. The only enclosed rooms on the main floor are the library (*Herrenzimmer*) and the kitchen. An open staircase leads from the hall to the bedroom level.

The spatial layout brings about a definitely theatrical effect. The route into the house consists of a sequence of spaces and directions that, as it were, physically prepare one for the arrival in the hall (figure 46). On two occasions visitors are exposed to the controlling view from the ladies' lounge: first as one approaches the front door; secondly as one climbs the steps. The ladies' lounge also overlooks the garden via the hall and the music room. All this gives it a privileged position—something that is reinforced by its wide horizontal window and the baylike projection in the front facade.

This street front has a severe symmetrical structure and its closed character gives the house the look of an isolated object (figure 40). The projection containing the lounge juts out at a low level above the front door giving the front facade a somewhat unbalanced, almost threatening appearance. The rear of the house, however, with its interplay of terraces and flights of steps, and larger windows, has a clear

Adolf Loos, Moller House,
music room seen from the
dining room.
(Photo: Albertina, ALA 2457.)

Adolf Loos, Moller House,
dining room seen from the music
room.
(Photo: Albertina, ALA 2454.)

45

Adolf Loos, Moller House,
stairs from the cloakroom
to the central hall.
(Photo: Albertina, ALA 2456.)

47

relation with the garden. The dominant feeling here is of a welcoming openness (figure 47).

Beatriz Colomina observes that with Loos, windows are not normally designed to be looked out of.[34] They function in the first instance as a source of light; what is more, they are often opaque or are situated above eye level. Moreover, Loos likes placing benches or divans under the windows, something that makes for ideal nooks for sitting and reading in, but where one really has to turn one's head to take a look outside. All this means that the interior is experienced as a secluded and intimate area. Nowhere does the space outside penetrate the house. While partition walls are often absent in the interior, replaced by large openings between two spaces, every transition to the outside is very clearly defined as a door and not as an opening in the wall. The transition between inside and outside is often modified by a flight of steps, a terrace, or a verandah.

The contrasts that give this house its character are fundamental to one's spatial experience of it. In the interior there is the contrast between the small oppressive entrance and the high-ceilinged, airy hall from which one gets a view of the whole main floor. There is also a sharp contrast between the small, informal ladies' lounge from where one can look out over the whole house, the formal inward-looking music room, and the light, open dining room with its clear relation with the garden. The exterior is distinguished by the explicit contrast between the front facade with its almost threatening character that seems to deny the visitor access, and the garden facade which is much more friendly, welcoming one in. The design serves to stress the split between the public realm of the world "outside" as represented by the street and the private "outdoor" domain of the garden.

The most striking thing in Loos's houses is the unique way that the experience of domesticity and bourgeois comfort is combined with disruptive effects. The different rooms that contrast so sharply with each other are linked together and kept in balance by the sheer force of the *Raumplan*; one does, however, constantly encounter influences that make for disunity. For instance, Loos makes a good deal of use of mirrors, particularly because they give one a sense of increased space. Their reflections in unexpected places are unsettling and disorienting. Sometimes mirrors or reflecting surfaces are combined with windows, serving to undermine the role of the walls, because their unambiguous function as partitions between indoors and outdoors is threatened.[35] There is a distinct interplay between the openness of the *Raumplan* that coordinates all the rooms and the completely individual spatial definition that distinguishes each room separately, due to the materials used and details such as ceiling surrounds, floor patterns, and wall coverings.[36] This, too, makes for an ambiguous experience of space; on the one hand one feels these are well-defined spaces, with clear protective boundaries, but on the other hand one is aware it is quite possible that one is under the gaze of an unseen person elsewhere in the house. The sense of comfort is not unqualified, but is upset at regular intervals by disruptive effects.

It was the same sort of ambiguity, combining straightforward aspects with others that are dissonant, that was responsible for the controversy around the Loos house in the Michaelerplatz (Vienna, 1909–1911) (figure 48). The lower part of this building was reserved for a firm of tailors, Goldman & Salatsch, who commissioned the project. The complex spatial structure of this part contains rooms with varying ceiling heights that relate to each other in different ways (figure 49). The 4-meter-high main room was entered directly from the street. A staircase that split in two at the landing took one to the mezzanine that served as the accounts office. From there several steps down led to the storage room while a few steps up led to the reception rooms and the fitting rooms just inside the front facade behind the English-style bow windows. The height of the ceiling in this "mezzanine gallery" was 2.6 meters; there was also an ironing room (4.8 meters high) and the sewing room, where the height was only 2 meters because the dressmakers sat at their work.

The *Raumplan* comes into its own in the treatment of the lower part of the facades. The main facade that looks out on the Michaelerplatz contains four nonstructural Tuscan columns in front of the entrance porch. A metal profile that is much too small by classical standards is placed on these marble monolithic columns. These extend upward with rectangular marble blocks that in turn link up with a modestly molded cornice. While the spaces between the Tuscan columns are left empty, the

48

Adolf Loos, house on the
Michaelerplatz, Vienna,
1909–1911.
(Photo: Albertina, ALA 2408.)

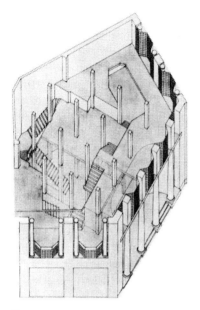

Adolf Loos, house on the
Michaelerplatz, axonometric
view of the *Raumplan* interior
of the tailor shop.

(From Hermann Czech
and Wolfgang Mistelbauer,
Das Looshaus [Vienna: Löcker
& Wögenstein, 1976], p. 107.)

49

equivalent spaces between the rectangular column blocks are occupied by the bow windows of the mezzanine gallery. The relation between the length of the columns and the rectangular blocks is roughly 3 to 1. With the side facades, on the contrary, the lower part of the facades are split up in a 2:2 ratio. At the same height as the metal profile in the main facade, however, there is an equally wide horizontal strip, splitting the bow windows in two; this has the effect of ensuring a certain continuity between the different facades. The large columns of the main facade are repeated on a smaller scale on either side of the bow windows on the side facades.

Over this commercial part of the complex there are offices and living accommodations that are reached via an entrance in the left-hand side facade. The dwelling area does not require any elaborate display and is a model of discretion, with its unpretentious windows in a bare whitewashed wall—something that Loos's contemporaries regarded as "nihilistic." The building's commercial functions, on the contrary, are intended to attract plenty of attention, and here the whole gamut of means that Loos regarded as the authentic repertoire of the modern architect was deployed: lavish-looking materials, large glass window panes, classical quotations, and an emphatic rhythm punctuated by unexpected dissonances. The marble columns do not support anything, but they serve to give form to the porch that in turn links the building up with the square, enriching the public domain. The Tuscan column is the simplest order in the classical repertoire. Rather than inventing a new form, Loos therefore exploits an already existing element in a new way. At the height

Adolf Loos, house on the Michaelerplatz, view of the Loos house together with the neighboring Herberstein palace.

50

Adolf Loos, house on the Michaelerplatz, view of a detail of the Loos house together with the Hofburg at the other side of the Michaelerplatz.

51

Adolf Loos, house on the Michaelerplatz, view of a detail of the Loos house together with the Michaelerkirche.

52

of the mezzanine the interior fills up the empty space above the porch: the top of the columns is indicated by a simple metal girder with the bow windows of the mezzanine above it between rectangular column blocks. In this way a transition is achieved from the columns with the spaces between them to the wall above that is completely filled in. The cornice marks the boundary between the lower and upper parts of the facade. The Tuscan columns are repeated on a smaller scale in the side facades, just as the iron girder is echoed in the wide horizontal strip in the bow windows on the side facades.

The rough ratios that determine the rhythm of the facade are partially dictated by the ratios of the other premises on the Michaelerplatz—the Herberstein palace, the Hofburg, and the Michaelerkirche (figures 50, 51, and 52). The contrast between the ratios of the lower part of the front facade (3:1) and that of the side facades (2:2) emphasizes their difference in importance. The use of materials in this commercial part is very rich: the columns are monoliths made of green veined Cipollino marble and the rest of the shop front is clad with the same material.

Loos's own comment on this design remains the best account of his intentions:

> In order to separate the commercial and living sections of the house on the Michaelerplatz, the design of the facade was differentiated. I meant to make use of the two main pillars and the smaller supports to accentuate the rhythm, without which there can be no architecture. The fact that the axes are not congruent emphasizes this split. To avoid the building becoming exaggeratedly monumental and also to stress that the occupant is a tailor by profession, albeit a leading one, I designed the windows as "English" bow-windows. The division of the windows into small elements was intended to guarantee the intimacy of the interior.[37]

What is emphasized is the way that architecture can design contrasts, the way that it distinguishes between different realms of life. Authenticity of expression has to do with the degree to which it succeeds in making these distinctions operative. This is accompanied by dissonances and nihilistic aspects, but it is precisely here that this architecture is true to life; rather than deceiving people with an illusory harmony, Loos chose a ruthless design that does not gloss over any discontinuities and moments of fissure but highlights them.

Discontinuous Continuity

The relationship with tradition is Loos's central theme, both in his writings and in his architectural work. He does not treat modernity as a new beginning, as a completely unique period that deliberately breaks with tradition. On the contrary, he sees modernity as a very specific continuation of the tradition. His ideas are not avant-garde in character: one does not find any rejection of the existing order in his work, any call for a tabula rasa or repudiation of our cultural inheritance. His attitude is programmatic in that he claimed to be the advocate of a correct notion of modernity as against the majority of his contemporaries, whom he saw as hypocrites and builders of cloud castles.

The continuity that he defended, however, bears the traces of fissures and discontinuities that were evidence that a cultural evolution was taking place. Modern culture in his view should be based on the realization that it is no longer a priori possible to guarantee any harmony between inner and outer: there is no such thing as a seamless link, or any automatic relationship of unbroken harmony between different moments of life. The self-evidence with which farmers used to cultivate their land in the mountains is not available to the modern city dweller, who has become uprooted and thus can no longer lay claim to his own culture without question. This is why it becomes necessary to draw up a program that makes it possible to react in an adequate fashion to this loss of self-evidence. Loos's program is based on the need for a mask. Modern human beings function in a complex society with a variety of social settings and possibilities; they are therefore obliged to resort to a cover that permits them to separate their own personality from the outward forms that it adopts. Only in this way can one respond to all these disparate demands without continually being obliged to expose one's whole personality. This "cover" for the personality consists in the first instance of the clothes one wears and in the second place of the architecture of one's dwelling.

The home must be shielded from the outside world. The surroundings of the metropolis, with the demands it makes in terms of social status, speed, and efficiency, goes counter to an idea of dwelling that is based on familiarity, intimacy, and personal history. A distinction has to be made between the world outside—the public world of money, and of all that is equivalent—and the indoor world, which is the private world of everything that is inalienable and nonequivalent.[38] Dwelling can only happen if it is insulated from the metropolis, not in relation to it. Anonymity and concealment are essential conditions if dwelling is to survive within the modern world— this is the implication of an analysis of Loos's houses.

It is clear that Loos is aware of a certain incompatibility between modernity and dwelling. Modernity does not allow for a dwelling that coincides with the totality of life. Dwelling no longer pervades every moment of life. It is obliged to retreat into a realm of its own that gives it protection from the demands of the public domain and the destructive forces of rootlessness and artificiality. Dwelling has to be entrusted to the interior: only there do the conditions exist for an unquestioning garnering of memories; only there can one's personal history take on form. Only through this retreating movement can dwelling realize itself and achieve authenticity.

This strategy provides an effective counterweight to the pernicious results of the loss of self-evidence that can be observed, for instance, in the choice of stylish interiors that are decorated by professionals. In such interiors dwelling is not experienced on the basis of personal memories and lived experiences; instead it freezes in an artificial outward show that has nothing to do with the individuality of the occupants. Loos uses the term "blasphemous" to denounce this stylish freeze. Imagine a domestic scene, he says, in which a young girl has just committed suicide and lies stretched out on the floor. If this floor is part of a van de Velde interior, then we are not dealing just with a tastefully furnished room, but with a "blasphemy of the dead."[39] Blasphemy occurs when dwelling is overwhelmed by "style" and "art." Style undermines dwelling, robbing it of its individuality. Art, moreover, has much too high a calling to become involved in the design of something that should be as self-evident as a house.

Loos's call for a radical repudiation of ornament is the corollary of this criticism. The absence of ornaments—the rejection of the deliberate creation of a new "style"—was in his opinion a correct response to the diagnosis of life as being rootless and fragmented. Ornament is that which people use to attempt to relate different aspects of life and to join inner and outer worlds in a coherent whole. By getting rid of ornament the illusion is destroyed that a harmonious unity of this sort is still possible. One can only remain true to tradition if one acknowledges that its continuity is not an unbroken one. Dwelling can only be saved by separating it from other aspects of life.

Loos's concept of modernity is therefore radically antipastoral. He does not conjure up any vision of a future in which all the different realms of life would merge in a harmonious unity. The belief in a single ideal uniting industrialists, artists, and craftsmen is completely foreign to him. In his view, the representatives of these different categories have different roles to fulfill on the stage of world history. He draws a clear dividing line between art and culture, between private and public, between dwelling and architecture. This division, he argues, is fundamental to the modern condition.

Walter Benjamin: The Dream of a Classless Society

In 1969, the year of his own death, Adorno wrote a final comment on the life and work of his friend Walter Benjamin.[40] The title of this text, "A l'écart de tous les courants," puts a finger on a major aspect of Benjamin's thought—the fact that it cannot be fitted into any specific philosophical or literary trend. Influenced by divergent currents of thought such as neo-Kantianism, the Jewish Kabbala, and dialectical materialism, Benjamin's philosophy preserves a curious individuality, precisely because it is permeated by different modes of thought.

Born in Berlin in 1892, the son of a Jewish businessman, Walter Benjamin studied philosophy, psychology, and German literature at various universities. In 1925 his *Habilitationsschrift* was rejected by the university of Frankfurt[41] and he resolved to earn his living as a freelance writer. After the Nazis came to power he went into exile and from then on his situation was extremely precarious. A minimal grant from the Institut für Sozialforschung[42] enabled him to live in Paris and work, until the war forced him to leave that city too. On the night of September 26, 1940, on his way to Spain—his plan was to go via Spain to New York and report to the Institute there—he committed suicide.

The work he left behind consisted of three books and a large quantity of essays, short and long. The *Passagenwerk* that would have been his masterpiece and on which he had worked during the last thirteen years of his life remained unfinished. Today Benjamin is acknowledged as one of the most important philosophers of modernity, even though recognition in his case came somewhat belatedly. The first edition of Benjamin's *Schriften*, edited by Theodor and Gretel Adorno, did not appear until 1955, and it was only in the sixties that his work finally became known in wider circles. Benjamin was a genuine cult figure for a while at the time of the student revolt of 1968. He was seen as a radical theoretician to whom one could refer in order to develop a materialistic theory about the relation between intellectual work and political engagement. The interpretation of his work that was fashionable at the time was based mainly on some of his most programmatic writings. These belong to a specific genre of Marxism; only occasionally do they give one an inkling of the theological-metaphysical mode of thought that was just as typical an aspect of Benjamin's philosophy.[43]

Gradually, as more of his work was published—a process only completed in 1989—the reception of his work became less lopsided. Within the large body of secondary literature,[44] the ambivalence that would seem to be a hallmark of his work has become a recurring theme. His writings are said to attest on the one hand to an insuperable melancholy and grief about what has been lost, and, on the other, to a radical and utopian belief in the power of the avant-garde that has paved the way for the realization of a genuinely humane society. A number of recent commentaries, however, have attempted to identify a certain coherence behind the variety, internal contradictions, and fragmented character of Benjamin's oeuvre and to define his ambivalence in terms of an underlying consistency or even of a system.[45] This would have to do with a number of philosophical intuitions that permeate his work even though they are not systematically stated in any explicit fashion. At issue here are some very specific—not to mention uncommon—notions about language, world, and history that do not belong to the standard categories of Western philosophy. They depend on a curious mixture of Jewish and materialistic concepts, combined with a theory of experience and an openness to revolutionary impulses in mass culture. In combination, these contradictory principles lead to a unique and multifaceted oeuvre.

In architectural theory there has been a fairly intensive, if somewhat ponderous, assimilation of Benjamin's concepts.[46] Attention has been paid in particular to his interpretation of modern architecture. Benjamin was convinced that this architecture of steel and glass fulfills the promises that are inherent in modern civilization, because it is an authentic expression of the "poverty" that is typical of this civilization, thus foreshadowing the realization of a transparent and classless society. It is in his vision of architecture that we find the quintessence of his ambivalent attitude toward modernity. For a proper understanding of his ideas on this subject it is first necessary, however, to look at his linguistic philosophy that underlies both his theory of experience and his views on the theory of history.

Mimesis and Experience

Benjamin's notions about language differ fundamentally from the ideas that are generally current in semiotics.[47] In his opinion language is not based solely on the conventional relationship between signifier and signified. In addition to this communicative dimension of language, which he calls "semiotic," he distinguishes a second, "mimetic" dimension that he sees as the origin of language. This mimetic level of language is less easy to locate than the semiotic one. The best way of describing it is as an extrapolation of the onomatopoeic character of language: just as words such as "cuckoo" and "tick-tock" resemble the thing that they denote, from a broader perspective language as a whole can be seen as a sort of imitation (mimesis) of the world.

Language as we know and use it, according to Benjamin, is a pale reflection of an original language that named things on the basis of similarities. The essence of this original language—and therefore of every language—is the name. This is the object of a mimesis, and is therefore linked by a relationship of similarity to the thing or person that bears this name. This mimetic structure, however, is no longer immediately recognizable and present in current language: it is no longer expressed in every individual word. Benjamin maintains nevertheless that, no matter how much it has been diluted and diminished, the mimetic structure continues to determine what language is. Not only can it be found between the spoken word and its meaning; it is also present between the written word and its meaning, and between the written word and the spoken. We become aware of this in the act of reading. Reading is more than just stringing together simple verbal meanings. In the act of reading a sort of abstract correspondence—Benjamin uses the term "unsinnliche Ähnlichkeit"[48]— can be observed in the similarity between text and reality that is "illuminated" at the moment one understands it. This nonsensuous similarity is embodied in the constellations that words form in combination with each other: just as the constellations of stars in the cosmos are interpreted by astrologers who can use them to make predictions, so words with their mutual relations and interplay create a correspondence with reality. Or, as Cyrille Offermans puts it:

> For Walter Benjamin, as for Adorno, a text is a sort of force-field: an exchange of semantic energy occurs in the words. A conscious use of language ... amounts to creating such a force-field.... The more

consciously a text is constructed, and the more motivated the words, the less arbitrary the words become, and their abstract and haphazard relation to things declines. The experience of things becomes tangible as it were in the text, although no separate word can be held responsible by itself for this presence.[49]

Human beings' faculty for mimesis, as Benjamin understands it, has two aspects: in its original sense it has to do with one's faculty for comparing or identifying oneself with something else, as a child at play will identify with a baker or a footballer, or with a train or a donkey; in a weaker derivative form it can be seen in our faculty for discovering correspondences and similarities between things that are apparently different. Genuine "experience," in the sense that Benjamin gives the term, should be seen as a mimetic gesture because "similarity is the organon of experience."[50]

This concept is crucial to Benjamin's theory of experience, in which he distinguishes between the two German words for experience, *Erlebnis* and *Erfahrung*. *Erfahrung* means life experience; it refers to an integrated stock of experience wherein the individual assimilates sensations, information, and events. The ability to establish such a stock of experience owes much to the existence of a tradition. In that sense experience can be said to be collective and unconscious. *Erfahrung* has to do with the ability to perceive correspondences and similarities and to act them out. *Erlebnis*, on the other hand, refers to sensations that are reduced to a series of atomized, disconnected moments that are not related to each other in any way and that are not integrated in life experience.[51]

These ideas play a role throughout Benjamin's work, but it is in his study on Baudelaire, which was a byproduct of his labors on the *Passagenwerk*, that he explores them in detail. Benjamin begins his argument by stating that the "structure of experience" has undergone a change: in the "standardized, denatured life of the civilized masses" in "the inhospitable blinding age of big-scale industrialism," true experience has become a rarity. For experience (*Erfahrung*) is "a matter of tradition, in collective existence as well as private life. It is less the product of facts firmly anchored in memory than of a convergence in memory of accumulated and frequently unconscious data."[52]

Whereas *Erfahrung* has to do with a gradual initiation into tradition, *Erlebnis* refers to superficial sensations. These are intercepted by an alert consciousness and responded to straightaway: there is an immediate response and the impression is more or less saved in conscious memory (*Erinnerung*); it leaves no trace, however, in the (unconscious) remembrance (*Gedächtnis*). Impressions that form part of remembrance, on the contrary, are the material from which *Erfahrung* is built. They are repetitive in character and often consist of impressions with a sensory content;[53] in the long run they have far more impact on the individual's experience than do the momentary and superficial impressions resulting from *Erlebnis*.

The hallmark of modernity is the decay of the subject's mimetic faculty and, with it, of the influence of tradition and of the significance of experience. The conditions of everyday life are increasingly unfavorable to the gaining of life experience. Newspapers, for example, present their information in such a way that their readers are obviously not intended to integrate it in their own experience. In fact, according to Benjamin, the opposite is the case: the whole aim of "news" is to keep current events from the realm where they might affect the experience of the reader. Processing information, therefore, is in a sense the opposite of acquiring experience; journalistic coverage has nothing to do with creating a tradition. City life with its rapid tempo and abundance of stimuli is the product of this development: the ephemeral, the sensational, everything that is continually changing is part of the order of *Erlebnis*; *Erfahrung*, on the other hand, is based on repetition and continuity.[54]

In his famous work of art essay, Benjamin describes this process of the atrophy of experience in terms of the withering away of the "aura" of the work. The status of the work undergoes a fundamental change as a result of the technical possibilities of reproduction by means of new audio-visual technologies (photography, film, tape recorders). What gets lost in reproduction is the uniqueness and the authenticity of the work of art—its unique existence in the here and now, the material substratum in which its history was acted out. Benjamin sums up this uniqueness and authenticity in the term *aura:*

> That which withers in the age of mechanical reproduction is the aura of the work of art. This is a symptomatic process whose significance points beyond the realm of art. One might generalize by saying: the technique of reproduction detaches the reproduced object from the domain of tradition. By making many copies it substitutes a plurality of copies for a unique existence.[55]

This withering of the aura is, in Benjamin's view, a socially determined event. It relates to the need of the masses to "get closer to things." The aura, however, consists of the "unique phenomenon of a distance, however close it may be."[56] It is this distance that is destroyed by the techniques of reproduction.

The process described here—that of the (reproduced) work of art becoming a commodity—is analogous to what Benjamin elsewhere calls "the atrophy of experience." In this essay he adopts a fairly optimistic attitude toward this phenomenon. He argues that the new mode of perception that results from the universal availability of reproduction techniques has a considerable potential for emancipation, bringing about a change in the attitude of the masses toward art from one that is retrograde to a progressive one. The experiencing of a reproduced work of art, such as a film, is no longer characterized by concentration and isolation, but by collectivity and distraction. As a result, what is involved is no longer an individual becoming immersed in a work of art as is the case, say, when one looks at a painting—it is rather the work of art itself that is immersed in the masses.

In Benjamin's view, then, modernity is characterized by a drastic change in the structure of experience. In some of his writings in which mourning and a deep sense of melancholy are the predominant feeling, he seems to regret this development.[57] In other writings, however, his tone is much less pessimistic. In these, the decay of experience is treated much more as a unique opportunity for humanity to begin all over again after the destruction of the false legacy of bourgeois culture. Benjamin's attitude seems to oscillate constantly between an approving tone and one that is mournful. His thesis about the decline of experience does not imply an exclusively negative diagnosis of modernity.

Particularly relevant in this connection is his essay "Erfahrung und Armut," written in 1933; this essay contains perhaps the most radical and intriguing formulation of Benjamin's liquidationist stance. In it he argues that the poverty of experience that he sees around him should be seized on as a new opportunity for humanity to make a completely fresh start. It brings a new barbarism into being, entailing a victory over a culture that can no longer be called human. That is what the most lucid avant-garde artists, such as Brecht, Loos, Klee, and Scheerbart understand. They wage a struggle against the traditional humanistic notion that prettifies humanity by dressing it up with elements of the past. Instead they turn toward their own naked contemporary, who is crying like an infant lying naked in the dirty diapers of the time. Their work is characterized by a "total disillusionment about the age and nevertheless an unreserved profession of loyalty to it."[58]

To Brush History against the Grain

The last text that Benjamin completed before his suicide in 1940 is entitled "Über den Begriff der Geschichte" (On the Concept of History). In the form of eighteen theses, this text contains in condensed form Benjamin's unorthodox ideas about history. In this essay he rejects the notion that history should be interpreted as the narrative of the progress of humanity against the backdrop of an empty, homogeneous time. In a famous passage, he unmasks the notion of progress as an illusion:

> A Klee painting named "Angelus Novus" [figure 53] shows an angel looking as though he is about to move away from something he is fixedly contemplating. His eyes are staring, his mouth is open, his wings are spread. This is how one pictures the angel of history. His face is turned toward the past. Where we perceive a chain of events, he sees one single catastrophe which keeps piling wreckage upon wreckage and hurls it in front of his feet. The angel would like to stay, awaken the dead and make whole what has been smashed. But a storm is blowing

Paul Klee, *Angelus Novus*, 1920.
(The Israel Museum, Jerusalem.)

53

from Paradise; it has got caught in his wings with such violence that the angel can no longer close them. This storm irresistibly propels him into the future to which his back is turned, while the pile of debris before him grows skyward. This storm is what we call progress.[59]

History is not the story of the advance of humanity but one of a heaping up of wreckage and debris. History consists of blood and suffering, and there is no such thing as a document of culture that is not at the same time a document of barbarism. Our cultural tradition is produced in a social setup that is rooted in exploitation and repression. One should never forget this when analyzing the past. The task of the historical materialist, therefore, is not to write history from the point of view of the victors (which is what is usually done) but from that of the victims. It is his task "to brush history against the grain."[60]

The past and the suffering of the past call for redemption. The present has a duty toward the past. This is because the different epochs do not relate to each other in a purely chronological order. There are, as it were, underground links that relate certain ages to each other. The French Revolution, for instance, experienced itself as a reincarnation of ancient Rome. Between different historical moments there is a relationship of correspondences and responsibility; but this is in fact an understatement—according to Benjamin, each specific moment of history contains *everything*, both the entire past and the virtual realization of the utopian final goal of history. It is the task of the historical materialist to make that plain. It is his task to freeze time with a constructive gesture, illuminating the subject of his research as a monad in which the potential for "blowing up" the historical continuum is already contained:

> Where thinking suddenly stops in a configuration pregnant with tensions, it gives that configuration a shock, by which it crystallizes into a monad. A historical materialist approaches a historical subject only where he encounters it as a monad. In this structure he recognizes the sign of a Messianic cessation of happening, or, put differently, a revolutionary chance in the fight for the oppressed past. He takes cognizance of it in order to blast a specific era out of the homogeneous course of history.[61]

In theory, then, the possibility of realizing the utopian final goal is implicit in every particular historical moment. Revolutionary classes are aware of this: it is their task to seize the opportunity of blowing up the historical continuum and making the leap forward into a new age. In this sense they are like the Jews for whom "every second of time was the strait gate through which the Messiah might enter."[62]

The theses on the theory of history constitute one of the few texts of Benjamin in which there is a deliberate interweaving of the theological-metaphysical mode of thought that formed such a powerful presence in his earlier work, with the explicit commitment as a historical materialist that colors much of his work during the thirties. This essay is clear proof that these two completely different approaches do not form successive phases in Benjamin's work, but are strata that simultaneously overlap and influence each other. Benjamin never cared to submit to the contradictions that, according to orthodox thinking, exist between historical materialism and a theological-metaphysical concept of the world. According to him, historical materialism is obliged to exploit theological thought if it is to achieve a genuine understanding of the past and the future. It is not surprising that Benjamin's version of historical materialism was as unorthodox for "real" Marxists as his messianism was for Jewish theologians.

And yet messianism remains a crucial element in the structure of his thought. Lieven de Cauter puts forward a convincing argument for the idea that Benjamin's entire oeuvre can be seen as consistent and comprehensible once we appreciate the fact that the notion of a messianic order underlies everything he wrote.[63] Implicit in this idea is that history should not be seen as a chronology of successive periods existing in a time that is empty and homogeneous, but as a triadic process consisting of an original paradisiac state, a period of decline (the fall) as the prevailing condition, and a utopian goal (redemption) as the supreme climax. The essential thing is that these three moments are not so much stages in a development as layers of meaning to be exposed by the historical materialist who is inspired by theology. Every historical moment contains all three moments in essence: the origins, however faint they may have become, can still be seen through all the evidence of the fall, just as redemption is also virtually present as a sort of messianic splinter.

Once we realize that this triadic figure of paradise, fall, and redemption constitutes the underlying structure of Benjamin's work, the ambivalence that characterizes his theory of experience and his diagnosis of modernity becomes more comprehensible. He describes what happens to experience as a process of decline: a falling off from a paradisiac state in which human language was synonymous with an Adamic naming of names and in which a mimetic attitude toward the world reigned unimpaired. In this process of decline, however, the germ of a possible reversal is contained. One can describe this fall from the point of view of mourning, of a melancholy for what has been lost and a concern to save as much as possible, even if only to preserve it through recollection. One can also—and this is the path he follows in his more radical texts—describe the fallen state in terms of its inherent potential for reversal (*Umschlag*), as a state, in other words, whose revolutionary possibilities should be recognized and exploited.

Architecture or the Physiognomy of an Era

It is in its architecture that the true reality of an era achieves its clearest expression: according to the *Passagenwerk*, architecture is the most important testimony to the latent "mythology" of a society.[64] Benjamin's aim is to read the character of the nineteenth century in the physiognomy of its architecture: by analyzing the "surface" of this culture—its fashions and its buildings—he hopes to identify its deeper, more fundamental characteristics.

This endeavor is crucial to his work. Benjamin sees the Parisian shopping arcades as the major architectural achievement of the nineteenth century. In these covered streets with their typical Parisian names—Passage du Pont-Neuf, Passage de l'Opéra, Passage Vivienne, Galerie Véro-Dodat (figures 54 and 55), Passage des Panoramas (figures 56 and 57), Passage Choiseul—an inexhaustible source of metaphors, analogies, and dream figures can be found that are at the same time grafted onto the tangible reality of an urban, metropolitan form. The *Passagenwerk* can be read, then, as an encyclopedic display of the historical potential that lies dormant in the word *Passage*, or arcade: Benjamin projects endless ramifications of meaning, associations, and connotations onto the object of his study.[65] He sees the arcade as a dialectical image—it is a momentary flash in which a number of fundamental aspects of history, of past, present and future, are synthesized in an extremely condensed form. Similar to a monad, it reflects the entire reality of the nineteenth century.

The arcades owed their existence to the rise of retail trade, particularly the trade in luxury articles, and also to new construction technologies: above all that of iron and glass architecture. This combination of developments gave rise to a new, typically nineteenth-century, urban form: the arcades form a transition zone between the "outdoor world" of the street and the interior space of the home. They really constitute an "inside" without an "outside": their form is only revealed from the inside; they do not have any exterior, or at least none that we can easily visualize. In this sense, according to Benjamin, they resemble our dreams:[66] one can know an arcade from its inside, but its exterior shape is unknown and even irrelevant to those who are inside.

The transparency of glass roofs is what gives the arcades their particular quality. It is this that makes the *Durchdringung* of inside and outside possible, giving them their character of a transitional zone between street and home. The glass roofs made the arcades a superb space for the *flâneur,* the aimless city stroller: if the street constitutes a sort of "living space" for the masses and for the *flâneur* who dwells in the midst of the masses, this metaphoric projection is achieved spatially in the arcade:

Galerie Véro-Dodat, Paris,
1823–1826.

(Photo: Annemie Philippe.)

54

Galerie Véro-Dodat.

(Photo: Annemie Philippe.)

55

56

Passage des Panoramas,
Paris, 1800.

(Photo: Annemie Philippe.)

57

Passage des Panoramas.

(Photo: Annemie Philippe.)

Streets are houses of the collective. The collective is an ever-vigilant, mobile being, that experiences, learns, and creates as much between the rows of houses as individuals do within the shelter of their four walls. This collective prefers the glossy enameled company signs to the oil paintings that decorate the walls of the middle-class salons. Walls with "Défense d'afficher" are its sleeping accommodation and the café pavements the bow window from which it observes its household. Its hall is where the road workers hang their coats on the fence and the exit leading to the dark back gardens is the corridor, the entrance to the room of the city. And the salon of the city is . . . the arcade. More than in any other place the street reveals itself here as the furnished and run-down interior of the masses.[67]

Even more suggestive than the arcades was the nineteenth-century iron and glass architecture of the huge halls where the great exhibitions were held. In both cases Benjamin sees a glorification of the phantasmagoria of the commodity: it is here that the urban masses revel in gazing at "nouveautés," it is here that the cult of commodities began. These huge exhibition palaces were "sites of pilgrimages to the commodity fetish";[68] "there is a rampant growth of the dubious flora 'commodity.'"[69] The commodity is enfolded in an almost fairyland aureole produced by the brilliant light during the day and by the flickering gaslight at night. They actually create an illusion, the "phantasmagoria of capitalist culture," that "reaches its most brilliant display in the World Exhibition of 1867."[70]

But this is not all. Benjamin treats the iron and glass architecture as a dream image in which contradictory aspects often play a role. This dream image shows the triadic structure of a messianic figure. Inherent in it is a fraudulent aspect—the glorification of the commodity fetish; at the same time it has a utopian aspect in that it provides an image of the classless society: "In the dream in which, before the eyes of each epoch, that which is to follow appears in images, the latter appears wedded to elements of prehistory, that is, of a classless society."[71] In Benjamin's view, the dreamlike character that is so typical of the architecture of the arcades and exhibition halls makes way in the twentieth century for a more sober reality.[72] A new architecture flowers in the twentieth century; with its qualities of transparency and spatial interpenetration, it anticipates the new (classless) society, the features of which are a clarity and openness that is much more pervasive than that of the preceding age.

Rolf Tiedemann sees this movement of awakening as a crucial point in the original aim of the *Passagenwerk*: Benjamin's aim was, by defining nineteenth-century cultural phenomena as "dream figures," to effect the awakening from the collective "sleep" of capitalism.[73] In his view this process of awakening has already partially taken place in the architecture of his time: in the architecture of the New Building and that of Loos, Mendelsohn, and Le Corbusier, he discerns a new concept of space containing qualities that correspond to the transparency of a classless society. This assessment of modern architecture is closely linked to his call for a new bar-barism, for a new start for humanity that has suffered so severely from the storms of modernity.

In the work of art essay, Benjamin states that architecture can be seen as the prototype for the new mode of reception of the work. Buildings are the object of a collective and distracted attention: the perception of architecture is tactile (through the use of buildings) rather than optical. This mode of perception is in keeping with the new conditions of life imposed by industrial civilization. The individual learns to adapt to these through a sort of absent-minded attention rather than through con-templation and close study: "The automobile driver, who in his thoughts is some-where else (for instance, with his car that has perhaps broken down), will adjust to the modern form of the garage much more quickly than the art historian, who takes a lot of trouble trying to analyze it stylistically."[74]

Benjamin ascribes a "canonical value" to this mode of reception: "For the tasks which face the human apparatus of perception at the turning points of history cannot be solved by optical means, that is, by contemplation alone. They are mas-tered gradually by habit, under the guidance of tactile appropriation."[75] Architecture functioned for him as the prototype of tactile reception, because it has to do with dwelling and therefore also with habits and habituation.

Benjamin understands dwelling as an active form of dealing with the reality that surrounds us, in which the individual and his surroundings adjust to each other. He refers to the grammatical connection in German between *wohnen* (dwelling) and *gewohnt* (customary, habitual), a connection that is found in English between "habit" and "inhabit." This connection, he says, gives a clue to the understanding of dwelling as a sort of hurried contemporaneity that involves the constant shaping and reshap-ing of a casing. This passage must be stated in the original German: "Wohnen als Transitivum—im Begriff des 'gewohnten Lebens' z.B.—gibt eine Vorstellung von der hastigen Aktualität, die in diesem Verhalten verborgen ist. Es besteht darin, ein Gehäuse uns zu prägen."[76]

It is because architecture responds to this "hurried contemporaneity" that it can serve as a model for what can be called a "politicizing of art," which, Benjamin argues in his work of art essay, is the only possible answer to the "aestheticizing of politics" as practiced by fascism.

Dwelling, Transparency, Exteriority

Benjamin's call in "Erfahrung und Armut" for a new barbarism should be seen in the light of his rejection of a superficial humanist approach—something against which he had been storing up ammunition for a long time. Opening moves for this intellec-tual strategy can already be seen in his *Ursprung des deutschen Trauerspiels*, the re-jected *Habilitationsschrift* of 1925.[77] With this study of the German *Trauerspiel* of the seventeenth century, his aim was not simply to make a contribution to literary history. His underlying purpose was to explore the notion of allegory with a view to shedding light on the approaches and strategies of contemporary expressionism. Benjamin was convinced that allegory had unjustly been classified as an artistic device of secondary importance, and that a study of this particular means of expression was also relevant to modern aesthetic forms.[78]

He deals with the difference between symbol and allegory via a critique of the attitude of romanticism. This attitude, based on idealist concepts, distinguishes between the two literary devices in terms of a hierarchical order in which symbols are qualitatively superior. The assumption is that a work of art that is conceived of as a symbol is founded on a unity, an inner correspondence between its outer form and its meaning. The beautiful merges, as it were, with the divine in an unbroken whole, so that it is possible to speak of an underlying unity of ethics and aesthetics. With the allegorical method, on the other hand, there is no intrinsic relation between signifier and signified: in allegory, divergent elements of different origin are related to each other and given a signifying relationship by the allegorist that remains extrinsic to its component parts. The symbol, which is ascribed a much higher position within the idealistic tradition of romanticism, is operative, for instance, in the ideal of *Bildung*. This ideal prescribes that individuals should be educated to be complete human beings in whom knowledge, aesthetic sensibility, and moral awareness merge to form the core of their personality.[79] The endeavor to achieve a symbolic totality is, in Benjamin's view, the fundamental characteristic of the humanism that derived from the romantic-idealistic tradition.[80]

Benjamin, however, does not accept this hierarchy. For him it is allegory that constitutes an authentic way of dealing with the world, because it is not based on a premise of unity but accepts the world as fragmented, as failed. Allegory refers to that which has been blighted in the bud, to everything that is a source of pain and is ruinous; it refers to a fallen state, and it is for this very reason that it is important, forming as it does an adequate expression of an experience which has entirely ceased to be comprehensive or total. Allegory operates externally while symbols base their meaning on a premise of unity, a presumed harmony between inner and outer. The difference comes down to the fact that the symbol derives its significance from its inner being, while allegory resolutely limits itself to the external. Symbols permit one to get a glimpse of totality and unity, while allegory reveals the world as a desolate landscape with ruins scattered here and there as silent witnesses of disaster.[81]

If we are to believe Asja Lacis that Benjamin thought of his study of the *Trauerspiel* as shedding light on a contemporary aesthetic problem, then, like John McCole, we will conclude that Benjamin is implicitly raising the question of a modernist aesthetics here. One can indeed discern significant parallels between his reevaluation of allegory and his later attitude toward modernistic culture. This is also the view of Rainer Nägele, who sees a remarkable parallel between Benjamin's treatment of the

opposition between allegory and symbol on the one hand and that between bourgeois interiority and avant-garde destructiveness on the other:

> What is at stake is not only the material substantiality of the world but
> the locality of the meaning-producing light: in the symbol it is "translu-
> cence," light emanating from an interior; whereas in allegory the ray
> comes from the outside. This is the essential topology that structures
> the rhetoric of the symbol-allegory opposition as well as that of bour-
> geois subjectivity and its interiority. Against it, a pathos of exteriority or
> of the surface emerges in Modernism: it revalorizes allegory in all its
> theatricality.[82]

Allegory—"the dissolution of the speculative synthesis of subject and object, visible
in the dismembered body and in the ruin"[83]—finds its counterpart in the preoccupation of the avant-garde with montage and construction. Instead of imitating an organic figure, the avant-garde opts for a mechanistic principle of design. This
modernistic principle has in mind a world in which the false ideal of the cultivation of
inwardness is liquidated in favor of a radical publicity. The goal of this publicity is
transparency as an unconditional revolutionary duty: in a genuinely classless society
in which collectivity reigns instead of individuality, privacy becomes an out-of-date
virtue that in no way should survive revolution.

The fact that there is such a striking similarity in Benjamin's work between his
critique of the romantic-idealist concept of the relation between symbol and allegory
and his interpretation of modernist aesthetics is not so strange after all. The rejection
of nineteenth-century tradition is an equally crucial element in modernist culture. It
should not surprise us, then, that Benjamin put special emphasis on this rejection.
What appeals to him in certain elements of the avant-garde movement is their "destructive character." He is convinced that these people in particular are the ones who
give a face to the age and who are capable of paving the way to the future: "Some
pass things down to posterity by making them untouchable and thus conserving
them, others pass on situations, by making them practicable and thus liquidating
them. The latter are called destructive."[84] It is these destroyers who have the most
to offer humanity. It is their work that is genuinely worthwhile. Benjamin quotes
Adolf Loos: "If human work consists of destruction, it is truly human, natural, noble
work."[85]

In Benjamin's view, destructive work is essential for the process that humanity is obliged to go through in its historical confrontation with technology and with
modern civilization. Only by way of a process of purification, with all the inevitable
pain that that involves—implying as it does the destruction of the old—will it be possible to create the conditions for a new humanity, a humanity that will be intrinsically
committed to the gesture of destruction:

The average European has not succeeded in uniting his life with tech-nology, because he has clung to the fetish of creative existence. One must have followed Loos in his struggle with the dragon "ornament," heard the stellar Esperanto of Scheerbart's creations, or seen Klee's New Angel, who preferred to free men by taking from them, rather than make them happy by giving to them, to understand a humanity that proves itself by destruction.[86]

Destruction is crucial because purification is essential for every form of vitality. To make something, to create it, does not have so much to do with originality or inven-tiveness but with a process of purification. Creativity is a false ideal, an idol. The real aim of those who have the concern of "true humanity" at heart can be found in the act of destruction that exposes pretense and illusions. Benjamin refers to Karl Kraus, who used quotations in a destructive fashion and thus succeeded in salvaging cer-tain vestiges from the ruins of history: "[Kraus] did discover in quotation the power not to preserve but to purify, to tear from context, to destroy; the only power in which hope still resides that something might survive this age—because it was wrenched from it."[87] Benjamin recognizes the same will to destruction and negation in people such as Loos, Scheerbart, and Klee. In these men, in their destructive work, the hope for the survival of culture lay concealed. This is because they understood that the be-lief in the "fetish of creative existence" prevents people from adapting their lives to the demands of the industrial era.

For Benjamin it is clear that the ideology of a false humanism subscribed to by so many people offers no prospect whatsoever of any mode of life that is equal to the challenge of the new conditions of existence, let alone one that would take full advantage of the political vision of a classless society that he regarded as being in-herent in technology. As John McCole puts it, Benjamin "remained adamant that the idealist tradition of humanism, and the classical ideal of humanity itself, were thor-oughly compromised. Not the preservation of these traditions, but only a purifying liquidating could hope to save what had once animated them."[88]

For Benjamin the activity of destructive characters was essential if revolution was to succeed. The destructive character explodes one's familiar environment and is averse to comfort, abandoning itself to the cold sobriety of glass and steel: "The destructive character is the enemy of the etui-man. The etui-man looks for comfort, and the case is its quintessence. The inside of the case is the velvet-lined track that he has imprinted on the world. The destructive character obliterates even the traces of destruction."[89]

Two different concepts of dwelling are contrasted here. In Benjamin's view, dwelling should basically be understood as a distant memory of one's mother's womb. The feeling of being protected and of seeking a protective casing is funda-mental to dwelling, but it was an idea that was pushed to an extreme in the nine-teenth century:

> The primal form of all dwelling is not a house but a case. This bears the imprint of its dweller. Taken to an extreme the dwelling becomes a case. More than any other age, the nineteenth century felt a longing for dwelling. It thought of dwelling as an etui and tucked the individual and all his belongings so far into it that it reminds one of the inside of a bow of compasses in which the instrument together with all its accessories is sheeted in deep, usually violet-colored velvet cavities.[90]

The romantic-idealist concept of dwelling resulted in the nineteenth-century interior claiming to be "the etui of the private person."[91] These interiors are so personal, so focused on property and ownership, that their message for every visitor is unmistakable—there is nothing for you here; you are a stranger in this house. Art nouveau pushed this notion of dwelling to an extreme, almost identifying the house with its inhabitant (or rather the inhabitant with its house—as might become visible in the way Henry van de Velde designed everything for the houses he built, up to the ladies' dresses that went along with it) (figures 58 and 59). In art nouveau, this conception of dwelling was culminating, and eventually brought to an end:

> About the turn of the century, the interior is shaken by art nouveau. Admittedly the latter, through its ideology, seems to bring with it the consummation of the interior—the transfiguration of the solitary soul appears its goal. Individualism is its theory. In van de Velde the house appears as the expression of personality. Ornament is to his house what the signature is to painting [figure 60].[92]

Art nouveau represents the last attempt of European culture to mobilize the inner world of the individual personality to avert the threat of technology. It is the culmination of tendencies that were already evident in the iron and glass architecture of the nineteenth century, in its arcades and its interiors. These architectonic figures are exponents of the dream that holds the collective in a trance: it is in the interior that the bourgeois registers his dreams and desires; in it he gives form to his fascination for the other—for the exotic and for the historical past. In the arcades, technology is applied not to confront the individual with the inevitability of his new condition but to display the material reality of capitalism, the reality of commerce, presenting it as a phantasmagoria. These tendencies are pushed through to their ultimate in art nouveau. In art nouveau the bourgeois dreams that he has woken up:[93] he has the illusion of having made a new beginning but in fact all that has occurred is a shift of imagery—from history to natural history.[94]

The historicizing masquerades of nineteenth-century interiors—with dining rooms furnished like Cesare Borgia's banquet chamber, boudoirs done up like Gothic chapels and "Persian"-style studies[95]—are replaced by an imagery that refers to flowers and vegetation, to the soothing undulation of an underwater world.[96] Tech-

Henry van de Velde,
Bloemenwerf, Uccle,
1895–1896.

(From Henry van de Velde,
Geschichte meines Lebens
[Munich: Piper, 1962], fig. 33.)

58

A dress for the lady of the house,
designed by Henry van de Velde
around 1898.

(From Henry van de Velde,
Geschichte meines Lebens,
fig. 50.)

59

nology is applied here to further the ends of the dream: art nouveau explores the technical possibilities of concrete and wrought iron within a concept where "art" is primordial. This strategy is doomed to failure: "The attempt by the individual to do battle with technology on the basis of his inwardness leads to his downfall."[97]

The endeavor to give expression to the inner personality does not tally with the reality of an industrial civilization that is characterized by a poverty of genuine experience. This poverty of experience means that the individual is not capable of constructing a personality for himself.[98] For this reason, art nouveau's bid to express this personality conflicts with the actual forces underlying the age. Only a new barbarism is in a position to give it form. Only a new barbarism is capable of saving what once had animated genuine humanism. A new barbarism is therefore the only appropriate answer to the challenges of technology.

While the nineteenth-century figures of the arcade and of the interior constitute a form of dwelling that is in decay, the new barbarism represents a radical change, bringing with it another notion of dwelling—one that is no longer founded in security and seclusion, but in openness and transparency: "The twentieth century, with its porousness and transparency, its longing for light and air, put an end to dwelling in the old sense of the word . . . Art nouveau shook the etui existence to its foundations. By now it is deceased, and dwelling is reduced: for the living by hotel rooms, for the dead by crematoria."[99] Dwelling as seclusion and security has had its day. Hotel rooms and crematories teach the individual to adapt to the new conditions of life that have more to do with transience and instability than with permanence and being rooted (figure 61). Things no longer allow themselves to be really appropriated; the notion of dwelling as leaving traces behind one withers away. Dwelling takes on

Henry van de Velde, interior
of a shop designed for the
Habana-Compagnie, Berlin, 1899.
"In van de Velde the house
appears as the expression
of personality. Ornament is
to his house what the signature
is to painting."

(From Henry van de Velde,
Geschichte meines Lebens,
fig. 57.)

Hannes Meyer, Co-op Zimmer,
1926—a visualization of a new,
nomadic way of living, based
on transience and instability
rather than permanence and
rootedness.

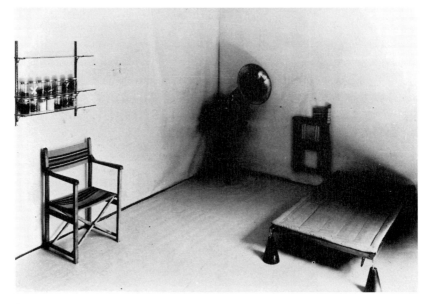

61

a "hurried contemporaneity" that is no longer recorded in ineradicable imprints but
which expresses itself in changeable constructions and transitory interiors with hard
and smooth surfaces (figure 62). This is not necessarily a negative development. On
the contrary, Benjamin perceives it as the fulfilling of an important promise. He links
the new coolness of dwelling with the openness and transparency that are characteristic of a new form of society (figure 63):

> For it is the hallmark of this epoch that dwelling in the old sense of the
> word, where security had priority, has had its day. Giedion, Mendel-
> sohn, Corbusier turned the abiding places of man into a transit area for
> every conceivable kind of energy and for waves of light and air. The
> time that is coming will be dominated by transparency. Not just the
> rooms, but even the weeks, if we are to believe the Russians, who want
> to abolish Sunday and to replace it with movable days of leisure.[100]

The motive of transparency has more than merely literal connotations for Benjamin. In this quotation he links spatial transparency in the sense that Giedion uses

the term with flexibility and adaptability in the individual who dwells in abiding places and transit areas, and with a flexibility in the structure of time as well. That time has become transparent amounts to a writing on the wall for Benjamin. It is a feature of revolutionary moments that the linear course of time is interrupted and that a new calendar is introduced or that the clocks are stopped. It is no coincidence, then, that he refers to Russia in this connection. Russia, which Benjamin had visited in the winter of 1926–1927, was, after all, the country where communism was gradually becoming a reality (this quotation dates from 1929) and which constituted the hope of many left-wing intellectuals, including Benjamin.

References to Russia appear elsewhere in his work. In his essay "Surrealism," for instance, he recalls an experience he had in a Russian hotel, where he was astonished by the number of bedroom doors left open by the guests. It made him realize that "to live in a glass house is a revolutionary virtue par excellence. It is also an intoxication, a moral exhibition that we badly need. Discretion concerning one's own existence, once an aristocratic virtue, has become more and more an affair of petit-bourgeois parvenus."[101]

Interior of one of the houses for the Bauhaus professors, built by Walter Gropius in Dessau, 1926.

(From Walter Gropius, *Bauhausbauten Dessau*, 1930, fig. 132, photo by Consemüller.)

Le Corbusier, project for a villa
in Carthage, 1928, drawing of
the interior.

"Corbusier turned the abiding
places of man into a transit area
for every conceivable kind of
energy and for waves of light
and air."

63

Nor is this reference to a glass house an isolated one. The motif recurs in his essay on Karl Kraus, as it does in "Erfahrung und Armut." There he talks of the example of the "adjustable flexible glass houses that Loos and Le Corbusier have in the meantime realized. It is not a coincidence that glass is so hard and smooth a material to which nothing can be fastened. It is also cold and sober. Things that are made of glass have no 'aura.' Glass is the enemy par excellence of secrecy. It is also the enemy of property."[102] Benjamin is implying here that, because it is inimical to secrecy and property, glass should be regarded as a material that literally expresses the transparency of the new society that would be founded on revolutionary lines. A society of this sort would have the political "radioscopy" of sexuality and the family, as well as of the economic and physical conditions of existence, as part of its program and therefore would be completely uninterested in protecting privacy in the home.[103]

Architecture, Modernity, and Dwelling

Benjamin's high esteem for modern architecture has to do above all with the metaphorical qualities that he discerns in it. Giedion's *Bauen in Frankreich* made a deep impression on him.[104] Giedion's use of the terms *Durchdringung* and transparency to describe the architecture of the New Building appealed to him considerably, as did the idea that the structure played the part of the unconscious. In addition to this, as we learn from the footnotes in the *Passagenwerk*, he was familiar with Adolf Behne's *Neues Wohnen, Neues Bauen* and Le Corbusier's *Urbanisme*.[105] As mentioned above, he frequently referred to Adolf Loos. In view of all this, it is somewhat surprising that he did not discuss the important activities in the field of public-sector housing that took place in the second half of the 1920s in Germany. As far as I know, there is not a word in his work about *Das Neue Frankfurt* or the activities of Martin Wagner and Bruno Taut in Berlin. Nor does Benjamin discuss the work of Hannes Meyer, the architect who went furthest along the road that he pointed to in "Erfahrung und Armut."[106] His idea about the role of architecture as the prototype of a new sort of art reception was therefore not verified against the practice of his contemporaries.

What is more, the radical thesis that he argues for with reference to literature in "The Author as Producer" is not explored in terms of its relevance for architecture. This thesis states that the hallmark of a progressive author is not so much the subjects he deals with as the way that he operates in production relations: a progressive author is one who transforms the hierarchical relation between readers, publishers, and writers and who educates the public in adulthood, so that the roles of reader and writer eventually end up being interchangeable. With respect to architecture this theme would be taken up later by Manfredo Tafuri and his colleagues of the Venice School, but Benjamin himself did not back up this claim in any detail anywhere in his work.

Benjamin's attitude toward the new architecture can in the end most appropriately be qualified as ambivalent—here too his ambivalence is a product of the triadic structure of his thought. Some passages in his work lend themselves to interpretation as a straightforward plea for a cold and ascetic architecture, appropriate to the new barbarism and therefore representing an adequate response to the omnipresent poverty of experience. In other writings his tone is more one of mourning. When, in his essay "Paris, Capital of the Nineteenth Century," he comes to describe the bourgeois interior, with its excess of knickknacks and furnishings—the interior that was familiar to him from his childhood[107]—he clearly betrays a nostalgia for this nineteenth-century form of dwelling, however much that manner of dwelling may be out-of-date and illusory. The prevailing tone here is one of the work of mourning (*Trauerarbeit*) that describes the withering of dwelling in order to rescue as much as possible of those elements that recall the original paradisiacal dwelling, the mother's womb. Elsewhere in his work another perspective prevails that focuses attention on the revolutionary potential concealed in the "decayed" form of dwelling.

It is unquestionably the case that Benjamin hoped for a revolutionary "reversal" (*Umschlag*) that would transform the life of the individual and of the collective by achieving a public openness, transparency, and permeability as conditions of everyday life. At the same time, however, as an individual subject he still clung to numerous memories of another sort of dwelling in another sort of time, the dwelling that made security and nurture possible in rooms that wrap round the individual like a shell.

The most striking feature in all this is Benjamin's strategic attempt to understand modernity and dwelling as things that are not in opposition to each other. He developed a complex vision of modernity that cannot be seen as unambiguously programmatic or transitory, but which aims to ignite the programmatic possibilities inherent in the modern—the new barbarism—in its most transitory aspects—fashion, mass culture, modern architecture—because of their transparency and instability. A similar strategy can be seen with regard to the idea of dwelling. Benjamin refused to embed dwelling unequivocally in tradition. Although he acknowledges that dwelling means leaving traces behind, it is also his view that a degree of *Umfunktionierung* is possible in this area: dwelling, that is, can be understood as a transitive verb, as a question of "habituation." This habituation, bound up as it is with a "hurried contemporaneity," is much more forcefully related to the modern condition of changeability and transparency than the notion of dwelling as leaving traces behind one. "Living in a glass house," therefore, is also a revolutionary duty par excellence. It can be seen as an instrument in the struggle for modernity, the struggle of those who want to exploit modernity for its revolutionary potential in order to fulfill the promises that had lain stacked up during thousands of years of suffering and oppression.

Building on Hollow Space: Ernst Bloch's Criticism of Modern Architecture

The whole work of Ernst Bloch (1885–1977), from his first publication, *Geist der Utopie* (1918) to the work that he wrote at an advanced age, revolves round the theme of utopia and hope. He approaches this theme from every angle—above all that of philosophy. In doing so he covers so wide a field that one is impressed by his exceptional erudition. In a language that is rich in imagery, his work throws light on the recurring importance of the utopian moment that one finds in daydreams, fairy tales, fantasies, works of art, and philosophical theories. Bloch considers hope to be an essential force in everyone's life, because being strives to fulfill itself by realizing that which is not-yet-being.

At quite an early stage in his life Bloch embraced the ideas of Marxism, and throughout his stormy career he never retracted. Fleeing from Nazi Germany, he arrived in America after years of peregrinations; not knowing the language, he was dependent on the earnings of his wife, Karola Piotrovskan, an architect. After the Second World War he returned to Germany. Rather than accept a professorship in Frankfurt, he took up a chair in philosophy in East Germany at the University of

Leipzig. The regime there was initially favorably disposed toward him, but after some time the tide turned and Bloch was forbidden to lecture or to publish. With the building of the Berlin Wall in 1961, he decided to apply for political asylum in West Germany. There he became professor once more, this time at the University of Tübingen, where he remained active until his death in 1977.

Heimat as a Utopian Category

Bloch's masterpiece is *Das Prinzip Hoffnung,* which he wrote during his American period and which was published in 1959. This imposing volume is a virtually encyclopedic survey of utopian aspirations, both in the personal realm and in the social and aesthetic fields. Bloch describes the most disparate phenomena as manifestations of the utopian moment. The whole is based on a philosophical ontology that understands being as essentially incomplete: according to Bloch, being necessarily contains a moment of not-yet-being. In every manifestation of being, therefore, one can see a tendency toward the self-fulfillment of a utopian ideal for the future.

According to Bloch, the fundamentally utopian character of being has usually been denied by philosophers. It is no coincidence that Terentius Varro, who was the first person to draft a Latin grammar, is said to have forgotten to include the future tense in his survey of the forms of the verb: Varro's omission is symptomatic of the neglect of the future that is typical of philosophical thought. Bloch's stated aim was to fill this vacuum: "A particularly extensive attempt is made in this book to bring philosophy to hope, as to a place in the world which is as inhabited as the best civilized land and as unexplored as the Antarctic."[108]

The basic theme of his philosophy, then, is "the still unbecome, still unachieved homeland [*Heimat*], as it develops outwards and upward in the dialectical-materialistic struggle of the new with the old."[109] *Heimat* is seen as the place where utopia is achieved, the homeland where human beings and the world are reconciled and where the dream of a better life is finally realized. This *Heimat* does not yet exist—nobody dwells there—but as children, we have all had a glimpse of it: an existence without deprivation, without alienation, and without expropriation.[110] The creation of this *Heimat* is the goal of all human endeavor.

It is also the fundamental concern of art. Bloch understands art as *Vorschein,* a prelude or "pre-appearance" that anticipates the realization of utopia. The best works of art present one with a foreshadowing of that utopian moment, not literally—because the future *Heimat* cannot be depicted in every concrete detail—but as the outline of a promise. Works of art direct one's gaze toward the attempt to make a better world, toward the desire for perfection, and for keeping hope alive. Art is like a laboratory in which events, figures, and characters are tested for their utopian potential.

In talking about utopia, therefore, one should not be understood to be referring simply to a concrete situation: "But to limit the utopian to the Thomas More variety, or simply to orientate it in that direction, would be like trying to reduce electricity to the amber from which it gets its Greek name and in which it was first noticed."[111] It is rather a question of constructions that contain all kinds of vistas of the future, wish fulfillments, and images of hope: the form in which utopia appears in art is multilayered and very diverse. Sometimes the utopian moment is only recognizable in the absence of a direct reference to a better future: a meditation on absence and void can, after all, imply the desire or hope for everything. However that may be, utopian thought consists in the first place of a critique of everything that is: the critical function of utopia is fundamental to it, and the same is true of art.[112]

For Bloch it is clear that Marxism is the embodiment of this philosophy of hope: he sees socialism as representing the praxis of utopia, and for a long time he believed that the political practice of the Eastern European countries was its concrete manifestation. However, he was not an orthodox Marxist in every respect.[113] His ideas about the relation between infrastructure and superstructure were too subtle for that. In *Erbschaft dieser Zeit* (1935), for instance, he puts forward the thesis that the legacy of bourgeois culture cannot be uncritically rejected when one is engaged in drawing up a socialist program for culture. On the contrary, it is necessary to investigate the utopian potential that it actually contains. The utopian content that is inherent in both existing practices and in those of previous ages should be understood as containing worthwhile stimuli for the development of a socialist culture.[114]

Bloch's vision of architecture also is based on these fundamental premises. He describes architecture as "an attempt to produce a human homeland."[115] The aim of great architecture is to build an image of Arcadia: it exploits the potential that is present in the natural surroundings of a site to create an environment that is in harmony with the aspirations of the human subject. Even when—in Gothic art, for instance—beauty and pleasure are infused with melancholy and a sense of the tragic, the promise of a better world can be discerned in its complex harmony:

> The encompassing element furnishes a homeland or touches on it: all great buildings were sui generis built into the utopia, the anticipation of a space adequate to man. . . . The better world, which the grand architectural style expresses and depicts in an anticipatory fashion, thus consists very unmythically, as the real task vivis ex lapidibus, of the stones of life.[116]

The anticipation of a better world—that is the achievement of the great architects of the past. Bloch discerns two prototypical styles that in his view constitute expressions of the utopian principle in contrasting fashions. Egyptian architecture embodies the longing for the perfection of the crystal: it is a frozen architecture, which in the sheer weight of the crystalline geometry of the pyramid expresses the desire for perfection by way of a symbolism of death. The Gothic style, on the contrary, makes use of the symbolism of the human body and the tree of life: in Gothic architecture, with all its flamboyance and dynamism, with its organic figures that intertwine as they strive upward, it is the longing for resurrection and for a transformation to a higher form of life that is the prime motif in its formal idiom. In contrasting fashion, then, both styles refer to utopia, to the promise of a better world—the Egyptian does it by striving for a perfect geometry that conforms to the order of the cosmos, while the Gothic extols the form of life itself in an organic and total design.[117] Most other architectures, in Bloch's view, are less extreme and contain references to both aspects—both the geometrical and the vitalist are present in them as utopian figures (*Leitbilder*). As for modern architecture, which he refers to as the architecture of the New Objectivity (*Neue Sachlichkeit*), he has nothing good to say. According to him, this is a manifestation of a culture that is completely bourgeois and which makes use of a thoroughly misguided image of utopia; with its sobriety and lack of ornament, all it does is glorify capitalism.

Washable Walls and Houses Like Ships

Right from the start, in his first book, *Geist der Utopie* (1918, 1923), Bloch attacked a number of the principles of what was to become modern architecture. He took up arms against the increasing dominance of technological culture that he saw as depriving things of their warmth and as surrounding people with cold appliances. Everything has become cold and empty; everything has to be "washable": "The machine knew how to produce everything so lifeless and inhuman in detail, just the way our new housing districts usually are. Its actual goal is the bathroom and the toilet that are the most unquestionable and the most original accomplishments of this era. . . . But now washing-up reigns. Somehow water flows from every wall."[118] An environment of this kind is typical of an age in which people seem to have forgotten what real dwelling means. They no longer understand the art of making their houses feel warm and solid: "At first, however, nearly everything looks empty to us. But how could it be different and where should the vital, beautifully formed utensil come from when nobody knows any more how to live permanently and has forgotten how to keep his home warm and solid?"[119]

Like Benjamin in "Erfahrung und Armut," Bloch states that humanity has to begin all over again: we are poor and have forgotten how to play. The conclusions that Bloch draws from this perception, however, are very different from those of Benjamin. He does not argue that the cold design that is typical of the age of machines should be elevated to a norm in order to clear the way for a new barbarism. On the contrary, it is his view that cold design should be confined to those things that by their nature are intended to be functional: "Surgical tongs for delivering babies must be smooth, but sugar tongs certainly must not."[120] There is a whole realm of human design, Bloch argues, that occupies an interim position between that which is strictly technical (obstetric forceps, chairs) and that which is art (statues). The applied arts have a crucial role here, even in the transitional phase to a socialist society.

Historically speaking, it was in the applied arts, the products of which were meant for the court or the church, that there was a relation between the construction of an object and its expressivity. Because of their lavish design these products—thrones, altars, and pulpits—transcend their immediate usefulness: they emphasize the spiritual assumption behind building in which the earthly aspect is no more than symbolic of another, heavenly world. This mode of perception has its relevance even in the twentieth century: "Hence, this third aspect still exists between chair and statue, perhaps even above the statue: 'applied arts' of a superior order; within it stretches a genuine, transcending carpet of purely abstract form instead of the comfortable, quasi-stale, purely luxurious carpet of daily use, assembled from resting-places."[121] It is here that ornament has its place. The new ornament with its linear arabesque design appears as a prelude, offering an alternative for the transcendent form of historical ornamentation. The reference to a heavenly life is continued here in a secular form, as the promise of a better future. For Bloch, ornamentation is always a token of something else: the reference to another form of life is always imprinted in decorative work—the utopian moment is indissolubly bound up with it, and it is here that ornamentation gets its meaning.[122]

In this text Bloch apparently is waging an implicit polemic with Adolf Loos. Although Loos's name is not mentioned, his criticisms are so clearly addressed to the theses about ornament and the applied arts advocated by Loos that there is every reason to assume that Loos was Bloch's direct target here. While Loos states that ornament in modern times is by definition false and even criminal, Bloch defends the point of view that it is ornament above all that keeps the promise of a better future alive. While Loos denounces the professors of the arts and crafts schools, whom he accuses of being completely superfluous, Bloch is of the opinion that it is the applied arts that make life tolerable, precisely because they offer a counterbalance for the coldness that emanates from technical objects and appliances.

Bloch's opinion of the new architecture has by no means been watered down by 1935 when he publishes *Erbschaft dieser Zeit*. He is particularly critical of it because it offers an outward pretense of rationalism, while society itself continues to develop according to the old models. The rationality of the New Objectivity is lacking in any concrete revolutionary potential, and for this reason it fits in perfectly with the capitalist mode of thought. The defenders of functionalism, who imagine that they can see the form of a future society in every sliding window, are profoundly mistaken. They exaggerate the impact of the purity and functionality of the New Building and do not see that hygienic dwelling has more to do with the taste of a young fashion-conscious bourgeois public, than with any desire to achieve a classless society. Apparently they do not notice that the absence of ornament is itself a decorative style; still less do they realize that the new estates that are built according to functional design principles often condemn their residents to live like termites.

For all these reasons, Bloch felt that the New Objectivity had no potential legacy to offer any future socialist society. It was in fact so much bound up with a bourgeois capitalist lifestyle that it was quite unsuited to designing a new society:

It goes without saying that communist functionalism is not synonymous with a version of late capitalist functionalism minus the element
of exploitation. On the contrary, when exploitation no longer exists . . .
the white blocks of rented flats in which our contemporary lower-class
beasts of burden are housed will become colorful and will have a
completely different geometry that will correspond to a genuine
collective.[123]

Bloch takes up a number of these arguments once more in the essay that he
devoted to modern architecture in *Das Prinzip Hoffnung*, entitled "Building on Hollow Space."[124] "Hollow space" (*Hohlraum*) is his term for the space of capitalism
where the glimmering surface is no more than an empty shell with no interior truth
corresponding to the hollow pretense of its exterior display. Capitalism hollows life
out, perverting the energy produced by hope into a meaningless pursuit of empty values. This can be seen in the architecture, which is the image of sterility: "These days
houses in many places look as if they are ready to leave. Although they are un-
adorned or for this very reason, they express departure. On the inside they are bright
and bare like sick-rooms, on the outside they seem like boxes on movable rods, but
also like ships."[125]

Modern architecture, in Bloch's view, was initially intended to create openness and to provide room for light and sun. Dark cellars should be broken open and
vistas opened up. The aim was to create an interchange between interior and outside; private space should be brought into relationship with the public realm. This
drive toward openness was premature, however. During the fascist period nothing
in the world outside was capable of enriching and improving the interior: "The broad
window full of nothing but outside world needs an outdoors full of attractive
strangers, not full of Nazis; the glass door right down to the floor really requires sun-
shine to peer and break in, not the Gestapo."[126] Under the social conditions of that
time, people's longing for intimacy and security was more than justified, and the
openness of modern architecture threatened to become a farce. Superficiality was
the result: "The de-internalization [*Entinnerlichung*] turned into hollowness; the
southern pleasure in the outside world did not, at the present sight of the capitalist
outside world, turn into happiness."[127] Since genuinely rational social relations that
might correspond to the rationalism of the New Objectivity do not exist, the "housing machines" of Le Corbusier will in all probability be things without history. They
exist, to be sure, and they impose their character on their environment, but they are
so abstract and schematic that the people who live in them cannot really engage in
any relation with them. "Even the townplanning of these stalwart functionalists is
private, abstract; because of sheer 'être humaine' the real people in these houses
and towns become standardized termites, or within a 'housing machine,' foreign
bodies, still all too organic ones, so remote is all this from real people, from home,
contentment, homeland."[128]

When architecture develops without any consideration of the social conditions within which it operates, it is inevitable that the "purity" it aims for is no more than an illusion. In the end this "purity" is no more than an alibi for a lack of imagination. Dualism, however, is also typical of this evolution, so that purely functional architecture still has a counterpart—in the exuberant expressionism of Bruno Taut and others. Bloch refers to Vitruvius, who taught that the three principles of architecture—*utilitas, firmitas, venustas*—should converge in the design. Here, however, they no longer cohere: *utilitas* and *firmitas* are aspects of functionalism, while *venustas* is allotted to expressionism, with the result that the essence of architecture is glossed over. Given the circumstances, however, this state of affairs is inevitable: "Precisely because [architecture], far more than the other pictorial arts, is and remains a social creation, it cannot blossom at all in the hollow space of late capitalism. Only the beginnings of another society will make genuine architecture possible again, one both constructively and ornamentally permeated on the basis of its own artistic aspiration."[129]

In 1965, when Bloch, together with Adorno, was invited by the Deutsche Werkbund to contribute to a seminar on "Bildung durch Gestalt" (Education by Design), he again returned to these arguments. His explicit question to the participants—whom, one may assume, were convinced functionalists—was whether the "honesty" that was the aim of functionalist architecture made any sense in a social situation that was by no means characterized by honesty: "The question remains unanswered as to whether the social forms that provided the context for the false enchantment of the *Gründerzeit* has in fact become that much more honest; whether the unornamented honesty of pure functional form might not itself turn out to be a fig leaf behind which a lack of honesty in the remaining relations lies concealed."[130]

It is possible that, because the social situation has evolved in the contrary direction, architecture cannot succeed in creating genuinely humane environments. Bloch does not doubt the integrity of the founders of functionalism or, for that matter, the legitimacy of their protest against nineteenth-century architecture with its ornament and kitsch; however, he considers that social developments have by now made this criticism superfluous, while the ruling class continues to exploit it for their own ends: "In *Maria Stuart* we read the words 'Count, the death of Mortimer came not untimely.' Something similar could be said, *mutatis mutandis,* of the death of ornament, which continues to be celebrated, and of the lack of fantasy, still being artificially produced."[131] For this reason, Bloch makes a case for a revival of fantasy in architecture. He draws a comparison between the current situation in architecture "which calls for wings," and in painting and sculpture "that should have shoes of lead."[132] This dualism, according to Bloch, has to be transcended. The functionalist architecture that has got rid of the legacy of the nineteenth century should now serve as a springboard for an architecture that could serve as *Stadtkrone* for all the arts.

Modernism as a Breaking Point within the Capitalist System

In using the image of the *Stadtkrone*, Bloch is clearly alluding to the expressionist architecture of Bruno Taut and others that received much acclaim around 1920 (figure 64).[133] Like the parallel tendencies in painting and literature, expressionist architecture tried to devise an alternative to tradition by concentrating on the power of imagery. It developed a plastic formal idiom that expressed utopian longings and visionary imagery. This imagery was outspokenly bound up with radical ideas of social renewal.

It is clear that this expressionist current in architecture was far more appealing to Bloch than the New Objectivity, which was the dominant trend after 1923. This was no coincidence. During his period in wartime Munich he had made the acquaintance of the artists of the *Blaue Reiter*—Franz Marc, Wassily Kandinsky—as well as representatives of the New Music. It was they who taught him to respect a willingness to experiment, the quest for the unknown, and the rejection of the indolence and complacency of the bourgeois order.[134] Bloch's own writings have an expressionist literary style—passionate, rich in imagery, asystematic, and sharp in tone. He continued to speak out as an advocate of expressionism even after Lukács and other Marxist intellectuals had denounced it as decadent.[135]

Expressionism, in Bloch's view, was an authentic response to the experiences of discontinuity and fragmentation caused by the modern condition. The world of capitalism is fissured, its spotless order is a mere pretense: behind its glittering surface there is nothing but a void. What expressionism does is simply to point to the

Bruno Taut, *Stadtkrone*, 1919.

(From Bruno Taut, *Die Stadtkrone*
[Jena: Eugen Diedericks, 1919].)

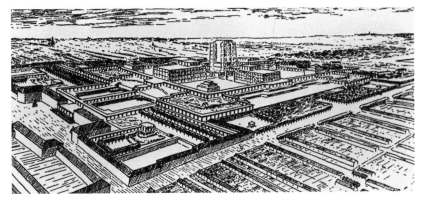

cracks in this surface in order to expose the void. Lukács's charge that expressionism is decadent is in a sense correct. But he is mistaken when he says that it should
be rejected: "So the Expressionists were the 'vanguard' of decadence. Should they
instead have tried to plaster over the surface of reality, in the spirit, say, of the Neo-
classicists or the representatives of Neo-objectivity [*Neue Sachlichkeit*] instead of
persisting in their efforts of demolition?"[136]

Bloch recognizes expressionism as a form of opposition to capitalism, a form
of criticism that according to him is not present in the New Objectivity. The same
goes for the technique of montage, which also exposes capitalist reality as fissured
and fragmented:

> In technical and cultural montage, the coherence of the old surfaces is
> broken up and a new one is constructed. A new coherence can emerge
> then, because the old order is more and more unmasked as a hollow
> sham, one of surfaces that is in fact fissured. While functionalism dis-
> tracts one with its glittering appearance, montage often exposes the
> chaos under this surface as an attractive or daringly interwoven fabric.
> . . . In this sense montage reveals less the facade and more the back-
> ground of the age than does functionalism.[137]

Montage, he states, is a technique that the expressionists also made use of. In their
best work, according to Bloch, they apply it in order to back up their personal intentions with fragments drawn from reality, and with archaic and utopian images. Montage allows one to turn the cultural legacy of the old system to advantage, isolating
the best fragments out of the existing order and deploying them in a new pattern; in
this way they are transformed (*umfunktioniert*) into elements that are fertile for the
establishing of a new mode of living. Montage is a way of forcing the old to produce
something new:

> This method has all the negative features of the void, but indirectly it
> also potentially contains something positive: the fragments can be
> used in another context to create something that works contrary to the
> normal order. In the context of the late bourgeoisie, montage means ex-
> posing the empty space of this world, while showing that this space is
> filled with flashes and cross-sections of a "history of appearances," not
> the correct one, but a hybrid form of it. It is also a way of assessing the
> old culture: from the point of view of journeying and bewilderment and
> no longer from the idea of "*Bildung*."[138]

Bloch, then, was an advocate of two typical aspects of modernism: expressionism and montage. It is all the more remarkable that he distanced himself so decisively from the New Objectivity. His stated reason was that he could not see

anything in functionalism that might be considered suspect by capitalism, let alone oppositional: the New Objectivity fitted in perfectly with capitalist logic and did not offer any hints of any other possible sort of culture.

Nonetheless, Bloch's judgment was extremely strict, not to say partisan. He clearly lost sight of the fact that utopian goals and radical political ideas played a role in the New Objectivity just as they did in expressionism. Of course, it is true that in the actual practice of construction, doctrinal purity did not always survive intact, but it was a considerable overstatement to say that the New Objectivity was simply a tool of capitalism. In this respect other Marxists such as Alexander Schwab had a more balanced opinion.[139] Schwab talked of the two-faced character of modern architecture, which he described as being both high bourgeois and proletarian, capitalist and socialist. It was responsible for emblems of capitalism such as department stores, office blocks, and villas, as well as for buildings that foreshadow a socialist society, such as the *Siedlungen*, factory buildings, schools, and clubhouses. For Bloch the latter category was apparently not really relevant; his criticism above all has to do with the fact that the aesthetic language of the New Objectivity is perfectly suited to the cool rationalism of the capitalist order. What he misses in it is not just everything that is fragmentary and fissured, but also the warmth and the fantasy that were present in expressionism.

In the end, Bloch's assessment of modernism differed fairly drastically from that of Benjamin—although in his comments on montage he approximated him very closely. The difference was that Benjamin had much more faith in qualities such as sobriety, transparency, and functionalism. Benjamin took the idea of *Umfunktionierung* much more literally than Bloch: he saw it as a definite possibility that stylistic coldness and rationality could lead to revolutionary change, and that it could contribute to building a genuinely humane society. For a radical thinker such as Benjamin, the modernist aesthetics of montage, which is concerned with exteriority and with surfaces, was intended less to "redeem" elements of the old order than to make room for a radically new form of living. Benjamin rejected the symbol, a mode that is based on an assumption of an intimate relationship between inner and outer. Instead he gave priority to allegory, montage, and destruction. He likewise disclaimed every appeal to creativity as well as all mention of warmth and security because he interpreted these qualities as representing a false humanism.

Benjamin's radical negativity and his posthumanist stance cannot be found to the same extent in Bloch's work. Bloch sees fantasy and creativity as vital qualities; warmth and seclusion are definitely positive values for him. The metaphorical opposition between full and empty that Benjamin wants to transcend remains an essential element in Bloch's discourse. He refers to capitalist space as being "hollow," its surfaces concealing nothing but an inner void. Pieces of technical apparatus with their cold shine and their lack of any adornment also have a "hollow" sound for him, and he considers the claim to rationality of the New Objectivity "hollow" too, since it failed to form any relationship with the warm glow of the revolution. The "fullness" of life was the aim of Bloch's utopian vision. Since every form of being is fundamentally incomplete, this notion of fullness always refers to the future.

Bloch's conception of modernity is clearly counterpastoral, in that he acknowledges the actual cracks and fissures that constitute the "hollow space" of capitalism. He contrasts this image of reality with the pastoral idea of a homeland-to-come. The images with which he invests this figure of *Heimat*, of a *Zu-Hause-sein*, are very eloquent. In *Spuren* (1930), for instance, he recalls an evening that he spent in the house of a friend:

> A delightful circular movement could be felt between inside and outside, between appearance and depth, energy and surface. "Listen," my friend said, "how good it is to feel the house at work." And you could hear the peace and how everything fitted precisely with everything else—and you feel a self-evidence in this trusty comradeship with things that every healthy human being is familiar with, the joy of life around you and the world charged with tao.[140]

Although he stresses that what he is talking about here is no more than a momentary experience, it is clear that for Bloch this image of harmony and solidarity expresses the very essence of *Heimat*: a condition where things lose their strangeness, and where reconciliation and identity prevail between subjects and objects. This has less to do with the rural context—Bloch was careful to contrast his idea of *Heimat* with the Nazi *Blut und Boden* ideology[141]—than with the feeling of oneness conjured up by both the atmosphere and the hour of the day. However that may be, *Heimat* remains a utopian category for Bloch; true dwelling, really feeling oneself at home, remains reserved for the future. Dwelling is not so much rooted in the past; it reaches out toward the future. It is true that one can discern elements in the past in which a utopian desire for dwelling take on a concrete form. These elements should be preserved: the memory of their utopian potential must not be forgotten, but should be made productive for the designing of a future society. That is the programmatic intent of his philosophy, which remains thoroughly connected with his emphasis on the utopian.

The Venice School, or the Diagnosis of Negative Thought

In using the term "Venice School," I am referring to a group of historians and theoreticians who were assembled in Venice around the figure of Manfredo Tafuri (1935–1994). Tafuri himself acquired an international reputation with the publication in 1968 of his first important book, *Teorie e storia dell'architettura*, in which he developed a critique of the "operative criticism" practiced by authors such as Giedion and Zevi. In 1973 *Progetto e utopia*, the most provocative and condensed statement of his views on modern architecture, was published in book form. Some years later these views were formulated more precisely in what has become a major work on the history of modern architecture, with Tafuri and Francesco Dal Co as authors. After the publication in 1980 of *La sfera e il labirinto,* Tafuri turned his back on the architecture of the modern period, reverting once more to his first love—the Renaissance. Nonetheless, he continued to serve as a catalyst in the detailed historical research that has been carried out in Venice on the history of architecture and urban planning in the nineteenth and twentieth centuries.[142]

The philosopher Massimo Cacciari, who holds the chair in aesthetics in Venice, has played an exceptional role in all this activity. Cacciari is a particularly productive author who is also active in politics and in the trade union movement. His philosophical studies, which initially focused on German urban sociology at the beginning of the century, bear witness to an increasing fascination with the work of Heidegger and Benjamin.[143] His analyses have been of crucial significance to the work of his colleagues in architectural history, most particularly through his concept of "negative thought." Like Cacciari, Francesco Dal Co also has carried out detailed research into the study of German architecture culture at the turn of the century, the period during which it "elaborated the most theoretically compact and significant ideas and underwent perhaps the most symptomatic experiences of 'modernity.'"[144] I will pay special attention to the contribution of these two authors because in my view they have come up with perceptions and working hypotheses that are of exceptional importance for the whole discussion around dwelling and modernity.

Architecture and Utopia

Tafuri's book *Progetto e utopia*, the first version of which dates from 1969, attempts to provide a "rereading [of] the history of modern architecture in the light of methods offered by an ideological criticism, understood in the strictest Marxist acceptance of the term."[145] With this end in view, Tafuri traces the development of architecture in relation to capitalist modernization since the Enlightenment. His central thesis is that the course of modern architecture cannot be understood independently of the economic infrastructure of capitalism and that its entire development occurs within these parameters. The whole aim of the book, then, is to demonstrate that this (ideological) subservience is present, even in situations that on the surface seem like explicit rejections of the model of bourgeois and capitalist civilization. The book discusses a number of moments in two centuries of architectural history, beginning with Laugier and ending with the role of structuralism and semiology. I will deal here mainly with the chapters on the avant-garde, because these are the ones that relate most closely to the material that is discussed elsewhere in this book.

Tafuri views the process of modernization as a social development that is characterized by an ever-expanding rationalization and a more and more far-reaching activity of planning. Within this process, he argues, the avant-garde movements perform a number of tasks that in fact further this modernization. For instance the "program" of the avant-garde includes the aim of trivializing the shock experience that is typical of the new, rapid tempo of urban life. The method adopted for this is the technique of montage. The principle of montage involves the combination of elements—theoretically of equal value—that are drawn from different contexts and related to each other in a nonhierarchical way. According to Tafuri, this process is analogous in structure to the principle that operates in the money economy. He describes the latter on the basis of a striking quotation from Georg Simmel: "All things float with equal specific gravity in the constantly moving stream of money. All things lie on the same level and differ from one another only in the size of the area which they cover." Tafuri goes on to ask: "Does it not seem that we are reading here a literary comment on a Schwitter 'Merzbild' [figure 65]? (It should not be forgotten that the very word 'Merz' is but a part of the word 'Commerz.')"[146]

What he is implying here is that the technique of montage that is used in avant-garde works of art derives from the relationship between things that is operative in the money economy. The development of this artistic principle, therefore, foreshadows a process of assimilation that every individual is subjected to—the transformation of the anxiety, provoked by life in the metropolis and by the "destruction of values," into a new principle of dynamic evolution. It is this process that took place in the rise of avant-garde art. "It was necessary to pass from Munch's 'Scream' to El Lissitzky's 'Story of Two Squares' [figures 66 and 67]: from the anguished discovery of the nullification of values, to the use of a language of pure signs, perceptible by a mass that had completely absorbed the universe without quality of the money economy."[147]

Tafuri believes, then, that there is a structural analogy between the laws of the money economy that regulate production and which govern the entire capitalist system on the one hand and the typical features of the avant-garde on the other. The latter, he argues, with its technique of montage, reproduces the "indifference to values" of the money economy, and in the rise and fall of successive -isms it replicates the mentality of permanent innovation that is typical of

Kurt Schwitters,
Merz column, 1930s.

65

Edvard Munch,
The Scream, 1893.

66

the process of social modernization.[148] This analogy forms the crux of Tafuri's thesis. Having in his view located the essence of the dialectics of the avant-garde, he goes on to state that "doing nothing other than interpreting something necessary and universal, the avant-garde could accept temporary unpopularity, well knowing that their break with the past was the fundamental condition for their value as models of action."[149]

The break with the past is materialized in the "destruction of the values" that forms the precondition for further development. The destruction of values is elevated by the avant-garde to the status of the only new value. This profanation is essential to the further development of the capitalist system: "The destruction and the rendering ridiculous of the entire historic heritage of the Western bourgeoisie were conditions for the liberation of the potential, but inhibited, energies of that bourgeoisie itself."[150] The avant-garde sees "destruction" and "negativity" as vital moments in capitalist evolution. The fact that they experiment with just these elements, rendering them, as it were, plausible for individual experience also has implications for the dissemination of the process of social modernization.

The avant-garde gives a form to the negative: "For the avant-garde movements the destruction of values offered a wholly new type of rationality, which was capable of coming face to face with the negative, in order to make the negative itself the release valve of an unlimited potential for development."[151] The particular part played by negativity, however, has never been the subject of an explicit discussion within the avant-garde itself. What the movement did discuss was the question of whether artistic-intellectual labor has a political character. Tafuri states that there were two different but complementary views within the avant-garde movement on this subject, the reverberations of which have continued to make themselves felt. On the one hand there were those who conceived of intellectual work as autonomous, as work on the language of art—a thesis defended by formalism as represented by Viktor Shklovsky—and on the other hand there were the advocates of a "committed" art, who posited artistic work quite simply as a political intervention. Tafuri cites Breton and the surrealist movement as a prime example of this position.

El Lissitzky, *The Story of Two Squares*, 1922.

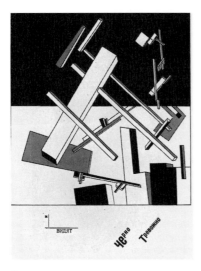

ВИДЯТ че́рно травоино

67

According to Tafuri, the most pressing question was the reconciliation of these two attitudes. Not only was it a vital problem for constructivism and for the urban development projects of the Social Democrat municipal authorities in the Weimar Republic; he also sees it as pivotal in the work of Walter Benjamin in the thirties. Tafuri argues that Benjamin's thesis about the "decay of the aura" in his work of art essay should be interpreted not only as a comment on the universal adoption of new methods of production, but also as the statement of a deliberate choice: to reject the sacred character of artistic work, and thus to accept its destruction.

The opposite choice, however, of attempting to preserve the autonomy of intellectual work, also responds to a quite specific need within capitalist development—the need, that is, to recover the notion of "Subjectivity" (the capital *S* is Tafuri's) that had become alienated by the division of labor. This, however, merely constitutes a rearguard action: the "disappearance of the subject" is historically inevitable due to the advance of capitalist rationalization. Every attempt to halt this development is, by definition, doomed to failure, according to Tafuri. And yet these "subjectivist" attempts have a specific purpose in terms of capitalist evolution in that they perform the task of providing a kind of comfort. In this sense too, Tafuri argues, a stance of this sort serves to prop up the system.

Tafuri considers that the constructive and destructive movements within the entire avant-garde movement are only seemingly opposed. They are both responses to the empirical everyday reality of the capitalist way of life; the former rejects it with a view to creating a new order, the latter responds by exalting the chaotic character of reality. The constructive tendencies "opposed Chaos, the empirical and the commonplace, with the principle of Form."[152] This "Form" originated in the inner laws of industrial production and was thus compatible with the underlying logic that gave this apparent chaos its structure. It is here that the significance of a movement like De Stijl is to be found: "The 'De Stijl' technique of decomposition of complex into elementary forms corresponded to the discovery that the 'new richness' of spirit could not be sought outside the 'new poverty' assumed by mechanical civilization."[153] The activity of the other, destructive tendencies had the opposite aim in view—to exalt chaos. Tafuri argues, however, that the tendency toward irony that was an aspect of this movement meant that a need for order was felt here too. "Dada instead plunged into chaos. By representing chaos, it confirmed its reality; by treating it with irony, it exposed a necessity that had been lacking."[154] Tafuri points, therefore, to an inner relationship between the constructive and destructive moments within the avant-garde. For this reason, he argues, it was no surprise that dadaism and constructivism merged after 1922.[155]

According to Tafuri, then, the whole concern of the avant-garde movements was to recognize and assimilate the dialectic of chaos and order that is fundamental to modern mechanized civilization: the dialectic between the apparent chaos of the constantly changing dynamic image of the city on the one hand and the underlying order of the de facto rationality of the system of production on the other—a rationality that in every case was deemed to be the decisive factor. The artistic labor of the avant-garde movements involved an assimilation of the new conditions of life that prevail in the modern city. This process of assimilation was a necessary precondition for a more thoroughgoing interiorization of these conditions by the people who were subjected to them. In Tafuri's scheme of things, the avant-garde movements are assigned the task of paving the way for a further proliferation and evolution of mechanistic civilization. They are, however, incapable of extending their assignment any further than this "vanguard" task: "The necessity of a programmed control of the new forces released by technology was very clearly pointed out by the avant-garde movements, who immediately afterwards discovered that they were not capable of giving concrete form to this entreaty of Reason."[156]

The avant-garde movements were incapable of genuinely influencing the course of capitalist evolution or of giving concrete form to the rationalization inherent in it. This task, Tafuri argues, was the work of architecture: "The Bauhaus, as the decantation chamber of the avant-garde, fulfilled the historic task of selecting from all the contributions of the avant-garde by testing them in terms of the needs of productive reality."[157] Architecture should be the mediator between the "progressive" demands in the work of avant-garde movements (including the demand for the planned control of the means of production) and the concrete reality of this production. According to Tafuri's diagnosis, however, architecture gets bogged down in this contradiction, because it is not prepared to accept its logical implication—that the contradiction can be solved only by a form of planning instituted outside of architecture, that would involve "a restructuring of production and consumption in general; in other words, the planned coordination of production."[158]

The fully planned control of production can be implemented only when there is a general socioeconomic form of planning that embraces all the sectors of social life and that is not confined to architecture. For architects to accept the consequences of this would mean disqualifying themselves: architecture would no longer be the subject of the plan but its object—and that is something that architects could not possibly accept: "Architecture between 1920 and 1930 was not ready to accept such consequences. What was clear was its 'political' role. Architecture (read: programming and planned reorganization of building production and of the city as productive organism) rather than revolution. Le Corbusier clearly enunciated this alternative."[159]

According to Tafuri, then, architecture attempts to take on the impossible task of being answerable for the technical organization of the restructuring of production and consumption. Instead of accepting the role of a participant in an overall plan, it presents itself as the author of this plan. This at least is how Tafuri understands the program of the New Objectivity, which accepts "all the conclusions on the 'death of the aura' with lucid objectivity" while at the same time completely failing to acknowledge the contradictory character of this assumption. If architecture undertakes to reorganize the whole field of social reality, in Tafuri's view it is by definition doomed to failure.

Implicit in the attitude of the architects of the New Objectivity, who accepted the "death of the aura," is a new attitude toward aesthetic experience: architecture no longer has the task of producing objects to be viewed and admired in a static fashion; rather, it must give form to a process—in other words, it must offer a dynamic experience. It is in these terms that Tafuri discusses Hilberseimer's book *Grossstadtarchitektur*, which treats the total structure of the modern city as an enormous "social machine." Hilberseimer starts out from the individual building as the first element in an uninterrupted chain of production that ends with the city itself: the city consists of a sequence of elements that no longer take the form of separate, individual "objects," but are endlessly reproduced in an abstract, elementary montage. Tafuri emphasizes this approach to illustrate that "in face of the new techniques of production and the expansion and rationalization of the market, the architect as producer of objects had indeed become an inadequate figure."[160]

Nonetheless, there were architects—the opponents of the New Objectivity—who remained bogged down in the "crisis of the object." Tafuri mentions Taut and Loos as well as Poelzig and Mendelsohn. While the architects of the New Objectivity movement accepted the destruction of the object and its replacement with a process, their opponents tried to counter this development by overemphasizing the object. But in that respect all they were doing was to carry out a rearguard action: they were responding to the secondary needs of the European bourgeoisie while knowing that they could not offer any comprehensive alternatives to the approach proposed by the New Objectivity.

According to Tafuri, the architects who subscribed to the credo of the New Objectivity had committed themselves to a concrete "politicizing" of architecture: May and Wagner, for instance, deployed their technical knowledge within a context of clear political and social-democratic options. In practice, however, this politicizing of architecture turned out to have a limited success: they did not manage to control developments throughout the city, nor could they restructure the system of production.

Furthermore, as Tafuri points out, the intervention model of the *Siedlungen* formed part of a broad anti-urban ideology that was rooted in a hostility toward the big city: "But the settlement itself openly set the model of 'town' against that of the large city. This was Tönnies against Simmel and Weber."[161]

In choosing this approach, Tafuri argues, these architects were opting for a fragmented and static organization of the city. This was the immediate reason for the limited success of this strategy: the modern city that is the product of capitalism does not permit any permanent balance; its internal dynamic undermines every attempt to impose a balance of this sort. The longing for a *Gemeinschaft* (community) as Tönnies had formulated it was continually forced to make way for the ever-encroaching reality of the *Gesellschaft* (society), and so the attempts of the New Objectivity to create a rational organization were doomed to failure: "Improbability, multifunctionality, multiplicity, and lack of organic structure—in short, all the contradictory aspects assumed by the modern metropolis—are thus seen to have remained outside the attempts at a rationalization pursued by central European architecture."[162]

Tafuri's set of hypotheses betrays the unmistakable imprint of Walter Benjamin—at least of the Benjamin who wrote the work of art essay and "The Author as Producer." While Benjamin analyzes the work of Baudelaire as the product of an interiorizing of the shock experience that is typical of modernity, Tafuri applies the same notion to the whole of the avant-garde and to different currents in modern architecture. The pivotal notion here is the idea that the principles that prevailed in the avant-garde movements—the destruction of values, the pursuit of the new, the quest for Form, the extolling of Chaos—are the same as those that underlie capitalist civilization. Tafuri shares this idea with other authors who were influenced by Marxism, such as Benjamin, Bloch, and Adorno. The problem is that they all draw different conclusions from this fundamental notion. Benjamin, for instance, continued to cherish the hope that an action of radicalizing capitalist rationalization might at a certain point bring about a transformation that would inaugurate a new form of society. For Bloch, on the other hand, the inner relationship that he perceived between the New Objectivity and capitalism was proof that modern architecture was incapable of designing a new society (he did not, however, include the whole avant-garde movement in this diagnosis). Adorno—as I will show later—sees this relationship as indispensable for developing an artistic practice that contains a genuine critique of the social system, while at the same time it has the effect of making this very critique marginal and inefficacious. The striking feature of Tafuri's analysis is that, unlike these other authors, he does not allow any margin for critical possibilities or for the hope of alternatives. Tafuri's critique of ideologies reveals *every* artistic and theoretical development—apparently without exception—as operating within the logic of the capitalist system and as being "historically necessary" to it. Tafuri attributes a monolithic character to this system that seems to be ineluctable.

As for the philosophical infrastructure of this diagnosis, Tafuri refers his readers to the work of Massimo Cacciari,[163] whose stance concerning "negative thought" is indeed of vital structural significance for Tafuri's set of hypotheses.

The Metropolis and Negative Thought

Cacciari's discourse on negative thought can best be understood by looking at his analysis of two texts: Simmel's "The Metropolis and Mental Life" of 1903 and Benjamin's study of Baudelaire that dates from the 1930s.[164] In Cacciari's view, negative thought represents a philosophical approach that stresses the irreducible nature of contradictions and the central position that the phenomenon of crisis occupies in capitalist development. He thus contrasts negative thought with dialectics, because the latter continually aims to achieve an ultimate synthesis of conflicting positions: "Negative thought registers the leaps, the ruptures, the innovations that occur in history, never the transition, the flow, the historical continuum."[165] Negative thought is operative within the process of capitalist development—in fact, it constitutes the most advanced moment in capitalist ideology. According to Cacciari, negative thought represents a crisis moment within capitalism; at the same time, he argues, this moment of crisis does not form any real threat to the system and is in fact favorable to its continued expansion.[166] The capitalist principle of development, after all, involves a depreciation of existing values by definition: capitalism is effectively synonymous for a situation where crisis follows on crisis.

It was Simmel's achievement, according to Cacciari, that he revealed rationalization—both in terms of human relations and of the money economy—as forming the basic structure of the Metropolis (figure 68). Cacciari understands Metropolis in an allegorical sense: it represents the modern condition and capitalist civilization—hence the capital *M*. Following Simmel, he states that the Metropolis is the seat of the *Geist* (spirit): and its hallmark is the process of *Vergeistigung* (spiritualization), understood as the process by which the personal and the emotional—both being forms of subjectivity—are abstracted to the benefit of a calculating and calculable functional rationality.

Cacciari extrapolates Simmel's discourse by pointing to an explicit relationship between this process of *Vergeistigung* and the increasing prevalence of the commodity system.[167] In small towns, he argues, one can still speak of use values and exchange values coexisting, without these two moments necessarily being in a dialectical relation with each other: it is perfectly conceivable that an object will simply be "used" without it being produced for the market. The Metropolis, on the contrary, is distinguished by an unrelenting cycle in which use values and exchange values are converted into each other uninterruptedly in order to ensure the continuity of production. In the Metropolis, people's behavioral patterns correspond to this continual transformation and are therefore eventually also subject to the laws of production.

By providing us with the tools for understanding the Metropolis, Simmel paves the way for an analysis of the Metropolis as a (necessary) instrument of domination in capitalist development. This development can take place only if the social domain is integrated in the logic of commodities. In Cacciari's view, an analysis like this belongs to negative thought. Even so, Simmel does not succeed, according to Cacciari, in following the logic of negativity through to its conclusions. Simmel argues that the metropolis, despite its being governed by the money economy, and by the principle that everything is calculable and quantifiable, remains the place par excellence for the development of individual freedom. The metropolis offers freedom of movement, freedom of action, a liberation from prejudice and traditional ties; all this creates an opportunity for everyone to develop unique personalities to the full. With this thesis, according to Cacciari, Simmel postulates a synthesis between "Metropolis and mental life" and refuses to accept the full consequences of his own analysis: "It is a synthesis that recuperates the value of community, of the *'Gemeinschaft,'* in order to reaffirm it in society, in the *'Gesellschaft'*; it recuperates the individualized freedom and equality of that *Gemeinschaft* and makes them the mainstay of the ideology of this *Gesellschaft*. But this synthesis is precisely what the theory of the negative would deny." [168]

With precisely those elements in mind that, in Cacciari's view, lead logically to the conclusion that every possibility of a "synthesis" is lacking, Simmel performs an operation that reduces them to sociohistorical circumstances. It is clear from this, according to Cacciari, that he is incapable of grasping the truly fundamental character of this crisis and of realizing that this makes any synthesis essentially impossible. He pursues the logic of negativity only to the point where it breaks decisively with every possibility of synthesis and control. At this point Simmel abandons his quest and instead undertakes an attempt to rescue nostalgic and superseded bourgeois values such as individuality and personal freedom. With this maneuver Simmel incorporates the negative in a system of thought that in the end serves the (ideological) function of achieving the transition from city to Metropolis, but without his being in any way aware of the ideological purport of his discourse. Cacciari considers that Simmels "synthesis" is symptomatic of the historical impossibility of capitalist development to achieve any understanding of its own character, the basic features of which are rationality, abstraction, and the rejection of the old values.

In his study of Baudelaire, Benjamin goes further than Simmel, according to Cacciari. Benjamin's central thesis is that Baudelaire's lyric poetry is a record of an experience of shock. The poet regarded it as his task to parry these shocks, no matter where they came from, with his physical and mental personality. In Baudelaire, moreover, the hidden presence of the metropolitan masses makes itself felt constantly, finding expression in the imagery and rhythm of his verse. The metropolis affects individuals in their deepest core. Both the shock experiences and the superficial encounters that are dealt with in Baudelaire's poetry are typical of the changing structure of experience. The form that his work takes is therefore also permeated with the process of rationalization, and with the feelings of hope and fear that accompany this process. Benjamin analyzes Baudelaire's poetry as being the epitome of the internalization of the basic features of the Metropolis.

In order to interpret Baudelaire in this tenor, Benjamin uses negativity as a theoretical instrument for achieving an adequate understanding of the reality of the Metropolis. What Benjamin emphasizes in Baudelaire is his way of dealing with the new structure of experience; this new structure is entirely bound up with the total *Entwertung* of values that occurs in the Metropolis. This process of the destruction of values no longer leaves any room for a synthesis or for the values of humanism:

> The negation of these very values is presupposed by negative thought in its hopeless understanding of the early forms of modern capitalist society. This negation is rationalization, is "*Vergeistigung*," and it moves in the same direction as this society, directly and knowingly sharing its destiny. But at the same time, it lays bare the logic of this society, negates its possibility of "transcrescence," and radicalizes its aims and needs; in other words, the negative reaches the point where it exposes this society's internal conflicts and contradictions, its fundamental problematics or negativity.[169]

This interpretation is something that Benjamin recognized in the work of Kafka, which he discussed in a letter to Scholem.[170] The most important point that Benjamin makes in this letter, according to Cacciari, is that there is a connection between the form that the experience of the metropolitan condition takes in Kafka's work and the discoveries of contemporary physics. Benjamin quotes a passage, from a book by a physicist, describing all the forces and counterforces involved in the simple action of someone entering a room: not only must he overcome the atmospheric pressure, but he must also succeed in putting his foot down on a spot that is moving at a speed of 30 kilometers per second around the sun. The feeling of alienation one gets from the extreme rationality of this fragment distinctly reminds one of the way that Kafka traces the logical consequences of a fundamentally incomprehensible system such as the law. In both instances, extreme rationality leads to alienation: analysis turns into tautology and there is no longer a way out of the maze to meaning. At the same time, one cannot help suspecting that there is a meaning; one can get a glimpse of it. This meaning, however, never becomes completely palpable. This is what emerges in Kafka's work—not so much a logic of the signs, nor an ultimate signification, but the fact that a difference exists, a difference between sign and thing, between language and reality. It is in the way that he insists on this difference that the meaning of Kafka's work is to be found: "The emphasis is no longer placed on the expression of the sign's logic, but on the expression of difference. Carried to its logical extreme, the rationality of the sign traps the sign within itself—as signifier without signified, fact without object, contradiction and difference."[171]

In Cacciari's opinion, Benjamin uses this comparison with scientific rationality to show to what extent Kafka's work is impregnated with the negative logic of the devaluation of all values. But even Benjamin does not take the final step by drawing the conclusions that should logically follow from his lucid perceptions. It is true that he exposes the essence of the Metropolis as a complex constellation of functions, interpretations, and machinations that regulate the entire system, including the domain of culture. But he does not succeed in grasping the function of the negative: he does not understand that the Metropolis is founded on negation.

It is difficult to avoid the feeling that Cacciari is carrying out a somewhat curious operation with his postulate of negative thought. Tomás Llorens points out that a certain *petitio principii*, a self-fulfilling premise, plays a role here:

> Cacciari seems to have set out to analyze the concept of metropolis as ideology—i.e. "as false consciousness"—and then, having found at its core the schema of "negative thought," he concludes that there is no true alternative, and therefore places his own search for truth under the aegis of the same schema. There is an element of self-contradiction here which cannot but affect the conclusion drawn from the analysis.[172]

It would indeed seem as though Cacciari is using his analysis of negative thought to provide arguments for a monolithic vision of modernity. Modernity—inseparably linked as it is with capitalist civilization—is described in his work as a phenomenon whose course is not in any way meaningfully affected by individual contributions in the form of theoretical or artistic currents. Cacciari seems to treat every intellectual interpretation, no matter how progressive, as in the end serving the evolution of a society whose less acceptable aspects it had set out to criticize. Less progressive theories are dismissed by him as "nostalgic" or "beside the point." Apparently he excludes the possibility that any form of critical thought could emerge that would do anything other than confirm the system it claims to condemn.

And yet this is not an adequate picture of Cacciari's work. In his concrete analyses he detects positions and strategies that do not entirely fit into a monolithic scheme like this. In the epilogue to *Architecture and Nihilism*, for instance, he distinguishes three possible ways of dealing with the condition of "nihilism fulfilled" that is his definition of modernity. In the first instance there is the absurd position of those who still aim at distilling a "culture" out of this nihilism—a position that he discerns in the nostalgic pathos of the *Werkbund* that remains determined to dress up the products of generalized rootlessness with quality and value. In the second instance there are those who aim to express the universal mobilization of the epoch in a symbol: while the specific character of the different places of the world disappears as the result of the leveling influence of modernity, they treat the whole world as a single specific place. This is typical, for instance, of the work of Paul Scheerbart or Bruno Taut in his expressionist phase. Finally, there are people like Loos who belong to a "school of resistance." Unlike the members of the first group, their resistance is not rooted in a nostalgic longing for coherence and harmony; on the contrary, it is based on a lucid and disillusioned grasp of the reality of nihilism. It is a resistance that materializes in design projects and which gives form to a critique and to a radical questioning. What is questioned and criticized is the oversimplification and one-dimensionality implicit in the attitude of "nihilism fulfilled." Loos's projects are based on the idea of composition as involving a listening to the differences. Meaning cannot be postulated as something that is universal and given in advance. What one can do is to create a suggestion of meaning by exposing the differences. In this stance Cacciari does apparently discern a possibility of reacting to the condition of modernity in an authentic and critical fashion.

Dwelling and the "Places" of Modernity

Francesco Dal Co comes to similar conclusions, if by a different route. In the first chapter of *Figures of Architecture and Thought*, a book that he dedicates to Cacciari, Dal Co investigates contrasting notions about "Dwelling and the 'Places' of Modernity." His point of departure here is Hermann Bahr and the ideal of reconciliation that Bahr proposes in his essay on "The Modern." According to Dal Co, this pastoral ideal of an integration between the self and the world, of an unbroken, harmonious transition between inner and outer worlds, is also the dominant tendency in modern architecture. Dal Co contrasts this ideal of unity and reconciliation with Nietzsche's diagnosis of modernity. Nietzsche talks of an irreparable rupture: with modern man there is no longer any correspondence between inner and outer; and this is a situation that cannot be remedied. A number of authors have gone along with this idea of Nietzsche's and have used it as a starting point for their interpretation of modernity. Hermann Hesse, for instance, constructs a notion of "home" on the basis of a reflection on the nomadic nature of existence in the metropolis. The *Heimat*, the homeland, belongs irrevocably to the past, and its image is cherished in memory: modern man is called to an adventurous existence of journeying and migrations. This journey does have a goal, but this goal does not have the fullness and sweetness of the *Heimat*. Nevertheless, the journey is guided by a longing for a home, as distinguished from the homeland, a "shelter within myself where my ego alone resides."[173] The longed-for home is based on a rejection of the rest of the world, on renunciation. The gap between world and home is unbridgeable; inner and outer are divorced from each other. Dwelling in Hesse's view is therefore seen not as an integration with the world but as separation from it.

Hesse's intuition that there is a distinction between home and homeland, according to Dal Co, has not been taken up in architecture, however. Modern architecture, Dal Co writes, attempts to create a space for dwelling that would reconcile tensions and where the original meaning of homeland—the sense of unity with one's country, with the soil, with the history of the nation and the spirit of the people—

would be recaptured in dwelling. Architectural culture has adopted this ideal from the work of Tönnies and Spengler, among others. In the work of these authors a rupture is discerned between the old social form of the *Gemeinschaft* and the new reality of the *Gesellschaft*. The *Gemeinschaft* is based on an organic link between people and their environment, on continuity and cohesion. The *Gemeinschaft* is the natural environment for *Kultur* and *Bildung*, both of which rely on a harmonious relationship between different domains of life (*Bildung* especially refers to those aspects of education that instill moral and social values). Dwelling has everything to do with taking root and with a feeling of oneness. The *Gesellschaft*, the social form that prevails in the metropolis, is based on difference and on rootlessness. Technological civilization can develop in the metropolis, but it is cut off from any possibility of cultural cohesion. The separating out of the different areas of life is the hallmark of the metropolis. Dwelling, therefore, also assumes another form there. No longer is the sense of oneness with a place or a social group the decisive factor. Dwelling in the metropolis has more to do with finding one's own place and with the negation of every organic connection with a community.

Dal Co considers that the concept of dwelling that most fully corresponds with life in the metropolis is to be found in the work of Levinas: "By understanding residence as an act foreign to taking root, Levinas indirectly confirms the negation of the organic value of the community environment as an expression of the telluric bond, while emphasizing that the essential character of the home lies with the wandering that makes dwelling possible."[174] In Levinas's work one encounters a demystified notion of dwelling, one that is based on a notion of extraterritoriality: a person chooses a house, dwelling means taking up residence somewhere; it does not originate in a preexisting link with a place or a community, but consists of an act of choosing. In this concept house and place are radically different. The house is the base from which the discovery and conquest of one's surroundings can take place. The house does not form any part of a harmonious relationship; nor is it part of a pacification process that brings about a reconciliation between people and their environment. On the contrary, the house is a border; it delineates a linguistic disharmony. Dwelling is the activity that produces this difference.

Dal Co sees a similar concept of dwelling in Heidegger's "Building, Dwelling, Thinking," which also takes the notion of an overthrow of the connection between place and dwelling as its point of departure. In the case of Heidegger, dwelling is not a harmonious expression of a relationship to a place that can be assumed in advance; on the contrary, it is that which makes a place a place. Dwelling is therefore a process of establishing meaning. Dal Co refers explicitly to Cacciari's interpretation in "Eupalinos or Architecture," in which Cacciari states that there is an analogy between dwelling and *poiēsis*—dwelling is an act of "waiting listening."[175] Dwelling confronts one with the destiny of "unconcealment" and emphasizes how far humanity has come from a time when unity and harmony were still possible. In dwelling, the poverty of human beings is made manifest.

Nonetheless, says Dal Co, modern architecture has failed to grasp this fact; indeed, it specifically adopts a stance of refusing to acknowledge this distance, this poverty. At the basis of this opposition is a utopian longing that desperately tries to bridge this distance, conquer the poverty, and restore the lost harmony.

In short, the experience of dwelling as exposure to unconcealment leads to the recognition of the condition of homelessness that is typical of the metropolis:

> Thus there is no harmony in dwelling, since no "fourfold" in modernity
> can recompose the wandering of which the home is product. Vanished
> for the modern project is the prospect of grasping, through its own
> forms, the full presence of a place . . . the point at which the divine
> traverses man's abode and manifests itself. If dwelling is nothing but
> the unresolved manifestation of the lacerations of living and hence an
> experience given to regret, then it is up to modern man to know
> this condition to its fullest extent, to the essence of metropolitan
> homelessness.[176]

Dal Co concurs with Cacciari, therefore, in interpreting Heidegger's text as an analysis of that which requires to be questioned (*Fragwürdiges*) at the heart of modernity. He too emphasizes the experience of homelessness as a basic condition of life in the Metropolis. Under these circumstances "dwelling" can only be defined as loss, as an exposure to the irrevocable consequences of the disappearance of the harmony and oneness that were typical of the *Gemeinschaft*. Modernity has severed the organic bonds between inner and outer realms, between dwellers and place, between individuals and the group, and there is no new wholeness that has taken its place. This is the reality that modern architecture has failed to see. It is the historian's task to clear up this misunderstanding and to show precisely how the illusory and utopian character of modern architecture attempts to justify itself. By adopting this stance, Dal Co is declaring his support for the aim—stated explicitly by Tafuri—of treating the writing of history as a critique of ideology.

History as Critique of Ideology

Manfredo Tafuri follows the Marxist tradition in treating history writing as a form of critique of ideology. In *Theories and History of Architecture* he opens a frontal assault on the approach known as "operative criticism," exposing its ideological character. He defines operative criticism as "an analysis of architecture (or of the arts in general) that, instead of an abstract survey, has as its objective the planning of a precise poetical tendency, anticipated in its structures and derived from historical analyses programmatically distorted and finalized."[177]

Operative criticism draws on history in order to give a certain direction to the future. In Tafuri's view, this is anything but an innocent activity. A renowned instance of a critical position of this sort is Sigfried Giedion—who consequently becomes the target of Tafuri's polemic. Giedion claimed that history is no neutral discipline but that it should make a contribution to overcoming the evils of one's own time. For this reason he deliberately embraced the cause of modern architecture, and his writings therefore have the character of an apology. His working method, however, leads inevitably to a selective history, which on a fairly subjective basis chooses to deal with a number of developments while omitting others. Furthermore, in Tafuri's view, Giedion's interpretation tends to distort the historical facts in order to fit them into an a priori pattern of development.[178]

This manner of writing history overshoots the mark, however, because "instead of making history, one makes ideology: which besides betraying the task of history, hides the real possibilities of transforming reality."[179] Since operative criticism hides historical reality behind an ideological veil, the possibilities of change that are genuinely present are not perceived. The resulting distortion of history means that rigorous analysis is replaced by mystification and prejudice. A procedure of this sort can only end in self-deception.

Tafuri opposes the notion of operative criticism with that of historic criticism: in his view, criticism and history are identical—in other words, architectural criticism should always be historic criticism;[180] what is more, there is a hiatus between architectural criticism on the one hand and architectural practice on the other.[181] Architectural criticism (architectural history, that is) cannot be expected to offer any ready-made solutions for the problems that occur in the practice of the profession. All that history and criticism can do is to help clarify the context—in the broadest sense of the word—within which architectural production is carried out; they cannot provide any guidelines for its future development.[182]

It is this idea, according to Jameson, that lies behind what is generally assumed to be Tafuri's "pessimistic" attitude toward the possibilities of contemporary architecture. Indeed, Tafuri's condemning the principle of operative criticism makes it by definition impossible for him to undertake the defense of any contemporary current or figure whatsoever. His notorious pronouncements about the impossibility for contemporary architecture to achieve anything more than "sublime uselessness"[183] should be seen in this light: rather than a carefully considered and definitive "position," they constitute a formal necessity within the broader structure of Tafuri's text.[184] Jameson in fact correctly points out that in his studies of specific cases, the Italian historian has a much more subtle and nonpartisan judgment than his sometimes rather extreme utterances would lead one to suspect. Like Cacciari, Tafuri tones down the radicalism of his theoretical position with the subtlety and philological detail of his concrete interpretations.

In the end, however, it must be admitted that both Tafuri and Cacciari seem to have a rather monolithic notion of history. They see modernity as an increasingly totalitarian, closed system within which concrete political and cultural practice appears to have no genuine impact on the course of historical development. Their theory displays a kind of materialism based on the primacy of the economic infrastructure—capitalism—which is viewed as the decisive factor in every area of social and cultural life. The relation between infrastructure and superstructure in their opinion is not unambiguous or mechanistic, but multifarious and layered. Even so, there is little scope in their theoretical position for practices that might have an effective critical influence in the direction of liberation and emancipation.[185]

Cacciari's discourse defines reality on the basis of the conviction that every form of "synthesis," every attempt to reconcile the contradictions, is illusory and has been superseded. Any theory that might promise a future emancipated society has therefore become impossible. And any critical mode of coexistence with the reality of capitalist civilization is unmasked in his discourse as a phenomenon of crisis that in fact ends up confirming the system. The only justifiable attitude, given this assumption, would seem to be that of a resistance originating in a completely disillusioned understanding of the reality of its own existence. A resistance like this cannot be ascribed any positive definition, because that would inadvertently take on the form of nostalgic or utopian desires, and thus be doomed to inefficacy. The only thing that is possible within this logic is to create the suggestion of a difference by demonstrating the existence of a plurality of languages—something that Cacciari perceives in the work of Loos and Kafka.

The notion of the existence of a "plurality of languages" that cannot be reduced to a single all-embracing synthesizing discourse is typical of the Venice School in another sense too. Patrizia Lombardo gives a lively description of the way that Cacciari and people like him link their intellectual research with their concrete political practice in the trade union movement and in—or in alliance with—the Communist Party. This is not a case of an unbroken, self-evident link: the language of professors is after all different from that of party militants. Lombardo sketches the movement between these different languages as a choreography in which synchronic and diachronic elements from contrasting registers coincide without forming any smoothly unified whole. There is a plurality of levels that corresponds to the actual preconditions of modern life. The realization of the ineluctable character of this fragmentation is what produces negative thought. According to Lombardo, this plurality explains why Walter Benjamin plays such a central role in Cacciari's intellectual universe: Benjamin also oscillated between different levels; with him, too, one can talk of a fascination with incompatible modes of thought, such as Marxism and mysticism.

Benjamin fills a similar role in Tafuri's work. It is by relying upon Benjamin's inspiration that Tafuri is able to give plausibility to an apparent contradiction in his work.[186] This contradiction has to do with the incompatibility between the Marxist concept of truth and that of poststructuralism, both of which form an active presence in Tafuri's work. Marxism in the strict sense of the word claims that there is such a thing as an "objective" reality which allows one to draw a distinction between ideology and genuine theory: it is only the authentic theory that offers an accurate account of objective reality, while ideology gives us a distorted and mystified picture. A similar assumption would seem to underlie the book *Architecture and Utopia*, which postulates a relatively unambiguous and monolithic interpretation of modernity. Although counterpastoral in its stressing of the unavoidable contradictions that are inherent to capitalism, the concept of modernity that is implicit in this book doesn't leave much space for an active intervention by intellectuals or artists that would really be capable of altering the course of things. Modernity is seen as a blind historical force that, though clearly programmed, is not programmatic in that it doesn't not come forth from any conscious project of emancipation and liberation.

In *Modern Architecture*, however, the emphasis is placed right from the outset upon the multifarious character of recent architectural history: "Obviously the intersection of all those manifold histories will never end up in unity."[187] The influence of poststructuralism, which takes as its point of departure the notion that reality cannot be grasped except through socially defined—and therefore distorted—categories, is more pronouncedly present here. Given a basis such as this, truth appears as diversified and impossible to define exhaustively. This stance, however, cannot easily be reconciled with the Marxist appeal to an "authentic theory." This contradiction is and remains a central epistemological problem for contemporary theory.[188] Benjamin, who was also familiar with this problem (though of course not in the same poststructuralist terms), solved it by postulating an alternative to the "history of the victors" in the form of a history that does not treat the historical facts as a series of causally connected moments, but rather as a constellation of monads in which the entire reality of history, with all its virtual revolutionary possibilities and hidden connections, crystallizes constantly, in a different form on each occasion. By defining history in this fashion the historian is also in a position to take the side of the losers, thereby increasing the chance that the fragile messianic power that is present in every historical moment can gain the upper hand.[189] Without adopting Benjamin's discourse in so many words, Tafuri develops a similar chain of argument in a text of 1980, "The Historical Project."[190] He points to the necessary plurality of languages that architecture and criticism have to deal with—the languages of design, of technologies, of the institutions, and of history—cannot be related by means of a universal hermeneutics. They remain fundamentally estranged, are in essence untranslatable, and their plurality is irreducible. This means that it is impossible for architectural criticism to link up directly with architectural practice. The two disciplines operate within different linguistic systems and their aims are not parallel. This radical counterpastoral stance prevents a truly programmatic attitude because its logic forecloses the possibility that the future could be consciously fabricated.

Tafuri thinks that a similar plurality is at stake in architectural history, which also cannot be described as a linear series of events that are linked in an unambiguous fashion. Writing history, therefore, is like working on a jigsaw puzzle in which the pieces can be combined in different ways. The form that emerges is in each case a provisional one. An intensive study of historical fragments leads one to a merely provisional conclusion. Tafuri describes the historian's work as a labor of Sisyphus that never ends definitively.[191] And yet that does not mean that it is a neutral or arbitrary form of work: the aim continues to be to produce an analysis that is "capable of calling into question at every instant the historical legitimacy of the capitalistic division of labor."[192] For this reason, history should be seen as a project, a project of crisis. The eventual goal is to subject the whole of reality to crisis: "The real problem is how to project a criticism capable of constantly putting itself into crisis by putting into crisis the real. The real, mind you, and not merely its individual sections."[193]

Cacciari might reply that subjecting reality to crisis is the driving force behind capitalist development, and that all Tafuri's history does is to find a language for the most extreme implications of negative thought. One is indeed led to the conclusion that the Venice School's idea of itself is subject to this kind of interpretation: the Venice authors assume that their analyses represent the only tenable position for a critical intellectual, even though they might not be capable of directly influencing the course of social development. Like Benjamin, they state that it is their deliberate aim to exercise a certain influence on reality. Like Benjamin again, they have no illusions about the actual impact their work may have. They still maintain, however, that it is necessary to continue this labor of Sisyphus and to do everything within their power to subject the standard narratives in the realm of history to a crisis. This stance originates in a combination of a "total disillusionment about the age and nevertheless an unreserved profession of loyalty to it." It materializes cautiously in the form of "projects." Both Tafuri and Cacciari use this term to indicate a mode and method for conceiving of a form of resistance. In the case of Cacciari, the term refers to the way that Loos in his designs makes a criticism of the self-fulfilling prophesy of nihilism. Tafuri calls history a project because it also has to do with a design: history is concerned with a continual redesigning of the past; it is continually engaged in reconstructing the theoretical framework within which historical events are to be understood. It is the activity of designing, we may assume, that for both authors produces a degree of freedom, which is absent from the calculating one-dimensional thought that is typical of the Metropolis. Neither for Tafuri nor for Cacciari does the term "project" have the utopian and programmatic connotations of immediate emancipation that lead Habermas to talk of "the project of modernity." For it is all too clear to them that a society that is governed by the regime of modernity does not easily respond to individual actions or analyses.

Beauty today
can have no other measure
except the depth
to which a work
resolves contradictions.
A work must cut
through the contradictions
and overcome them,
not by covering them up,
but by pursuing them.

Theodor W. Adorno, 1965

Architecture as Critique of Modernity

4

Avant-Garde versus Modernism

When in 1949 the Swiss artist Max Bill, a former student at the Bauhaus, was commissioned by the Scholl Foundation to design a group of buildings for a school in Ulm, he persuaded his clients that the curriculum of the new school should be modeled on that of the Bauhaus. After he built the school he was appointed its director. Bill saw a direct line from the concerns of Morris and Ruskin via the Werkbund and van de Velde down to the aims of the Bauhaus of Gropius—and thence to the system of his own Hochschule für Gestaltung (School of Design). The theme running through this tradition was the desire to achieve *gute Form* (good design): according to Bill, the promise of a widespread distribution of high-quality articles for everyday use was inherent in the industrialization of society; this promise, he said, had not been fulfilled—partly because of the bad taste of the public, continually reinforced by advertising and publicity; and partly because of the inadequate links between existing educational institutions and the needs of industry. The new school was intended to respond to this need. Its aim was to guarantee that industrial designers got an education that would enable them to fulfill their social responsibilities and produce designs for the rational manufacture of high-quality products:

> The school is a continuation of the Bauhaus. . . . Its underlying principle is the combination of a broad but thorough technical training with a sound general education on modern lines. By this means the enterprise and constructive spirit of youth can be infused with a proper sense of social responsibilities and taught that cooperative work on important problems of modern design is a major contribution to the most urgent task of the modern age: the humanizing of our increasingly mechanistic civilization.[1]

Behind Bill's educational system was a functionalist credo that stated that rationality and the use of modern materials were the basic elements of good design. The attempt to respond to the requirements of industry and the improvement of the quality of the products formed the *Leitmotiv*. The artistic input of the individual designer was put at the service of the integration of design with industrial mass production. Bill's ideas reflect a pastoral and programmatic concept of modernity and are in that respect comparable with those of Giedion. Like Giedion, Bill felt a great admiration for Robert Maillart, the Swiss engineer, on whose work he edited a book.[2] Bill, however, represented a generation of architects and designers whose commitment to arts took a very specific form. For this generation functionalism was an evident requirement. They accepted the need for an enrichment of life through "good design"; their notion of design, however, was dominated by the needs of industry and mass production. This idea was in the end radically different from the avantgarde position that aimed to abolish the distinction between art and life by organizing life on the basis of art.

As in design, the prevailing trend in postwar modernist architecture no longer had much in common with an avant-garde idea: functionalism was now smoothly incorporated into the logic of postwar reconstruction that had as its program the speedy and efficient production of a large number of dwellings. The socially critical position that modern architecture had stood for in the years between the wars was thus replaced by an institutionalized and officially recognized approach.

This development did not pass unnoticed, however. Max Bill encountered some opposition, for instance, when he founded the Hochschule für Gestaltung. This came first from Asger Jorn, the Danish painter who together with Constant and Dotremont was one of the figures behind the Cobra group of artists.[3] In 1953 Jorn initiated the International Movement for an Imaginist Bauhaus. He accused Max Bill of having reduced the revolutionary ideas of the Bauhaus into a soft academic discourse and of misusing them for a reactionary strategy. The Bauhaus's, argued Jorn, was instituted first and foremost in response to the question of the position of the artist in the age of machines. The Bauhaus's answer was to work on the education of the artist. According to Jorn, however, experience has proven that the solution did not lie there: "The direct transfer of artistic gifts is impossible; artistic adaptation takes place through a series of contradictory phases: Stupefaction—Wonder—Imitation—Rejection—Experience—Possession. . . . Our practical conclusion is the following: we are abandoning all effort at pedagogical action and moving toward experimental activity."[4] Jorn therefore emphasized the experimental character that was inherent in the practice of art. In his view, this laboratory function by which different artists stimulated each other to research and innovation was the most vital contribution of the Bauhaus experience of the 1920s. It was this quality that he aimed once more to restore to prominence in his Movement for an Imaginist Bauhaus and in his critique of functionalism.

In the conflict between Bill and Jorn, a rift emerges that is very similar to the one Bloch had observed between functionalism and expressionism. Bill emphasizes functionality and rationality in construction, while ascribing a subordinate role to the imagination. In Jorn's view the validity of all activity in the field of design lies in the imagination—in innovation and experiment; the requirements of function and rationality are entirely secondary categories for him.

Jorn was not alone in his views. He found allies and fellow spirits in various groups and individuals who saw themselves as the legitimate heirs of the prewar avant-garde movements. They opposed the integration of artists in a commercial circuit, insisting on the role of the artist as social critic and innovator. This avant-garde in fact operated to the left of modernism in architecture. The symbiosis that had existed between progressive architects and artists before the war had ceased to be self-evident.

In 1957 various groups, among them the Movement for an Imaginist Bauhaus, decided to merge in the Situationist International. In their early years most of the activities of the situationists formed part of the program for a "unitary urbanism" that consisted of a vigorous critique of current modernist urbanism. Unitary urbanism rejected the utilitarian logic of the consumer society, aiming instead for the realization of a dynamic city, a city in which freedom and play would have a central role. By operating collectively, the situationists aimed to achieve a creative interpretation of their everyday surroundings, and they created situations that subverted the normal state of affairs.

A striking feature of international situationism was its pronounced theoretical content. An active exchange developed between situationist theory and the discussions of Marxist groups such as Socialisme ou Barbarie. Lucien Goldmann and Henri Lefebvre in particular exercised an unquestionable influence on the theoreticians of this movement. As a result international situationism formed one of the moments in the twentieth century where the trajectory of the artistic avant-garde merged with a theoretically informed political activism.

International situationism was the last of the avant-garde movements that explicitly strove to overthrow the status quo by dissolving the boundaries between art, social praxis, and theoretical reflection. Its aim was an immediate revolution which would be performed on all levels of society and which would permeate the whole experience of life. Thus, it opposed all instances which could be identified with the establishment—including the contemporary praxis of architecture and urbanism. For the situationists, it was clear that modernist architecture had long ceased to oppose tendencies toward rationalization and conformism that were part of a capitalist consumer culture. Thus, an attack against the prevailing functionalism was one of their priorities. This criticism found its most concrete manifestation in New Babylon, a long-term project by Constant that originated in situationist experiments.

New Babylon: The Antinomies of Utopia

By the time that Constant (born 1920) embarked on his New Babylon project, he had already acquired a reputation as a painter and member of the Cobra group.[5] The event that marked the beginnings of New Babylon was the meeting of a group of avant-garde artists in 1956 in Alba, Italy, where Constant delivered a lecture entitled "Demain la poésie logera la vie" (Tomorrow Poetry Will Be the House of Life). The meeting in Alba was instrumental in setting up the Situationist International, which was officially established in London in 1957.[6] A central figure in this operation was Guy Debord, who was active in one of the constituting groups—the Lettrist International—which revolted against the commercializing of art and strove to bring about creative situations through collective actions. The cooperation between Debord and Constant would be a key factor in the initial development of unitary urbanism.

Constant, New Babylon,
bird's-eye perspective of group
of sectors I, 1964.

(Collection Gemeentemuseum,
The Hague.)

As an example of the program for a "unitary urbanism," New Babylon is the most fully developed counterpart of functionalist architecture (figure 69). It is a utopian scheme for a new mode of dwelling and a new society that took the form of a vast series of maquettes, charts, sketches, and paintings. New Babylon offers a consistent critique of social modernity—it was not without reason that Constant called his project an "antithesis of the society of lies."[7] New Babylon is a simulation of a situation of total liberation—of an abolition of all norms, conventions, traditions, and habits. The project radicalizes and idealizes the transitory aspects of the experience of modernity. It imagines a world in which all that is fleeting and transient has acquired the force of a law; a world of collective creation and absolute transparency where everything is exposed to the public gaze. In New Babylon imagination is in power and *homo ludens* is sovereign. At the same time the project testifies to the paradoxes and contradictions inherent in visions of this kind. In New Babylon, therefore, the tragic character of utopia comes to the surface.

Unitary Urbanism and the Critique of Functionalism

The key text that describes the fundamental aims of unitary urbanism dates from 1953 and was first published in June 1958, in the first issue of *Internationale Situationniste*, the periodical of the movement. Written by Gilles Ivain (the pseudonym of Ivan Chtcheglov), it was originally intended as an action program for the Lettrist International. The text condemns the boredom and utilitarianism that prevail in standard urbanism. Ivain devised strange images of symbolically charged urban scenes and magic sites where, he argued, imagination is stimulated. A new architecture is called for, an architecture that would banish boredom: no longer a cold and functional architecture but a flexible, constantly changing décor. In this way the unity between the individual and the reality of the cosmos can be achieved. Houses should be flexible, their walls adjustable, vegetation should enter life. The future lies in change:

> The architectural complex will be modifiable. Its aspect will change totally or partially in accordance with the will of its inhabitants. . . . The appearance of the notion of relativity in the modern mind allows one to surmise the EXPERIMENTAL aspect of the next civilization. . . . On the basis of this mobile civilization, architecture will, at least initially, be a means of experimenting with a thousand ways of modifying life, with a view to a mythic synthesis.[8]

In the cities of the future there will be ongoing experiments in new forms of behavior. Architectural forms will be charged with symbols and emotions. City quarters might be built to harmonize with specific feelings: Bizarre Quarter, Happy Quarter, Noble and Tragic Quarter. The inhabitants' most important activity will consist of constant loitering and drifting. This will bring about a disruption of banality that will create the possibility for a freedom of play.

This essay by Chtcheglov provided guidelines for the Situationist International in its early years. A key practice in this respect is the *dérive*, an aimless drifting, theorized by Debord.[9] The situationists converted this technique of traversing frequently changing urban environments into an instrument for investigating the "psychogeography" of cities. Psychogeography, Debord states, explores the influence of the geographical environment, consciously organized or not, on the emotions and behavior of individuals. The term suggests that one might make a relief map of the city, indicating the constant currents, fixed points, and vortices by which urban environments influence the emotions of passersby and inhabitants. Debord provides detailed instructions for carrying out a *dérive* properly: it should take a fixed amount of time (preferably twenty-four hours) and involve a small group of people whose path is determined by a combination of system and randomness. The aim is to move through the city without purpose, thus provoking unexpected occurrences and encounters.[10]

In the "Declaration of Amsterdam," a manifesto of 1958, Debord and Constant describe unitary urbanism as "the uninterrupted complex activity through which man's environment is consciously recreated according to progressive plans in all domains."[11] Unitary urbanism is the fruit of a collective creativity of a completely new kind. It cannot be produced by the activity of individual artists, but calls for the combined efforts of all creative personalities. This will bring about a fusion of scientific and artistic activity by which the development of transitory small-scale situations is accompanied by the creation on a larger scale of a universal, relatively permanent environment in which playfulness and freedom are the prime features.

The "Declaration of Amsterdam" emphasizes the synthetic and collective character of "unitary urbanism." It is based on the thesis that the most urgent task of the artist is to implement this program: "It is the immediate task of today's creatively active people to bring about conditions favorable to this development."[12] The original French version has more resonance than the English. Instead of the neutral word "conditions," the French uses "ambiances," meaning "atmospheres" and suggesting the creation of specific situations. The declaration also states that the individual practice of any branch of art whatsoever is out of date and reactionary, and that it will not be tolerated by members of the Situationist International. Given the basic goal of creating a unitary urbanism, it is the task of everyone to collaborate in order to achieve a spatial and collective art.

With his New Babylon project, Constant was offering a quite specific response to the aims of this manifesto. Whereas he started working on New Babylon under the umbrella of the Situationist International, publishing the first articles on New Babylon in the journal of the movement,[13] it soon became clear that he and Debord would part company. Constant put all his energies into developing New Babylon as a concrete model of how the world would look after the realization of unitary urbanism. The group around Debord, on the other hand, considered that Constant was too exclusively concerned with what they called "structural problems of urbanism." According to them, one should rather engage in activities emphasizing "the content, the notion of play, the free creation of everyday life."[14] For Debord unitary urbanism was only a point of departure, a potential catalyst in the struggle for a total social revolution, which he believed was waiting just around the corner. To develop a critique on various fronts, moreover, it was necessary to involve not only artists and intellectuals but also students and proletarians. New Babylon, conceived of and elaborated in artistic terms and media, was, for Debord and his partisans, clearly limited in scope. They even accused Constant of functioning as a public-relations officer for capitalism because his project tried to integrate the masses in a totally technified environment.[15]

Constant, for his part, did not expect this social revolution to take place in the near future. As a sort of strategy for survival in hard times, he considered that it made sense to get involved in the concrete design of "une autre ville pour une autre vie" (a different city for a different life). In the course of 1960 this difference of opinion became increasingly apparent, and Constant resigned from the group in the summer of that year.

The remaining situationists continued to work on unitary urbanism but in a different way from Constant. They did not produce any maquettes, drawings, or paintings; instead they wrote articles that criticized urban planning and development as it actually was.[16] They denounced the existing practice of urban development as serving the ideological purposes of capitalism: current urbanism, in their view, has as its aim to organize life in such a way that people are discouraged from thinking that they might have anything of their own to contribute. By emphasizing the question of transport, contemporary urbanism isolates people from each other, preventing them from using their energy for genuine participation. Instead they are offered the spectacle: "That participation has become impossible is compensated by way of the spectacle. The spectacle is manifest in one's residence and mobility (personal vehicles). For in fact one doesn't live somewhere in the city; one lives somewhere in the hierarchy."[17]

The fact that they are part of the spectacle turns people into passive individuals who are alienated from their own existence. This is why the situationists saw it as their first task to free people from their identification with their surroundings and with codes of behavior imposed by a capitalist society. Unitary urbanism therefore involves a permanent critique of the manipulation exercised by existing urban structures. This criticism can be activated by the tensions and conflicts of everyday life. The aim of unitary urbanism is to provide the basis for a life whose driving force is continuous experimentation.

The situationists were concerned, however, that unitary urbanism would not lead to the creation of "experimental zones" that would be isolated from the rest of the world. Their strivings, they claimed, had nothing to do with the designing of yet another holiday resort. On the contrary, "Unitary urbanism is the contrary of specialized activity; to accept a separate urbanistic domain is already to accept the whole urbanistic lie and the falsehood permeating the whole of life."[18]

A fertile method for criticizing urbanism is that of deliberate distortion, *le détournement*. This technique aims to present a certain matter in a different light than is officially intended, so exposing its fraudulent character. According to Kotanyi and Vaneigem, it is possible to subject the lies in urbanist theory to a *détournement* in order to counter its alienating effects. In this way one can trigger a process of disalienation. What is necessary is a reversal of the rhythm of the discourse of urbanism. This causes a subversion of its power of persuasion and a diminishing of the resulting conditioning. The appropriate strategy for achieving this goal of destruction is the creation of *situations*. These can liberate currents of energy that will permit people to make their own history. Unitary urbanism is therefore indissolubly linked with the revolution of everyday life: "We have invented the architecture and the urbanism that cannot be realized without the revolution of everyday life—without the appropriation of conditioning by everyone, its endless enrichment, its fulfillment."[19]

This evolution within unitary urbanism, from experiments in the visual arts to an involvement with agitational literature and activities, formed part of the general trend in the Situationist International. The movement was becoming increasingly preoccupied with political and socially subversive actions and was distancing itself from any artistic practice. Right from the start of the movement, it was already argued that the individual practice of art should be rejected in favor of a collective approach. At that moment, however, the conclusion was not yet drawn that *all* artistic activity was reactionary. This notion only began to get the upper hand after 1960 when artists who had doubts about this strategy, such as Constant, were expelled from the movement. From 1962 onward the situationists were dominated by activists such as Guy Debord and Raoul Vaneigem, whose contribution to the revolutionary struggle took the form of articles and pamphlets. Vaneigem stated explicitly:

> It is a question not of elaborating the spectacle of refusal, but rather of refusing the spectacle. In order for their elaboration to be artistic in the new and authentic sense defined by the SI, the elements of the destruction of the spectacle must precisely cease to be works of art. There is no such thing as situationism or a situationist work of art or a spectacular situationist. . . . Our position is that of combatants between two worlds—one that we don't acknowledge, the other that does not yet exist.[20]

The argument behind this statement goes as follows: the whole social system is organized in such a way that people are reduced in every way to being passive consumers, alienated from their own needs and desires. In order to maintain this generalized impoverishment, people are offered solace in the form of leisure activities. These are organized in a "spectacular" fashion; in other words, they are conceived of in such a way that people partake in them passively, without genuinely participating. This system, which is totalitarian and hierarchical, prevails in every area of social existence, including the art world. This can be seen in the commercial organization of the art market, where the work of artists who have made a name can be sold for a great deal of money. Artists who collaborate with this circuit are surrendering to the system and are therefore guilty of an antirevolutionary attitude. The simple fact of creating products that are labeled as "art" and that are marketable means that artists effectively help to prop up the system. The revolutionary artist, who aims to prevent the system from regaining control of play and creativity, can only be consistent if he abandons all complicity and stops producing works of art. This is why the situationists can state that "we are artists only insofar as we are no longer artists: we come to realize art."[21]

Debord developed this theory in *La société du spectacle*. This book contains a detailed critique of society based on the ideas of Hegel, Marx, Lukács, and the Socialisme ou Barbarie group. Debord proposes the thesis that capitalist society is essentially different from what it was in the nineteenth century. Instead of the dominance of the commodity, one now has the dominance of the spectacle. Debord begins his book with the statement that "in societies where modern conditions of production prevail, all of life presents itself as an immense accumulation of spectacles. Everything that was directly lived has moved away into a representation."[22] The image has become autonomous and the entire social system is dominated by the monopoly of representation. The real world, life that is directly lived, has become nothing more than images; as a result these images have acquired the power of reality, and they are now the active motors of hypnotic behavior. The spectacle is the nightmare of imprisoned modern society. It is maintained because individuals are seduced into preferring the amnesia of sleep to the intensity of a genuinely experienced reality.

Debord relates the mechanism of the spectacle to separation and expropriation. The retreat into representation is in his view one of the sources of the universal alienation that is typical of the capitalist system. The spectacle is both cause and result of the loss of unity in the world. This diagnosis takes up a number of criticisms that had earlier been developed by Henri Lefebvre. In an influential book of 1947, Lefebvre argued that everyday life suffers from very powerful forms of alienation. Life is no longer experienced in its entirety, but disintegrates into disconnected and unrelated moments. Individuals are alienated from their own desires. Their work, their social identity, their leisure, and their public lives, even the way they relate to their families—none of this has anything to do with their essential being, but is produced by the control and conditioning of a social system that has other ends in view.[23]

Debord's *Society of the Spectacle* is primarily concerned with analyzing the *societal* mechanisms that maintain alienation and dispossession. The counterpart of this book is Raoul Vaneigem's *The Revolution of Everyday Life*. Starting out from similar theoretical premises, Vaneigem's work discusses the possibility of revolutionary changes in the *everyday life* of individuals. He states the aims of the revolution as follows: "In its chaotic underground development, the new society tends to find practical expression as a transparency in human relationships which promotes the participation of everyone in the self-realization of everyone else. Creativity, love and play are to life what the needs for nourishment and shelter are to survival."[24]

The situationist ideas in these two books were fertile soil for the revolutionary movement that culminated in the student uprising of 1968, in which the situationists played an important part. The Provos and Kabouters in Amsterdam were also inspired by the situationists.[25] Many of the notions of the movement for participation that prevailed in the architectural scene in the 1970s sound like an echo of the situationists' appeal for participation and self-realization.[26] "Alienation" was the key word for social criticism in this period, and architecture and urbanism were seen as crucial fields where the self-realization of the individual could be achieved. Functionalism was rejected because it played into the hands of alienation and nonparticipation: instead of genuinely considering the real desires of individuals, functionalism was thought to respond only to manipulated and abstract needs that did not relate in any way to the concrete inner experience of individuals.

New Babylon: The Antithesis of the Society of Lies

After his break with the situationists, Constant continued to work on his New Babylon project, in which he traced a new form of society and dwelling. Its point of departure is the idea that a thoroughgoing automation of production can reach a point where work becomes unnecessary so that people can enjoy endless free time. The surface of the earth gradually becomes covered with sequences of "sectors," gigantic structures built on high supports that tower over a landscape used for fully mechanized agricultural production and covered with lanes of fast-moving traffic (figure 70). The typical feature of life in the "sectors" is that people are totally liberated: they are freed from all ties, norms, and conventions; they stay in an environment that

Constant, New Babylon, group of
sectors, photomontage, 1971.

is entirely free of oppression and which they have full control of. By pressing a button they can adjust the temperature, the degree of humidity, the density of smells, and the intensity of light; with a few simple operations they can change the shape of a room and decide whether it is to be closed or open. They have a choice between a large number of "atmospheres" (light or dark, warm or cool, stiflingly small or frighteningly large) that can constantly be altered or manipulated. There are specific areas for erotic games, for experiments in filmmaking or radio, and for scientific tests; there are other areas set aside for seclusion and rest. New Babylon is a dynamic labyrinth that is continually being restructured by the spontaneity and creativity of its inhabitants. These people lead a nomadic existence based on a continual rejection of convention and any form of permanence: "The sectors change through all the activities within them, they are constantly evolving in form and atmosphere. Nobody therefore will ever be able to return to a place that he visited previously, nobody will ever recognize an image that exists in his memory. This means that nobody will ever lapse into fixed habits."[27]

"It is a matter of achieving the unknown by a derangement of the senses." It is no coincidence that Constant chooses this sentence of Rimbaud as a motto for his description of "The New Babylonian Culture."[28] He deliberately situates himself in the lineage of the avant-garde that links upheavals in art with social and political revolution. The distinctive feature of the avant-garde, in his view, is its critical struggle against existing society and culture.[29] This programmatic aim, he states, was typical of prewar groups such as the Arbeitsrat für Kunst. It was, however, revised by some artists and groups that ended up being involved in reactionary or conservative practices. The urgency with which these artists endeavor to bring about a direct relation between art and "reality" meant that they were seduced into accepting commercial society. This was what happened to functionalism, which, according to Constant, implied the surrender of the artist to the demands of a utilitarian society. Artists have to understand that this can never be their role. Reconciliation with existing society can never be their aim; instead they must keep alive the awareness of another possible world. Art is dead—its social role is finished—but if one gives up the struggle, one is giving up on everything, including the future. For the time being, a genuinely new culture is unattainable; for this reason one should opt for experiment as a delaying tactic. It was with this strategy, Constant comments, that Cobra picked up the threads of the avant-garde once more. The experiments of Cobra, however, also turned out to be prone to commercialization, and therefore unitary urbanism was developed. And so the last episode of individualistic culture was brought to a close. Zero point was arrived at. Art is dead, but creative man—*homo ludens*—rises up. Now that economic development has reached a point where a potential for virtually unlimited production makes compulsory work superfluous, the prospect of a new, playful culture begins to emerge. The last artists, in Constant's view, have the task of paving the way for this culture of the future and of giving a lead to the revolt of *homo ludens*.

Culture has always been created in the margins of the system, he argues. In previous ages it was not the masses who produced culture, but creative spirits whom the system of patronage reprieved from the obligation to work every day. Creativity and a desire for play can only flourish when one's total energy is not swallowed up by the essential work of commodity production. Automatization will ensure that the masses will also have these opportunities. This means that the conditions will exist for a genuine mass culture, a collective culture that will take on a totally different form from the existing one. This form of culture can come into existence only in a free society where nobody has any power over anyone else. In a situation like this, each individual will be able to enjoy his creativity to the full, and norms will lose their meaning. New Babylon should be thought of as foreshadowing this future. It is an artificial paradise, a world in which human beings as such can fulfill their destiny as creative beings, in accordance with their deepest longings.[30]

Constant has illustrated this future situation in numerous maps, maquettes, drawings, and paintings. The maps show a whole series of linked structures stretching out across the landscape. They exist on various scales, starting with a quasi-European dimension—as, for instance, with the map for the Ruhr area of New Babylon—and continuing with models simulating the development of concrete cities or city districts (Amsterdam, Antwerp, Paris) (figure 71). Sometimes they are set in a completely abstract, neutral background. On other occasions, existing contemporary or historical maps serve as a background.

One intriguing series is that of the collages where "sectors" are created out of parts of other urban plans. For instance, there is a symbolic representation of New Babylon dating from 1969 in which fragments of existing maps of cities are pasted on to a background showing minimal evidence of roads with thicker parts for intersections (figure 72). Things like street names can still be read on the fragments of the maps, so that they vaguely refer to specific cities. It is possible to discern a piece of London and another piece of Berlin, side by side with a district of Amsterdam and a chunk of a Spanish city. It is as though Constant is using this *détournement* to suggest that New Babylon will unite the qualities of all these cities. It is quite clear that he gives primacy to open, public space. He argues repeatedly that 80 percent of New Babylon will consist of collective spaces and that private space will be reduced to an absolute minimum.

The fact that he attaches great importance to the public quality of space can be seen in the collection of his lectures and articles, *Opstand van de homo ludens*, in which he states that public space is the area where people meet each other, and that this means that it is the area for play. Without public space, he argues, no culture is possible. The forum in classical times, the market squares of the Middle Ages, and, more recently, the boulevard—these were the places where cultural life developed.[31] The covered, large-scale structures of New Babylon are clearly thought of as a continuation of this tradition. Constant is stating implicitly here that he sees New Babylon as a fulfillment of Lefebvre's *droit à la ville*. In coining this expression, Lefebvre is referring not so much to a definite physical city context, but rather to the presence of an urban atmosphere that has to do with freedom, complexity, and limitless possibilities.[32] With New Babylon, Constant is placing himself in a real tradition of urbanity, as is evident from his close collaboration with the Amsterdam Provos in the 1960s, one of whose demands was to reclaim the street from the automobile. At one point the Provos even proclaimed Amsterdam as the first sector of New Babylon.[33]

Constant, however, did not see New Babylon as a plan that was technically viable or capable of immediate implementation. He repeatedly stated that the conception of New Babylon is based on two assumptions that are far from being realized: the collective property of the land and the total automatization of production. Fundamental revolutionary social changes would have to take place before the project could be realized. For this reason, New Babylon should rather be seen as a visualization of a possible future world, as an illustration of the living conditions of *homo ludens* after finally taking over the baton from *homo faber*.

Constant, New Babylon over
Amsterdam, 1963.
(Collection Gemeentemuseum,
The Hague.)

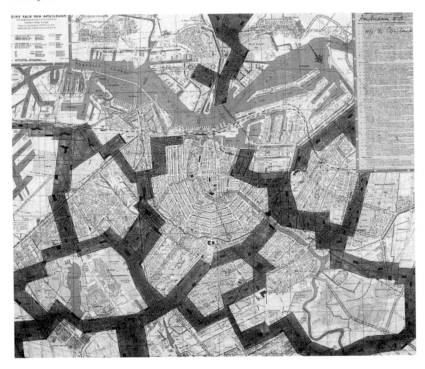

71

During the first years of New Babylon, Constant made a large number of maquettes that come in a variety of forms. The first of them dates from 1956 and is meant as a design proposal for a Gypsy encampment in Alba. An umbrella-shaped transparent construction partially covers a space in which one can vaguely discern a spiral shape. By means of screens and palings, the Gypsies were invited to create their own site. The two spatiovores of 1959 and 1960 take up the circular form once more, but here they are transparent, shell-shaped structures raised high above the ground (figure 73). Inside the shell there are sections of floor made of perspex that are suspended in the air by means of rods and wires. Judging by the size of the objects on the ground in the spatiovore of 1960, these maquettes must represent gigantic constructions covering a considerable area and towering many meters above the ground, being supported at only three points. There are no notes to indicate the precise function of these gigantic shells, which one, it seems, could compare with space stations that accidentally have landed on earth.

Constant, symbolic representation
of New Babylon, 1969.

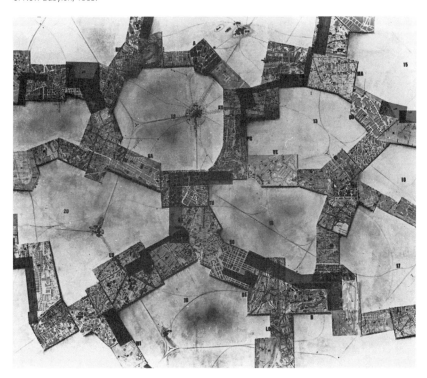

Constant, New Babylon,
spatiovore, 1960.

73

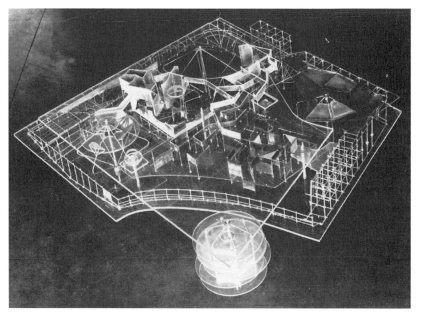

74

Constant, New Babylon, yellow
sector, 1958.

(Collection Gemeentemuseum,
The Hague; photo: Bram Wisman.)

Constant, New Babylon, interior
view of the yellow sector, 1958.
(Collection Gemeentemuseum,
The Hague.)

75

76

Constant, New Babylon, mobile
ladderlabyrinth, 1967.

In terms of their form, the spatiovores are autonomous elements, something that makes them quite exceptional within the overall framework of New Babylon. The other maquettes are thought of rather as parts of sectors that can easily be linked to each other. This is the case, for instance, with the maquette for the yellow sector (1958), which is the one Constant described in *Internationale Situationniste* (figure 74).[34] The construction is held up by a few massive pylons, with a sort of frame construction propping up the floor and roof slabs. In one of the corners there is a circular structure that has become separate from the rest and which has six floor slabs on top of each other with short gaps between them, in contrast to the two slabs of the main structure. The whole is held together by a flat yellow roof slab that apparently also explains the name of this section. On the different "stories" one can see a collection of folded collapsible walls that are used to demarcate different spaces (figure 75). It is not a matter of enclosed volumes here, but of spaces of various sizes that interpenetrate.

Another striking feature are the maquettes of labyrinthine spaces, such as the small labyrinth of 1959 or the mobile ladderlabyrinth of brass, perspex, and wood that dates from 1967 (figure 76). This one reminds one of a wire maquette for one of van Doesburg's counterconstructions with their floating surfaces and interpenetrating volumes. In the case of the maquettes for New Babylon, one can never clearly ascribe definite functions to specific parts of the building, or accurately calculate any scales or other concrete details. Above all, the maquettes give a picture of an artificial world that is dominated by technology and in which artificial materials and ingenious construction techniques are used to make a type of dwelling that exists separate from the landscape and whose typical features are interpenetration and indeterminacy. The atmosphere of an airport or a space station is often suggested, something that occurs explicitly in a maquette of 1959, which Constant dubbed *Ambiance de départ*. A nomadic mode of life is thus suggested that is made possible by technology.

The real problem with the maquettes, however, is that the tension between the larger structures that are fixed and the small-scale interior structures that are flexible and labyrinthine is not always fully worked out. Constant himself declares that "the real designers of New Babylon will be the Babylonians themselves,"[35] but this cannot be seen very clearly in the maquettes. In this sense the maquette-sculptures are a limited form of representation, and perhaps this was why Constant relied increasingly on drawings and paintings as his work on New Babylon progressed.[36]

The least appealing drawings are the architectural perspectives—"Bird's eye perspective of group of sectors I," for example, which dates from 1964 (figure 69). These drawings can be interpreted simply as fairly detailed depictions of large-scale constructions that form a sort of chain that undulates through the landscape. This simplicity means that they have far less poetic power and intensity than the other sketches. A small group of drawings reminds one of technical blueprints. The em-

Constant, New Babylon,
drawing, 1962.

(Collection Gemeentemuseum,
The Hague, T44-X-1974.)

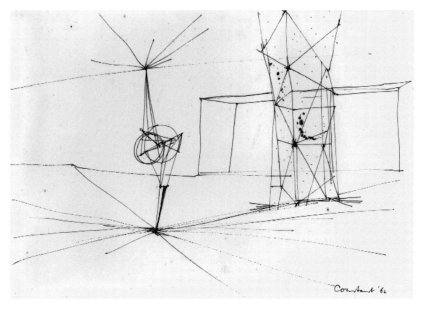

77

phasis here is often on constructional aspects and the artist's aim is apparently to persuade the public of the viability of his proposal.

More interesting than these drawings are the numerous sketches that evoke the construction principles of New Babylon rather than showing them in technical detail. It is in these drawings that Constant is most successful in expressing the tension and poetic power of structural forms. For instance, there is one striking drawing (figure 77) that plays two structural principles off against each other: on the one hand there is a lattice column that covers a considerable area with its narrow connecting rods and points of intersection, and on the other hand we see an extremely slender element that looks like a vertical version of the logic of a three-pointed arch. Whether the latter element really can have a supporting function is doubtful, but that is not the point here. It is the interaction that gives this drawing its character—the interaction, that is, between these two forms and the pattern of lines of force they suggest. Similar remarks might be made about a sketch from 1962 (figure 78) that illustrates a lattice construction for a sector of New Babylon set in a hilly landscape. Here too there are slender structures and minimal suggestions of lines of force and support points. An *Aufzug* is mentioned, suggesting an elevator linking the inhabited areas with the ground.

Constant, New Babylon,
drawing, 1962.
(Collection Gemeentemuseum,
The Hague, T95-83.)

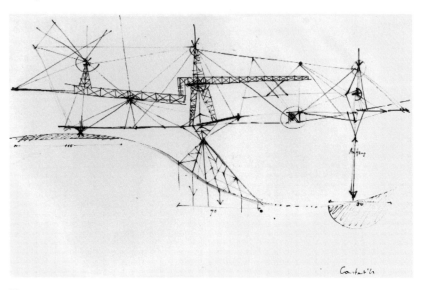

78

79

Constant, New Babylon,
Labyratoire, 1962.
(Collection Gemeentemuseum,
The Hague.)

Constant, New Babylon, labyrinth
with stairs, drawing, 1960.

(Collection Gemeentemuseum,
The Hague.)

The prints and drawings in which Constant gives an impression of the spatial character of New Babylon are also numerous. Features suggesting dynamism and mobility are frequently emphasized here—stairs, ladders, elevators, adjustable walls (figure 79). Many of the views of the interior give an impression of a somewhat suffocating labyrinthine space, a boundless area in which one can lose one's way ad infinitum (figure 80). There are staircases and passages that lead nowhere, and heavily emphasized shadows with Piranesi-like spaces outlined against them. Now and then one sees blobs that look roughly like human silhouettes. In drawings where a larger number of these silhouettes appear, it is striking that there is no interaction between them: in each case what we see are figures who traverse the labyrinth alone.

A typical feature of the drawings is the tension they convey. This tension is often created by graphic means—fragile shapes are opposed to compact ones, dark is opposed to light, dynamic lines are contrasted with static volumes. Sometimes tension is produced by the rhythm of the walls that give structure to the space depicted, or it issues from the movement of the human figures or from the distortions of perspective. This tension can be seen as indicative of the continual oscillation between the liberating and disturbing impressions that the viewer is subjected to. On the one hand, New Babylon fulfills one's expectations of an absolutely free space, where the individual can construct his own environment as he pleases, exploiting to the full its creative possibilities. Movable walls, ladders, elevators, and stairways suggest a possibility of endless journeys and constant new encounters. The individual can project himself onto his environment within a general structure that harnesses the poetic potential of technology to the full. On the other hand, these drawings also betray a feeling of unease. The indifference with which the earth's surface has been stripped, the huge scale of the structures supporting the sectors, the endlessness of the interior spaces that never seem to permit any contact with the outside world: these features also seem to appear, even if Constant did not intend them to. In this sense, the drawings—more than the maquettes—form a sort of modification of Constant's discourse on a utopian world that is free of oppression and inequality.

The same is true of the paintings that Constant produced during his New Babylon period. Initially, in his most radical phase, Constant avoided painting for reasons of principle, viewing it as a bourgeois and reactionary art. Nevertheless, he never entirely abandoned his brushes, even if he

Constant, *Fiesta Gitana*, 1958.
(Collection Centraal Museum, Utrecht.)

81

Constant, *Ode à l'Odéon*, 1969.
(Private collection, on loan to
Gemeentemuseum, The Hague.)

82

ceased to exhibit or sell any canvases. The works of these years also take up the themes and motifs of New Babylon—labyrinths, ladders, *homo ludens*—but they should perhaps not be seen as direct illustrations of life in New Babylon. Rather, they provide a reflection at a distance accompanying and possibly commenting on the work on New Babylon.

Typical of some of these paintings are their vivid, brilliant colors, suggesting scenes of joyous festivities. The element of play here comes to the fore in the form of carnival-like figures in scenes that teem with activity. In *Fiesta Gitana*, from 1958, fiery and colorful splashes of paint dominate like explosions of joy (figure 81). There is, however, an unmistakably somber undertone, as though Constant was acknowledging in his paintings that festival and violence, joy and chaos, creation and destruction, are ineluctably linked. *Homo Ludens*, for instance, a painting from 1964, is

83

exuberant in its range of colors and its festive atmosphere. The figures are painted
in garish, definite colors that spill over into the surrounding areas. But here too the
somber, dark undertone is noticeable, both in the black background that rejects the
expansive joy of the merrymakers and in the attitude of the human figures to each
other—as though no real contact exists between them.

In the "labyrinthine" paintings this conflict is even more pronounced. *Ode à
l'Odéon* (1969) depicts an unending space in the manner of Piranesi, an interior without any world outside consisting of a large number of walls, palings, and ladders
(figure 82). Transparent screens, gridlike surfaces, and sections of floors are
crisscrossed—supported?—by horizontal, vertical, and diagonal lines. There is no
longer any definite perspective here, no central point from which the spatial organization can be grasped as a whole. One experiences this space as ambiguous and

Constant, *Terrain vague*, 1973.
(Collection Gemeentemuseum,
The Hague.)

84

opaque; human silhouettes wander across it apparently aimlessly and without any interaction. The colors are shades of gray and beige, with white brightening the scene from time to time. In *Ladderlabyrinth* (1971) the dominating color scheme is a sort of yellow with orange hues, combined with pink and bright yellow (figure 83). The spatial organization is even more confused than in *Ode à l'Odéon* because there are no longer any long sight lines here; a deliberate ambiguity seems to be built into the placing of surfaces and lines. The two indistinct pink and gray silhouettes dominating the painting would seem to be linked with each other by invisible threads of desire. Sexual connotations make an appearance here—something that is lacking in the previous New Babylon work.

Constant's gesture of farewell to New Babylon might be found in a painting from 1973 entitled *Terrain vague* (figure 84). An almost apocalyptically vacated space is set against a horizon black as night. The foreground and edges of the visual field are patched and cut with lines. Barely recognizable in the distance is a structure out of New Babylon. A few walls and screens point one's gaze toward the depths. On closer inspection, the monotonous yellow-white surface that occupies the greater part of the painting turns out to overlay a more complex background collaged from newspaper and other imagery. Is this a palimpsest representing the end of history? The painting's title means "wasteland," but it is clear that this land is not really empty: it is covered with traces and scars that inscribe a very specific history. Considering that New Babylon elsewhere is pictured as the place of an eternal present (because no place in it can ever be recognized by its inhabitants), this proves a strange compilation of images. One is tempted to see *Terrain vague* as emerging from an understanding of the incompatibilities between the reality of a wasteland that is always occupied by hidden memories and the impossible utopia of New Babylon where memories and history are declared irrelevant. And one wonders whether, after all, Constant does not rather opt for history than for an eternal present.

The Tragedy of Utopia

New Babylon depicts a world where people are liberated from all norms, forms, and conventions. All oppressive ties are dissolved, and there is no longer any fixed pattern of social obligations or of loyalties to family or to a specific place. The law of the transitory prevails in New Babylon—immediate situations have primacy over permanent structures. The commonplace—the ordinary, everyday framework that gives life its form and that permits one to postpone indefinitely any question about the ultimate meaning of life—has been abolished. With it, it would seem, the possibility of "dwelling" has also disappeared. For dwelling (inhabitation) has to do with developing habits, with habituating oneself to a certain pattern, which is exactly what Constant tells us is impossible in New Babylon. As a utopian vision of the future, New Babylon therefore arouses feelings of dread rather than of desire: dwelling in a situation of pure indeterminacy apparently does not respond to our deepest wishes and desires.

In a certain sense, New Babylon is the fulfillment of the logic of negation that was characteristic of the avant-garde: in order to achieve the goal of total liberation from all norms and conventions, all habits and traditions had to be destroyed. According to this logic, poetry and the commonplace are mutually exclusive moments. On the side of the commonplace one finds banality and mediocrity, the whole body of petrified outward forms that is purely conventional and that with its sheer weight crushes to death any inner experience. For this reason the commonplace is considered intrinsically *false* by the avant-garde. Behind this screen of conventionality, one hopes to find the real, the genuine, and the authentic. This moment of authenticity is equated with purity and openness, with what is most personal and spontaneous. Within this logic, poetry is about peeling away all the layers of conventionality to reach the pure kernel of authenticity. The heart of poetry can be reached only if one strips off the rough exterior of the commonplace and banal. One can achieve real individuality, it is assumed, only by breaking out of the straitjacket of convention. This is the conviction that underlies the world of New Babylon.

New Babylon is a visual version of the dream of ultimate transparency that Benjamin detected in the avant-garde of the 1920s. It presents an image of a social form in which the desires of the individual and the requirements of the community are inseparably entwined. As Constant describes it, it is a society where there is no longer any necessity for secrecy and possessions; it is an absolute collectivity in which the general interest coincides automatically with the sum of individual interests. New Babylon, it would seem, is a society without power relations. It is the concretization of Benjamin's longing to reach the programmatic promise of modernity by igniting its transitory aspects. A utopia like this, however, is full of internal contradictions, which surface involuntarily in Constant's drawings and paintings. It is indeed impossible to imagine a society existing that is so harmonious and free of stress without its individual members being subtly coerced to adapt and conform—an oppression that implies the opposite of genuine freedom. Dynamism, permanent change, and flexibility are in fact ineluctably in conflict with qualities such as peace, repose, and harmony.

Constant argues that New Babylon is intended for postrevolutionary society, for the *homo ludens* that will be born of the revolution. Until this revolution takes place, however, the existing type of human being—*homo faber*—will continue to be corrupted by an untruthful society that imposes its norms and values, forcing the individual to conform, imprisoning him in a straitjacket of conventions and suppressing his creativity and autonomy. The revolution will bring about a total liberation; authenticity and individual commitment to the collective will be the basic characteristics of the new society. This faith in the revolution and in the human race's real potential for change is characteristic of the intellectual climate of the sixties in which New Babylon is rooted, but it does not take into account what has in the meantime became known, in Foucault's phrase, as the "micrology of power." It ignores the finely meshed interplay between the principles on which the social system is founded and the psychological mechanisms that guide individual behavior. There are in fact few reasons for assuming that a fundamental change in the organization of society would immediately result in an equally fundamental change in the nature of human beings. In other words, there is no guarantee whatsoever that the disappearance of the social struggle for existence would mean that violence and conflicts between individuals would disappear like snow melting in the sun. The human condition is probably a bit more complicated than that.[37]

This point is precisely what Constant's imagery suggests. The drawings and paintings indeed seem to convey a much more in-depth understanding of the human condition than the texts. The images are hardly open to being interpreted as foreshadowing an ideal future; they appear as a multilayered commentary on the impossibility of giving utopia a concrete form. In the complexity suggested in the drawings and fully realized in the paintings, the "dark side" of the world of New Babylon also is depicted. Drawings and paintings show a condition in which wanderlust and the lack of permanent ties are untrammeled, but they also make it clear that this condition is inseparably bound up with the death drive, with groundlessness and indeterminacy. A painting, as Constant said way back in his Cobra period, is an animal, a night, a scream, a human being, or all of that together. This notion continues to have its repercussions in the work of his New Babylon period. As a result, the paintings make visible something that Constant was still able to conceal in the maquettes and the narratives—the fact that this utopian world is not perfect and harmonious, that the dismantling of all the conventions leads to a zero point of human existence in which the authenticity that is striven for is reduced merely to a torrent of perceptions and sensations; it is no longer an ideal but a caricature. In this sense New Babylon is a striking proof of the impossibility of giving utopia a concrete form and of making poetry the only moment of reality: one cannot "dwell" in New Babylon.

To the extent that New Babylon represents the social criticism of the situationists in a concrete form, these remarks can also be applied to them. Debord, for instance, in his criticism of urbanism states that the proletarian revolution will lead to individuals and communities constructing their own environment and appropriating their own history. The land as a whole will be restructured according to the needs of the workers' councils. Space will become flexible to provide possibilities of play.[38] Here too the relation between revolution and utopia was short-circuited, as though the proletarian revolution and the establishment of workers' councils would be sufficient guarantees for the realization of a condition in which alienation is abolished.

The basic misunderstanding here has to do with the interpretation of the concepts of "alienation" and "authenticity," which are seen as opposites. Both are difficult categories to pin down. It is questionable, however, whether they would really be mutually exclusive, as the avant-garde logic assumes. The avant-garde had elevated the achieving of authenticity to a fundamental aim, reacting to the empty display and insincerity that characterized nineteenth-century culture.[39] History has shown, however, that the figure of authenticity is one that is constantly receding and eludes one's grasp. The authenticity that the avant-garde imagined winning by its repeated iconoclastic gestures proved to be momentary and intangible. The quest for authenticity always had to start all over again, because the result lent itself all too easily to commodification, to recuperation, that is, by the logic of consumption, the very thing against which the whole quest was set up. This led in the long run to an impasse, which is responsible for the antinomial condition of art and architecture today.

No Way Out: Adorno's Aesthetic Theory

In his *Aesthetic Theory*, Adorno states that the commitment of art to utopia is the source of the most important of the antinomies that govern its present condition: "At the center of contemporary antinomies is that art must be and wants to be utopia, and the more utopia is blocked by the real functional order, the more this is true; yet at the same time art may not be utopia in order not to betray it by providing semblance and consolation."[40] This is exactly what becomes clear in Constant's New Babylon project. As a project that aspires to embody the utopian goal of history, it is based on a negation of all that is false and fraudulent in present society; it therefore highlights the necessity of putting an end to oppression and domination. The quality of the project, however, does not lie in the fact that it offers a harmonious or idyllic image of this final goal. On the contrary, New Babylon does not lend itself to use as an instrument of illusion or consolation. Its truth lies in its negativity and in the dissonances that continually pervade its image of harmony and well-being.

Adorno's *Aesthetic Theory* provides us with remarkable tools with which to examine an ambivalent project such as New Babylon. It can properly be called one of the most elaborate attempts to describe the major contradictions that art is faced with in modern conditions, and in my view the book has lost little of its relevance, even if some of Adorno's ideas may well be dated in certain respects.[41]

Adorno (1903–1969) belonged to the first generation of the theorists of the Frankfurter Schule. On his father's side he was of Jewish origin. Like so many others, he was forced to emigrate from Germany in the early thirties, first to England and later to America. In 1950, he returned to Frankfurt, but the shock caused by the Holocaust lingered on, permeating his later work. His texts are dominated by the question of how it is possible for the ideals of the Enlightenment, the ideas of reason, progress, and universal emancipation, to turn into their opposite when they are put into practice. He views modernization as leading to repression and manipulation rather than to liberation, and he poses the question of why and how this development took place. The most explicit treatment of these questions is to be found in the famous book that he wrote with Max Horkheimer during the war, *Dialectic of Enlightenment*. His other major works—*Negative Dialectics* and *Aesthetic Theory*— also are steeped in this sense of the paradoxical and contradictory character of modernity. His approach is original and unusual in that he combines an analysis of the philosophical question about the nature of the Enlightenment and modernization with an intense interest in contemporary artistic developments. This dual approach, embracing both philosophical and aesthetic aspects, is responsible for the presence in his work of a programmatic as well as a transitory conception of modernity. The purpose of his work is to clarify the complexities of modernity, to analyze its different manifestations, and to determine the relations between them.

Constellating the Nonidentical

Martin Jay introduces Adorno's thought by describing it in terms of a constellation of five primary points of light and energy that have had a decisive influence on his work.[42] The first and brightest star in this constellation is that of nonorthodox, nonaligned neo-Marxism. Adorno's Marxism is characterized by its negative opinion of the possibility of political action and its refusal to recognize the proletariat, whether or not represented by "the Party," as the authentic collective subject of the revolution. His thought is, however, unquestionably materialist and dialectical (even though his dialectics is a "negative" one), and his writings attest to a characteristically Western Marxist insistence on the utopian potential of modern society.

The second of the five stars is that of aesthetic modernism. Right from his early years Adorno was interested in modern music; he thought seriously about becoming a composer and studied for some time under Alban Berg in Vienna. Modern art always had a convinced advocate in him against the accusations of orthodox Marxists that it was decadent and "bourgeois."

Jay identifies Adorno's mandarin cultural conservatism as the third star in the constellation. With this term he is alluding to the often regressively oriented romantic anticapitalism that was a dominant tendency in Germany before the First World War. Leading exponents of this tradition were authors such as Tönnies and Spengler. While Adorno himself did not subscribe to this mandarin tradition—quite the contrary, in fact—he was influenced by some of its ideas. The distinction, for instance, between "culture" and "civilization" recurs in Adorno's work, albeit in a modified and more balanced form. His biases that are sometimes elitist, his dislike of mass culture, and his hatred of instrumental thought can in Jay's view also be traced back to this tradition.

The fourth force in Adorno's field comes from his being part Jewish. A large number of his friends and intellectual colleagues were Jews, including Walter Benjamin, Max Horkheimer, Herbert Marcuse, and Leo Löwenthal, and the course of Adorno's own life was deeply influenced by his Jewish identity. As a non-"Aryan" he was deprived of his right to teach at the University of Frankfurt after the Nazis came to power, and this forced him to emigrate. The awareness of the Holocaust—as summed up in the symbolically loaded term "Auschwitz"—was crucial to the whole of his postwar oeuvre.[43]

His Jewishness did not only influence the course of his life. Traces of some motifs from Jewish philosophy also can be found in Adorno's thought. Sometimes these themes emerge due to the influence of Benjamin, whose notion of language as mimesis, for instance, was clearly influenced by the Jewish Kabbala; sometimes, however, their origin was more direct, as with the theme of the ban on images. In Jewish tradition, the banning of images means that the one and only true God—Yahweh—cannot and must not be depicted, because no image or name is capable of doing justice to His infinity and truth. Adorno takes up this motif in his treatment of the topic of utopia. According to him, utopia cannot directly be named, described, or depicted. When it is given a concrete form—as in Thomas More's book for instance—it at once takes on a totalitarian and dogmatic character, so that one of its aspects becomes the absence of freedom, which is the opposite of what the unattainable ideal notion of utopia really implies.

The final star in Adorno's constellation is identified by Jay as "deconstruction-ism." While there is obviously no question of a direct exchange between Adorno's work and that of Derrida, Jay does discern a certain correspondence between them.[44] It was Adorno's intention to apply "immanent criticism" to Western meta-physics, dismantling it from within with an extremely rigorous reading of the texts, thus identifying its contradictions and false premises. This aim displays unmistakable similarities with Derrida's concept of "deconstruction."

Marxism, modernism, mandarin conservatism, Jewish self-identification, and a certain anticipation of deconstructionism—all these different poles are integrated in Adorno's work in a manner that makes it unique. Unlike Benjamin, who moved back and forth between the different stars in his constellation and who did not always succeed in mediating between them effectively (something that explains why the interpretations of his work differ so sharply), Adorno's writings possess a very high degree of consistency, with few or no fundamental shifts in his philosophical as-sumptions.[45] Some questions are more effectively stated in his later work—in that respect "Auschwitz" is decisive; broadly speaking, however, there is a remarkable consistency between the early texts and the later ones.

Consistency, however, by no means implies one-dimensionality. Adorno's work is in fact characterized by constant conflicts and paradoxes. His thought oscil-lates between conflicting poles, and this has implications for his writings. His style is deliberately nonsystematic and he is not afraid of paradoxes. This way of writing should be seen in light of his view of reality, which he regards as being contradictory at every point; thus, discourse about it must also be prepared to risk being contra-dictory. As Susan Buck-Morss puts it: "Given the premise of an essentially antago-nistic, contradictory reality, it is clear why Adorno felt that knowledge of the present demanded the juxtaposition of contradictory concepts whose mutually negating ten-sion could not be dissolved."[46] The fact that his work is contradictory does not make it gratuitous: although truth is never simple or without contradictions, one must not assert just anything. The truth content of thought and writing remains a decisive fac-tor, even if this criterion itself is ambivalent. With Adorno, truth always has a twofold content: on the one hand it refers to the actual situation (the classical notion of truth as *adequatio rei et intellectus*); on the other hand—and this is certainly no less im-portant—"truth" refers to something that is always out of reach, to a utopian con-tent. For Adorno "truth" corresponds not only to the world "as it is," but also to the world "as it might be."

The whole of Adorno's work testifies to his opposition to the dominance of a mode of thinking that endorses the world "as it is," to what he calls "identity think-ing": the thought that maps out reality by means of unambiguous concepts and which in the act of cataloguing concrete and specific phenomena makes an abstrac-tion of their particular character, thus standing in the way of any perspective that of-fers something "other." Like Benjamin, Adorno sees the "other" as concealed in the concrete and the particular; it can be rendered visible only by an analysis that gives an account of the specific and contradictory character of concrete phenomena. It is this aim that forms the core of the numerous essays and analyses that Adorno devoted to concrete phenomena.[47] In his principal philosophical work, *Negative Dialectics*, he attempts to support these aims with an epistemological basis. His purpose is to employ a strictly philosophical approach to elucidate the "nonidentical," that which cannot be contained within the conceptual grid of identity thinking. Adorno states explicitly that *Negative Dialectics* is an attempt to make a consistent use of logic in order to trace that which escapes the hegemony of the unity principle and of a hierarchically organized conceptual apparatus.[48]

In Adorno's opinion, reality is nonidentical: reality is not simply what it is, it does not entirely coincide with itself, but continually refers to something else, to something more than itself: "That which is, is more than it is. This 'more' is not something that is annexed to it, but is immanent in it, because it consists of what has been repressed. In that sense, the nonidentical would be the thing's own identity as opposed to the identifications imposed on it."[49] While the principle of nonidentity is therefore in a certain sense rooted in reality itself, the nonidentical only becomes manifest in language. It only acquires a clear outline through the relationship that language creates with reality. When language casts its network of concepts over reality, "identifying" the phenomenon, the nonidentical falls through this net. It does not permit itself to be defined by a single concept, but this only becomes apparent because the concept attempts to do just that: "Whatever part of nonidentity defies definition in its concept goes beyond its individual existence, because it is only in polarity with the concept, in staring at the concept that it will contract into being."[50] The "nonidentical," that which cannot be grasped by an identifying gesture, can be approximated in language only by hemming it in with a constellation of concepts, each of which on its own is not able to identify the matter completely; through the tensions generated by their force field, however, they give form—mimetically— to that which cannot directly be grasped. Adorno states this concept of language as follows:

> Language offers no mere system of signs for cognitive functions. Where it appears essentially as a language, where it becomes a form of representation (*Darstellung*), it will not define its concepts. It lends objectivity to them by the relation into which it puts the concepts, centered about a thing. Language thus serves the intention of the concept to express completely what it means. Only constellations are capable of representing, from without, what the concept has cut away within: the "more" which the concept is so eager to grasp without ever being able to.[51]

In Adorno's thought, therefore, language occupies an extremely important position. Through its use of constellations, language enables us, even if only for a moment, to escape the identifying, totalitarian aspect of thought. This is also why Adorno registers a protest against Wittgenstein's celebrated statement that one should be silent about that which one cannot speak: "Wittgenstein's formulation closes its own horizon against expressing mediately, in a complex manner, and in constellations, what cannot be expressed clearly and immediately."[52] It is Adorno's view, moreover, that there is a close kinship between the principle behind identity thinking and the exchange principle that in the guise of the commodity structure dominates the social system: both principles in their own way set up a form of equivalence and exchange, thus suppressing the heterogeneity and particularity of individual phenomena that are nonidentical and nonexchangeable:

> The exchange principle, the reduction of human labor to the abstract universal concept of average working hours, is fundamentally akin to the principle of identification. Exchange is the social model of the principle of identification, and without the latter there would be no exchange; it is through exchange that nonidentical individuals and transactions become commensurable and identical. The spread of the principle of identification imposes on the whole world an obligation to become identical, to become total.[53]

For Adorno, criticism of identical thought ipso facto also implies a criticism of the exchange principle and vice versa.

Adorno's concept of language has a profound impact on the style in which his essays are written. He declares his preference for the essay as form.[54] The essay is concerned with analyzing something that is concrete and particular; the fact that it is fragmentary and incomplete makes it the ideal instrument for "reading" the fragmented reality. But even Adorno's longer texts still preserve an essay-like character: the text consists of blocks of twenty or thirty pages without any interim headings or separate sections. There is no concession to make his readers' task easier by providing a clear, didactic division into chapters and paragraphs.[55]

This antisystematic working method is the correlative of the call to revolt against the identity principle, which asks for a clear and systematic form. The result is that for a reader who comes to them unprepared, Adorno's texts are often very recalcitrant. They do not conform to the requirements of a clearly constructed discourse that develops a sequence of arguments starting with a clearly stated point of departure and ending with a logical conclusion. His texts are "composed" rather than logically constructed, so that contradictions and ambivalences must be viewed as basic ingredients of their composition.

Modernity as the Unfolding of the Dialectic of Enlightenment

In the *Dialectic of Enlightenment* a theory of modernity is developed that Adorno continues to adhere to in his later writings as well. The crucial problem here is that of the self-destruction of the Enlightenment: "We had set ourselves nothing less than the discovery of why mankind, instead of entering into a truly human condition, is sinking into a new kind of barbarism."[56] Given the programmatic ideals of the Enlightenment—the "project of the modern," as Habermas would later call it—and given the progress made in the fields of technology and science, and the links between the two phenomena (the Enlightenment, after all, was the signal for the start of the industrial revolution and thus of the flowering of scientific thought), how could humanity end up in a situation so far removed from the ideals of the Enlightenment as to be its complete opposite?

Horkheimer and Adorno see part of the answer to this question in an ambiguity that is inherent in Enlightenment itself. In order to explain this ambiguity, they make an implicit distinction between critical rationality—reason, that is, in its most authentic and unqualified guise—and instrumental rationality, which is thinking reduced to purposes of utility or to mere calculation. While instrumental rationality is solely concerned with deciding on the most appropriate means to achieve a given goal, critical rationality also aims to subject to reason the goals aimed for. These two forms of rationality resemble each other, but they are opposites too, since instrumental rationality can be deployed to achieve goals that from the point of view of critical-rational thought are anything but reasonable.

The dialectic of Enlightenment consists precisely in the fact that through the process of rationalization, critical rationality—the rationality that was at the origins of the project of Enlightenment as a project of emancipation—is being reduced to instrumental rationality. This reduction implies that it is no longer the project of emancipation that guides development. It is rather the efficiency of the system itself that becomes the sole guiding principle. Enlightenment thus ends up as its own opposite: the programmatic attempt to give reason priority over myth in fact leads to the dominance of an efficiency that upholds the system, while this efficiency is mythical rather than rational. Thus, Horkheimer and Adorno stress the counterpastoral tendencies that are inherent to the dialectic of the Enlightenment and that foreclose the possibility of realizing its programmatic intentions.

A similar dialectical process takes place in the individual who acts as an enlightened subject: the rational mode of behavior that is a requirement of enlightened thought turns out to be possible only when one's inner, natural impulses are repressed; the result is an aporetic figure by which people can fashion an identity for themselves as rational beings only by betraying their identity as natural beings.[57]

Adorno and Horkheimer see Enlightenment, therefore, as connected with a tendency to dominate, that has as its object as well nature outside man as man's repressed inner nature. And yet the authors do not reject Enlightenment. Despite the destructive effect of the dialectic of Enlightenment, meaning that genuine progress and emancipation risk becoming illusory, they consider that there is still no other course that can be taken: however inadequate Enlightenment may be, it remains the only possible road to freedom.

Dialectic of Enlightenment is open to being read as a thoroughly pessimistic book that leaves no room for any justifiable hope of progress and emancipation.[58] According to Horkheimer and Adorno, modernity actually tends to become monolithic in character: Enlightenment has violent and totalitarian traits, and these have inundated almost every area of reality. The authors substantiate this diagnosis on the basis of developments such as the proliferation of positivism in science and philosophy, the degradation of the individual to the level of being a mere supplier of labor or a consumer, and the media's continuous belittling of the public.

The most notorious chapter of their book, "The Culture Industry: Enlightenment as Mass Deception," is devoted to this last theme. The producers of popular entertainment, state Horkheimer and Adorno, pervert culture by turning it into a manipulated, uniform, and utterly predictable commodity. The technological rationality of the mechanisms of reproduction, and the commercial logic of consumption, hold such a sway over the culture industry that there is no longer any room for anything that does not obey the norm, for anything critical. The laws of the cliché prevail to such an extent in this industry that everything that does not conform to it is automatically twisted into being an exception that confirms the rule.

The culture industry, they argue, is occasionally characterized by a subtlety that reminds one of an avant-garde artwork. The difference lies in the fact that the works of the avant-garde serve truth, while the culture industry is dominated by commodification. This can be seen in the continual reproduction of the same thing: despite appearances to the contrary, the genuinely new, the unpredictable, and the unashamed are excluded in a highly calculated manner.

The culture industry implies a short-circuiting between the categories of light and serious art, and it is precisely here that the fraudulence lies. For the separation between these two forms of art is in fact the correlative of defective relations in the social domain:

> Serious art has been withheld from those for whom the hardship and oppression of life make a mockery of seriousness, and who must be glad if they can use time not spent at the production line just to keep going. Light art has been the shadow of autonomous art. It is the social bad conscience of serious art. . . . The division itself is the truth: it does at least express the negativity of the culture which the different spheres constitute. Least of all can the antithesis be reconciled by absorbing light into serious art, or vice versa. But that is what the culture industry attempts.[59]

According to the authors, the culture industry derives its power from managing to bring the leisure time of individuals under the same rules as their working time. To respond without thinking and to be entertained without having to make an effort—these are the logical consequences of a social development of which every aspect is completely governed by the laws of rationalization.

With this chapter about the culture industry, Horkheimer and Adorno have written a classic that has set the tone for the whole postwar discussion about mass culture. The somewhat rigid premises and the strict dichotomies that they apply are not received with much sympathy nowadays, but their ideas continue to play a vital role in representing a radical-critical position.

It is not here, however, that the relevance of the *Dialectic of Enlightenment* for our discussion is to be found. What I find still fascinating about this book has rather to do with the ambivalent attitude that the authors maintain toward modernity. They link their idea that Enlightenment is totalitarian and monolithic with the conviction that there is nevertheless no other course that can be followed:

> We are wholly convinced—and therein lies our *petitio principii*—that social freedom is inseparable from enlightened thought. Nevertheless, we believe that we have just as clearly recognized that the notion of this very way of thinking, no less than the actual historic forms—the social institutions—with which it is interwoven, already contain the seed of the reversal universally apparent today.[60]

Thus they continue to adhere to the necessity of Enlightenment—that is, to a programmatic conception of modernity—despite the distorting logic that they perceive in it. They are aware that the logical structure of this position is aporetic. The aporia lies in their using the means of enlightened thought to expose the destructive tendencies that are inherent in this very thought. They are unable—and unwilling—to escape from this vicious circle.

It is here that one can see how their position differs from that of the so-called postmodernists. Horkheimer and Adorno emphatically acknowledge their debt to the tradition of Enlightenment and they aim, as it were, to carry out a sort of enlightening of the Enlightenment. An author such as Lyotard goes one step further, taking his leave from Enlightenment altogether. While Lyotard states that there is no reasonable excuse for the confusion of reason,[61] it is precisely this "reasonable excuse" that Horkheimer and Adorno are trying to find in the *Dialectic of Enlightenment*. Their quest results in a position that holds two points of view that are not entirely compatible: belief in enlightenment on the one hand and a rejection of the distorting mechanism inherent in it on the other.

A similar tension between incompatible conceptions recurs in Adorno's interpretation of the new. In *Minima Moralia*, a book that was written at almost the same time as the *Dialectic of Enlightenment*, he devotes a short but fascinating reflection to it, under the heading of "Late Extra." The new emerges here in the first instance as the false appearances behind which the old, that which is always the same, conceals itself: "The new, sought for its own sake, a kind of laboratory product, petrified into a conceptual scheme, becomes in its sudden apparition a compulsive return of the old."[62] Things that are proclaimed as new are merely reproductions of the same old scheme foisted on us by the prevailing demands of the cycle of consumption and production. There isn't, in fact, anything that is genuinely new. On the other hand it is equally clear to Adorno that "the cult of the new, and thus the idea of modernity, is a rebellion against the fact that there is no longer anything new," and again, "the new is the secret figure of all those unborn."[63] In other words, no matter how perverse the forms of the new may be, no matter how false are its claims, in the constant appeal to the new, in the fascination for the transitory—almost like a charm that is repeated—the hope is concealed that something really new will emerge one day, and that the ignition of the transitory might lead to the realization of the project of emancipation.

Adorno's concept of modernity is characterized, therefore, by a recurring tension between contradictory aspects. He sees modernity as on the one hand tending toward a monolithic, unambiguous control over both the individual and over social life as a whole, while on the other hand it represents the promise of a *different* future and provides the means and potential to achieve it. As far as its transitory aspect is concerned, Adorno recognizes the new, the fleeting, and the constantly changing as a false semblance behind which the old and the eternally returning are concealed, but in which the figure of rebellion and hope is also inscribed.

Mimesis and Negativity

The concept of *mimesis* plays a crucial role in Adorno's *Aesthetic Theory*.[64] It is a concept that he rarely describes in precise terms, but which definitely has a much broader connotation in his work than do the traditional notions of art as an imitation of nature. Adorno's interpretation of this concept is undeniably indebted to Walter Benjamin and his mimetic theory of language. Benjamin's influence can already be perceived in the passage in *Dialectic of Enlightenment* in which Horkheimer and Adorno explain how during the course of history the character of language underwent radical change. Originally, they claim, sign and image formed, under the form of the symbol, a unity in language, as can be seen from Egyptian hieroglyphs in which signification is the result of the merging of abstract reference in a sign and imitation in an image. This original unity dissolved and both modes of signification developed separately. The sign became decisive for the development of language as denotation—in science and scholarship—whereas the realm of the image has been reduced to that of art and literature:

For science the word is a sign: as sound, image and word proper it is distributed among the different arts, and is not permitted to reconstitute itself by their addition, by synesthesia, or in the composition of the *Gesamtkunstwerk*. As a system of signs, language is required to resign itself to calculation in order to know nature, and must discard the claim to be like her. As image, it is required to resign itself to mirror-imagery in order to be nature entire, and must discard the claim to know her.[65]

Horkheimer and Adorno see the divorce between sign and image as a disastrous development, because reason in the fullest meaning of the word cannot be reduced to pure calculation: in that case it degenerates into a purely instrumental rationality, with the irrational consequences that follow. The same goes for the image: when the image becomes pure depiction and is no longer governed by a rational impulse, it is also inadequate and cannot bring about any genuine knowledge of reality. Nevertheless, "The separation of sign and image is irremediable. Should unconscious self-satisfaction cause it once again to become hypostatized, then each of the two isolated principles tends toward the destruction of truth."[66] According to Horkheimer and Adorno, it is possible both in art and in philosophy to confront this fissure between sign and image, and to attempt to bridge the gap. Philosophy operates at a conceptual level, the level of the sign, whereas artworks at the level of aesthetic appearances, that of the image. Inasmuch as art and philosophy both aspire to provide knowledge of truth, however, they may not hypostatize their own form of knowledge as absolute: philosophy cannot only operate with concepts, while art is obliged to be something more than pure depiction, more than just a reproduction of what exists.

Adorno returns to this motif in *Aesthetic Theory*. In this book he refers to "mimesis" as meaning a kind of affinity between things and persons that is not based on rational knowledge and which goes beyond the mere antithesis between subject and object.[67] The mimetic moment of cognition has to do with the possibility of approaching the world in a different way than by rational-instrumental thinking. For him mimesis is something else than a simple visual similarity between works of art and what they represent. The affinity Adorno refers to lies much deeper. To him it is only stating the obvious to say that an abstract painting can, in mimetic fashion, say something about reality—for example about the alienation and reification that are typical of that reality.

According to Adorno, it is characteristic of art that it endeavors to create a dialectical relation between both moments of cognition, mimesis and rationality—"image" and "sign," to use the terminology of *Dialectic of Enlightenment*. A work of art comes into being on the basis of a mimetic impulse that is regulated by a rational input. Rationality and mimesis, however, are opposed to each other in a relation that is antithetical and paradoxical: the two moments of cognition cannot easily be reconciled. The work of art, therefore, is not able to resolve the contradiction by simply mediating between rationality and mimesis because they are in a way incompatible, and this incompatibility cannot be denied. The value of a work of art in fact depends on the extent to which it succeeds in highlighting the antithetic moments of both rationality and mimesis, without eliminating their opposition through some kind of unity that purports to reconcile the two.[68] This is why Adorno regards tensions, dissonances, and paradoxes as basic attributes of modern works of art.

Adorno is convinced that art entails a form of criticism. The critical character of art is in several respects related to its mimetic quality. In the first instance, art is one of the few realms of society where the mimetic principle is still privileged. Generally speaking, society tends to forbid mimesis, and social practice is increasingly dominated by instrumental rationality. In view of this situation, the existence of art as a domain not totally permeated by rationality provides in itself a critique of the domination of rationality. Adorno argues that the uselessness of art, its refusal to be "for-something-else," unmistakably implies a form of criticism with regard to a society where everything is forced to be useful.[69]

Against the prevailing dominant mode of thought—identity thinking, which constantly subsumes the heterogeneous under the heading of sameness and, in Adorno's words, is "schooled in exchange"[70]—the principle of mimesis embodies a "resemblance of artworks to themselves"[71] that makes room for the nonidentical and the opaque. Art is thus perceived by Adorno as one of the last refuges where real experience, the experience of the nonidentical, is still possible. He concurs with Benjamin in his opinion that modernity has provoked a crisis of experience by increasingly destroying the conditions that allow individuals to develop their capacity for genuine experience. Modern art, he states, provides a way to deal with this crisis and to express it.[72]

The very modernity of art in fact depends on how it relates to this crisis. Art cannot escape this condition: "*Il faut être absolument moderne*," says Adorno, thus repeating Rimbaud's maxim. For Adorno, however, the statement does not mean that one should simply accept one's historical condition; it also implies a need to resist the historical trend. Adorno interprets Rimbaud's phrase as a categorical imperative that combines an honest assessment of social reality with an equally consistent opposition to its continuance. If one wants to resist repression and exploitation, one should not ignore them but recognize them as the actual conditions of existence; only by doing so can one take action against them. From an artistic point of view, this means that modern art needs to employ advanced techniques and methods of production; it also means that it is obliged to incorporate contemporary experiences.[73] At the same time, however, the implication is that art contains a significant degree of criticism and opposition to the existing system.

It is this shading that gives Adorno's aesthetic theory its specific character: Adorno says modern art *as art* is critical. The critical value of a work of art is not embodied in the themes it deals with or in the so-called "commitment" of the artist, but in the artistic process itself. Adorno is convinced that the mimetical potential of art, if it is rightly applied—"right" not in political but in disciplinary, artistic-autonomous terms—vouches for its critical character, even apart from the personal intention of the artist. Works of art yield a kind of knowledge of reality. This knowledge is critical because the mimetical moment is capable of highlighting aspects of reality that were not perceivable before. Through mimesis, art establishes a critical relation with social reality.

Because art in Adorno's view plays the role of an oppositional activity, Michael Cahn calls his concept of mimesis "subversive": "According to Adorno, art must differ from the social in order to remain art. At the same time, however, it must be similar to its opposite in order to be possible as critique, since only the mutual involvement of critique and its object avoids the Hegelian double-bind in which two conflicting statements oppose each other unresolvably."[74] In order to carry out a genuine critique, it is necessary for works of art to identify to a certain extent with what they are in revolt against. This notion can be seen, for instance, in a passage in which Adorno states that works of art are in a certain sense allied to the death principle. Because they remove that which they objectify from the immediacy of life, they submit by way of mimesis to reification, which, as a social realization of instrumental thought, nevertheless constitutes their own death principle. It is precisely here that Adorno sees the precondition for genuine critique: "Without the admixture of poison, virtually the negation of life, the opposition of art to civilizatory repression would amount to nothing more than impotent comfort."[75] In order not to fall back into useless consolation, in order to serve as genuine critique, art is obliged to enter into a relation of similarity with reality, against which it levels its criticism. Art must become "Mimesis an ihr Widerspiel" (mimesis of its opposite): "Art was compelled to this by its social reality. Whereas art opposes society, it is nevertheless unable to take up a position beyond it; it achieves opposition only through identification with that against which it remonstrates."[76]

This is also why Adorno states that works of art can exercise a critique of the dominant thought only inasmuch as they at least in part have made this dominant thought their own: "The opposition of artworks to domination is mimesis of domination. They must assimilate themselves to the comportment of domination in order to produce something qualitatively distinct from the world of domination."[77] Cahn compares the strategy that Adorno describes with the medical principle of inoculation: in order to give the patient immunity to a certain sickness, he is infected with it, but in a controlled manner. In the same way art should be "infected" with the reification that it in fact opposes. The control organ that according to Adorno is employed in art (to round out Cahn's metaphor) is reason: art is not simply mimesis; through reason it becomes a controlled form of mimesis. It is precisely this interplay between mimesis and reason that puts art in a position where it is able to exercise criticism.

The mimetic impulse, according to Adorno, has to do with a gesture of negation: the work of art does not produce a positive image of reality or a positive image of what a utopian, ideal reality might be. On the contrary, the image it produces is a thoroughly negative one, showing as it does the negative aspects of what is called reality. With the gesture of negation that it uses in order to reflect societal reality mimetically, it reveals something about that reality that usually remains hidden. This hidden essence of reality is exposed as something that is unacceptable, a non-essence, while at the same time the need for something else, for a real essence, is suggested: "Even while art indicts the concealed essence, which it summons into appearance, as monstrous, this negation at the same time posits as its own measure an essence that is not present, that of possibility; meaning inheres even in the disavowal of meaning."[78]

Adorno firmly insists on giving the negative a privileged status because he is convinced that only by a gesture of negation does one have the right to appeal to the "other," to the "utopian."[79] To him the objective of modern art is to make people aware of the terrifying character of everyday reality. Under these circumstances, negativity is the only way to keep the idea of the utopian alive. Indeed, the utopian is inconceivable in a positive form, for no image is powerful enough to illustrate the utopian in a positive way without making it appear ridiculous and banal.

The utopian element in Adorno's work is essentially negative—utopia, after all, means "nowhere." While it still refers to the notion of the existence of the "other," this "other" cannot and must not be named, because then it runs the risk of no longer remaining the "other" but of becoming "the same." Utopia, then, can only acquire form in a negative manner, by continually confronting reality with what it is not: "Insofar as we are not allowed to cast the picture of utopia, insofar we do not know what the correct thing would be, we know exactly, to be sure, what the false thing is. That is actually the only form in which utopian thinking is given to us at all."[80]

Works of art create a privileged field for the dialectic operations of negativity. This is because they assume a concrete formal shape. This means that they go a stage further than abstract negations, which have little persuasive power because they are not very determinate. Adorno takes Samuel Beckett's work as an example. Its value lies in the way his texts take the form of a determinate negation of meaning. It is not a case here of absence of meaning—in that case Beckett's texts would be irrelevant rather than illuminating. Meaninglessness is given form in them through the concrete negation of meaningfulness. As a result it is possible to preserve the memory of what meaning is capable of being. It is precisely here that the value of his work is to be found.[81]

This complex interplay of mimesis, negativity, and utopia underlies various of Adorno's definitions of modern art. He states, for instance, that "art is modern through mimesis of the hardened and alienated; only thereby, and not by the refusal of a mute reality, does art become eloquent; this is why art no longer tolerates the innocuous."[82] While the modern social system is characterized by reification and alienation, art is able to register a protest against it only by relying upon mimesis to make this reification its own. In doing so it carries out an operation of determinate negation by exposing reality as a combination of broken fragments. As a result something emerges that normally is not visible: "By determinate negation artworks absorb the *membra disjecta* of the empirical world and through their transformation organize them into a reality that is a counterreality, a monstrosity."[83]

Following a similar rationale, Adorno argues that in modern art, dissonance takes the place of the harmonious model: only dissonance can give an adequate picture of a reality that is the opposite of harmonious; in fact, it is only by means of a dissonant form that one is able to evoke the memory of the genuinely harmonious.

> The attraction of the charming can only survive where the powers of refusal are the strongest: in the dissonance that refuses to believe in the deception of the existing harmony. . . . While formerly ascesis suppressed the aesthetic appeal to desire in a reactionary way, today the same ascesis has become the characteristic of progressive art. . . . It is in this negative fashion that art refers to the possibility of happiness, a possibility that through a purely partial positive anticipation at present is frustrated in a pernicious fashion.[84]

Art indeed refers to the harmonious—Adorno maintains that in one way or another art is also a *promesse du bonheur*[85]—but it can only point to it effectively by means of a mimesis of its opposite. This is what Adorno means when he states that dissonance is "the truth about harmony."[86]

The Dual Character of Art

In Adorno's view, art has a double character: on the one hand, it is *fait social* and socially determined; on the other, it is autonomous, and obedient only to its own styling principles. Art is *fait social* because it is the product of a form of societal labor. Art is socially determined not because of any direct influence of the societal structure of production forces and production relations, nor because of any social commitment in the themes that it deals with. In Adorno's view, the social factor is present in art because history is sedimented in the "material" used by the artist. Adorno uses the word "material" in a very broad sense: it includes both the concrete materials used to make the work, and also the techniques at the artist's disposal, his arsenal of images and memories, the influence of the context on the work, and so on. This material is undeniably socially formed and this social aspect therefore permeates the work as a whole.

Works of art are also autonomous, however: the artistic process, the mimetic-rational way of giving shape to this material, is an entirely autonomous affair. The autonomous character of art, according to Adorno, does not prohibit its critical content. Indeed, the artistic discipline largely *owes* its critical potential to its autonomous character. First-rate works of art are always critical; each of them in its own fashion exposes by means of mimesis an aspect of reality which would remain concealed but for this gesture. In his analyses of specific artworks—his particular interest was modern literature and serious music—the purport of his text was invariably to show exactly how the social determination of the material, combined with its autonomous artistic processing, enabled the artist to produce a work that contains a critical attitude toward social reality.

In an essay about *Commitment* he clarifies his position further. Committed art, art that endeavors to win over the public to a certain way of thinking, is based in Adorno's view on false premises. To the extent that it can be called art, it is subject to the autonomous formal principles of the medium that it uses. In this constellation the intention of the artist is only one moment in the whole process, and that moment cannot be the only one that determines the final result. A work such as Picasso's *Guernica* is in the first instance an autonomous work: it is not made with the sole aim of denouncing the evils of war. Effectively, however, this is what it does, precisely because as a work of art it reflects critically on the given reality:

> Even autonomous works of art like the *Guernica* are determinate negations of empirical reality: they destroy what destroys, what merely exists and as mere existence recapitulates the guilt endlessly. . . . The artist's imagination is not a *creatio ex nihilo;* only dilettantes and sensitive types conceive it as such. By opposing empirical reality, works of art obey its forces, which repulse the spiritual construction, as it were, throwing it back upon itself.[87]

It is in this complicated relation with reality that the critical power of art is implied—not in the explicit commitment of the artist. Adorno even sees a danger in the latter: "Hidden in the notion of a 'message,' of art's manifesto, even if it is politically radical, is a moment of accommodation to the world: the gesture of addressing the listener contains a secret complicity with those being addressed, who can, however, be released from their illusions only if that complicity is rescinded."[88] The fact that one wants to convey a message means that one is conforming to the norm of what can be communicated and understood, to the norm of identity thinking. This implies a betrayal of art's singularity, the essence of which is precisely not to conform, thus offering through its resistance a sanctuary to the nonidentical. Only by remaining faithful to itself can art genuinely exercise criticism and keep alive the hope of something different: "An 'it shall be different' is hidden in even the most sublimated work of art. If art is merely identical with itself, a purely scientized construction, it has already gone bad and is literally preartistic. The moment of intention is mediated solely through the form of the work, which crystallizes into a likeness of an Other that ought to exist."[89]

Adorno had already expressed this view much earlier. Traces of it recur in his discussion with Benjamin about the latter's essay on works of art.[90] Adorno does not agree with Benjamin that little can be expected of autonomous art with regard to possible revolutionary social developments. He also does not share Benjamin's belief in the progressive character of the new reproduction techniques. As far as the first point was concerned, Adorno thought that Benjamin was perhaps correct in diagnosing a "decay of the aura" of the work of art, but that this process of decay also had to do with internal artistic developments and therefore could not be attributed only to the influence of reproducibility. Adorno stresses that "*l'art pour l'art* is just as much in need of a defense"[91] and that Benjamin is mistaken in attributing a counter-revolutionary function to the autonomous work of art.

He has similar difficulties with the potential for emancipation that Benjamin perceived in the new medium of film. He accuses Benjamin of having an undialectical approach in that he condemns the domain of high culture in an unqualified fashion while uncritically lauding everything that pertains to "low" culture: "Both bear the stigmata of capitalism, both contain elements of change. . . . Both are torn halves of an integral freedom, to which however they do not add up. It would be romantic to sacrifice one to the other."[92] Adorno shares with Benjamin the belief that history is sedimented in the materials and techniques that the artist employs in his work: it follows for him that the artist, precisely through the fact of using these materials and techniques, can reveal the true face of history. It is due to this belief that for Adorno the truth content of a work of art does line up with its artistic significance.

Adorno's *Aesthetic Theory* describes the condition of modern art as a situation that is dominated by antinomian structures and expectations from which there is no definitive escape. The whole aim of modern art is to give concrete form to utopia (in one way or another it remains a *promesse de bonheur*), but on the other hand art is not in a position actually to become a utopia because if it did so it would lose its efficaciousness and degenerate into an empty form of consolation. Modern art is radically autonomous in its attitude toward social reality but remains nevertheless tied to it through its hidden strands of negation and criticism. Modern art is the result of a combination of mimesis and reason, with these two moments of cognition being essentially incompatible, and the work of art not really capable of mediating between them. A definitive solution, a genuine reconciliation, a satisfactory harmony, would seem to Adorno not to be within the bounds of possibility. At the same time, art does occupy a privileged position in his eyes precisely because it succeeds in giving form to these incongruities without detracting from either of the two polarities. In its best moments art succeeds in referring to the utopian form while at the same time exposing its inaccessibility under present societal relations.

Contradictions and paradoxes, according to Adorno, also govern social reality in a broader sense. That is how *The Dialectic of Enlightenment* interprets modernity: Enlightenment is supposedly founded in reason but is transformed into myth; the new is desirable because it represents the promise of the radical other and yet at the same time it is only a flimsy mask for the return of the old. Horkheimer and Adorno give us a tragic picture of the Enlightenment, with the tragic element lying above all in the fact that people in general are not aware of the contradictions and absurdities that determine their condition. In Adorno's opinion one can speak of a *Verblen-dungszusammenhang*—people are blinded by the idea that the world is as it is. As a result, the possibilities for real change that objectively exist do not get through to their consciousness and therefore have no chance of succeeding. The thesis of the "totally administered world" postulates that people are imprisoned in a network of social relations of production and consumption so that they unconsciously allow themselves to be manipulated, with the result that the system can continue to exist fundamentally unchanged. In contrast with Tafuri, Adorno does in fact see possibilities of resistance in the face of these developments. He, too, is clear that radical political change is not something that is going to take place overnight, but he does allow some margin for criticism, more than Tafuri does. He sees, for instance, possibilities for genuine criticism in the domain of art and philosophy in particular, however marginal this may be in terms of society. It is the way in which he explores these possibilities that gives his work its relevance for today.

Some precautions, however, should be formulated. Although Adorno's work offers a wealth of stimulating ideas and perceptions, there are also some problematic aspects to it. In terms of this book they can be summed up under two headings: Adorno's unilinear notion of history[93] and his pronounced preference for autonomous art.[94] With regard to the first point it should be stressed that Adorno assumes that history is characterized by an increasing exacerbation of the process of reification and an increasing prevalence of identity thinking. As a result, the social system with its blind logic proliferates, permeating more and more the whole fabric of individual and collective existence. It is in the context of this evolution that he interprets the maxim *"il faut être absolument moderne"* as meaning the obligation of art to use the most advanced materials and techniques: only in this way will it be able to preserve its critical content. If, however, one does not share Adorno's notion of history as a one-way street, if one is rather inclined to see the evolution of history as a complex of disparate, uneven, and contradictory developments that are characterized by a lack of synchronicity and continuity rather than by a strict logic of reification, then one is no longer obliged to interpret this maxim in such a unilinear fashion. Criticism and resistance remain in my view an obligation; but these need not be confined to the most advanced materials and techniques: in a situation where it is not clear precisely what progress is and what techniques can be called the most advanced, a limitation like this is no longer relevant.

The second series of objections have to do with Adorno's obsession with autonomous art, an obsession that means that he has never paid much attention either in his *Aesthetic Theory* or elsewhere to heteronomous forms of art such as architecture. Adorno's aesthetic sensibility is most outspoken in the fields of music and literature—he has never devoted much attention to the visual arts, to dance and theater, or to architecture. His texts sometimes give the impression that the whole realm of cultural production is by definition split into two domains: autonomous art (good, critical art) and the products of the culture industry (bad, reified art). The reality is of course much more complicated. It is statements of this kind that have led Adorno's critics to accuse him of being an elitist, and in some ways they are right. Adorno certainly did not have much of an eye for the inventive and critical use that has been made of some of the products of mass culture in everyday practice. That, however, does not mean that suggestions do not occur now and then in his work that permit such material to be read as a form of cultural production that consists of more than just commodification and the urge to conform.[95]

Another consequence of his preference for autonomous works of art is that he adopts a position that according to Peter Bürger is quite simply anti-avant-gardist.[96] Adorno himself does not make any distinction between modernism and the avant-garde, but if one concurs with Bürger's line of argument and assumes that what the avant-garde was concerned with was the abolition of the institution of "art," then it makes sense that Adorno could not go along with this aim. For him it is clear that the distance between actual social reality and the promise of a different future inherent in autonomous works of art is so great that there is no question of the abolition of art being able to achieve the desired goal, namely genuine emancipation and liberation. On the contrary, in Adorno's view it is only by preserving its autonomy that art can remain critical.

In my opinion, it is above all Adorno's dual purpose as evidenced in *Aesthetic Theory* that gives his work its relevance today: the aim to see works of art in the perspective of their social definition and social relevance on the one hand (in other words, in terms of their character as denouncing social reality) and on the other hand in the perspective of their autonomy as aesthetically shaped objects. Adorno's dual definition of the work of art and the way in which he describes the mutual relation between these two aspects remains in my mind a fascinating departure point for analyzing specific works of art—or architecture.

Mimesis in Architecture

It is by no means self-evident that architecture can be approached as a mimetic discipline. As long as one thinks of "mimesis" as a literal copying or imitation, as a depiction or reproduction of a given reality, it is difficult to discern its presence in architecture. This is also the reason that Heidegger states in *The Origin of the Work of Art* for relying on the model of the Greek temple. In this text Heidegger attempts to identify what is the essence of art; according to him, it has to do with truth, but not with depiction or "representation":

> We now ask the question of truth with a view to the work. But in order to become more familiar with what the question involves, it is necessary to make visible once more the happening of truth in the work. For this attempt let us deliberately select a work that cannot be ranked as representational art.
>
> A building, a Greek temple, portrays nothing.[97]

For Heidegger the Greek temple is an appropriate vehicle for clarifying his ideas on art precisely because mimesis in the sense of *Darstellung* or representation does not play a role.

Once one departs from this narrow notion of mimesis, however—as Benjamin and Adorno do—the thesis that architecture is nonmimetic loses its validity. When one's definition of mimesis no longer coincides with faithful copying, but refers rather to more general figures of similarity and difference, to certain affinities or correspondences, then there is no longer any reason for excluding architecture from the realm of mimesis. In architecture, too, forms are constructed and buildings designed on the basis of processes of correspondence, similarity, and difference. The reference points here are extremely varied in character: the program of demands, the physical context, a typological series, a particular formal idiom, a historical connotation. All these elements lend themselves to being treated mimetically and thus to being translated in the design.

When discussing mimesis in architecture, however, the reference to Adorno and Benjamin is not the sole productive one. In French poststructuralism, there is also considerable discussion of the extent and significance of mimesis. This concept plays a crucial role in the work of Lacoue-Labarthe and Derrida in particular.

Mimesis in Contemporary Theory

For Lacoue-Labarthe, the reflection on mimesis is the pretext for his confrontation with Heidegger that he sees as the main task of contemporary philosophy.[98] In "Typographie," his contribution to the book *Mimesis. Désarticulations*,[99] his argument pivots on the curious observation that Heidegger, who devoted a thorough discussion to virtually all the basic concepts of Greek philosophy, never reflects on mimesis as such. By way of a deconstructivist reading of the writings in which Heidegger comes closest to dealing with this problem, Lacoue-Labarthe argues that Heidegger ignores mimesis because of its "constitutive undecidability." This lacuna in his thought means that Heidegger to a certain extent continues to follow the path of Western metaphysics, even though it is a tradition that he aims to break with.

Mimesis is characterized by a "constitutive undecidability," according to Lacoue-Labarthe. This he explains by referring to Plato's treatment of mimesis. In Plato's *Republic* it is explicitly stated that poets, writers, actors, and artists should be excluded from the ideal state because their work makes no contribution whatsoever to truth and goodness. Their exclusion is first formulated in the chapter that deals with education. According to Plato, the spiritual education of small children must not be determined by listening to stories (as is usually the case), because stories are largely based on fantasy and are therefore untrue. Thus, the state should keep a careful eye on the production of texts, permitting only those that serve the truth and propagate elevated principles. That means amongst other things that a writer can only tell his tale in indirect speech because the use of direct speech means that he is pretending to be another, and that results in confusion and a disguising of truth. For the same reason actors are also not welcome in Plato's republic, and music is required to be restrained and lacking in emotion.

Only in a much later chapter about art and censorship is the fundamental reason for this exclusion stated. Here Plato compares the making of a painting or sculpture with the way that reality is reflected in a mirror. The image that appears in a mirror is not real; it is clear that what is involved is a derivative form, a copy of the truth. Plato concludes from this that works of art are far removed from the truth and that the wise man should therefore be on his guard against them.

Lacoue-Labarthe points out that something quite curious is going on in this passage. Apparently Plato is able to defend his rejection of mimesis only by way of the trope of the mirror—in other words, by means of a comparison, by a mimetic gesture. The exclusion of mimesis, the control of mimesis, apparently can only be achieved by appealing to a means that is proper to mimesis:

> It remains fragile. And, in fact, if the entire operation consists in trying to go one better than mimesis in order to master it, if it is a question of circumventing mimesis, though with its own means (without which, of course, this operation would be null and void), how would it be possible to have even the slightest chance of success—since mimesis is precisely the absence of appropriate means, and since this is even what is supposed to be shown? How do we appropriate the improper? How do we make the improper appropriate without aggravating still further the improper?[100]

We are faced with a crucial dimension of mimesis here—namely its connection with the conflict between the self and the other, between the authentic and the inauthentic, between the proper and the improper. If one does not succeed in unambiguously separating the categories of truth and mimesis—without, that is, making an appeal to comparisons or metaphors—then it is indeed difficult to determine what it is that is "proper" about the truth. When mimesis is brought in to help achieve an understanding of the distinctive features of certain entities, the specific character of this operation consists in the fact that these features can be highlighted only by means of a comparison with something else, something different. Therefore, one can succeed in grasping the "proper" only by way of the "improper," something that inevitably complicates one's notion of the proper.

Seen in this light, Heidegger's caution with regard to mimesis comes as no surprise. In Heidegger's thought, the concept of authenticity, of what is proper, is a decisive category, and it is precisely the stability of this category that is cast in doubt by a reflection on mimesis.

Elsewhere, however, Lacoue-Labarthe points out that Heidegger's interpretation of art basically remains a mimetology.[101] Heidegger certainly does not thoroughly explore the theme of mimesis in any depth—he apparently understands it in a Platonic sense and sees mimesis as a secondary figure that is subordinate to the truth in the sense of *adequatio* (identity between statement and fact). Heidegger nevertheless regards art as a privileged locus where a world takes on form and where the truth is revealed again and again in an ever new way. Art *gives shape* to truth and it is in this giving shape—in this inscription of a form, in this typography—that one finds a mimetic moment, even if Heidegger himself does not use this term.

Lacoue-Labarthe thus argues that mimesis is in fact the essential figure of Heidegger's concept of truth as *alētheia*. Heidegger conceives of the truth as a game in which the similarity of being to itself is exposed, a play of concealing and revealing, a play by which something is exposed and becomes visible, whereas something else withdraws or is concealed. Mimesis underlies this process of revealing and concealing because it has to do with elucidating similarities and differences.

The fact that mimesis is ineluctably linked to every philosophical claim to truth is also a recurrent theme in the work of Jacques Derrida. In "White Mythology," a text from 1971, he discusses the scope and impact of metaphors in philosophical thought. In the philosophical tradition that began with Aristotle, metaphor is seen as a trope that produces a transfer between a noun that means something different and a specific matter to which that noun is newly applied. Metaphor thus operates in the realm of mimesis: it exposes a hidden resemblance that can be observed between two entities which belong to different fields. The remarkable thing is that on closer analysis all "concepts" would appear to derive from a metaphorical origin: they are "faded" metaphors as it were, figures of speech in which the mimetic origin can no longer clearly be read. In this text Derrida traces a number of fundamental philosophical concepts, explaining their mimetic roots. As with Lacoue-Labarthe, the question that inevitably occurs is that of the decidability of categories such as "proper" and "improper": if a metaphor tends to shed light on a matter in a way that is improper (being figurative) and if one cannot but grant that concepts in the end are reducible to faded metaphors, how then is it possible to explore the "proper" meanings of a concept or the "essential" properties of some matter?

Derrida points out that in philosophical tradition a certain strategy is adopted to avoid this difficulty. An axiology is set up by which a distinction between "proper" and "improper," between essence and accident, is *postulated*. This distinction, which is not "proven" but merely elucidated by metaphors or similes, in fact props up the whole philosophical discourse in the tradition of metaphysics.

As Mark Wigley shows, the figure of the house plays an important role in this constellation. Derrida refers to the classical description of the metaphor in which it is stated that the word used in the metaphor dwells, as it were, in a borrowed house. This figure "is a metaphor of metaphor: an expropriation, a being-outside-one's-own-residence, but still in a dwelling, outside its own residence but still in a residence in which one comes back to oneself, recognizes oneself, reassembles oneself, outside oneself in oneself."[102] The association between the figure of the house (*oikos* in

Greek) and the problem of the proper (*oikeios*) is self-evident. According to Wigley, it has everything to do with the fact that the house represents a basic experience that enables one to make a distinction between inside and outside. This distinction is in the end fundamental to the forming of concepts in philosophy:

> The house is always first understood as the most primitive drawing of a line that produces an inside opposed to an outside, a line that acts as a mechanism of domestication. It is as the paradigm of interiority that the house is indispensable to philosophy, establishing the distinction between the interiority of presence and the exteriority of representation on which the discourse depends.[103]

Put this way, it is clear that the house as a basic metaphor accommodates the hierarchic distinction between presence on the one hand and representation on the other, between a direct and primary presence and an indirect, secondary representation, between the truth as immediate presence and mimesis as mediated imitation. (One should note that, once again, this distinction is being explained via a mimetic gesture.)

The hierarchy accorded to these terms is responsible for the antimimetic attitude that prevails in the philosophical tradition. This attitude has everything to do with the threat that comes from the feminine. Plato associates the mimetic in the first place with the tales that women tell little children. He considers their influence to be dangerous because in these stories the clear distinction between truth and lies is dissolved. Lacoue-Labarthe argues that a sort of male urge to rebel against the primary control of the mother is underlying Plato's text at this point. A child's first surroundings are defined by women who are by consequence always associated with the stage in which the subject is not yet completely developed. As Lacan has shown, a child, an infant (*infans* in Latin means without speech) gradually becomes a subject by making its entry into language, by learning to speak. The human condition is such that the emergence of ego-consciousness does not coincide with physical birth. There is a considerable period in which a child is not yet a subject. The child is not capable either of achieving the status of a subject all by itself: it has to go through what Lacan calls the "mirror stage."[104] It learns to see itself as an entity and as differing from its environment, due to the fact that it identifies itself with its mirror image and with the name it has been given by its parents. The identity of the subject is in other words not established in a completely autonomous way, but is formed on the basis of elements that come from outside and that are mimetically appropriated.

According to Lacoue-Labarthe, here is the ground for the antimimetic attitude that one encounters so often in philosophy. Antimimesis refers to nothing else than the ultimate Hegelian dream of philosophy, the dream of an absolute knowledge, of a subject that understands its own conception perfectly, thus also controlling it perfectly. The dream of a perfect autonomy is constantly threatened by the confusing plurality that mimesis represents. It is, in other words, threatened by instability, by feminization.[105]

The Issue of Critique

The question that now emerges is that of the critical content of mimesis. For Adorno, as we have seen, the critical potential of artworks is closely linked to their mimetic character: in his view the thing that is specific to works of art is their implementation in mimetic form of a concrete negation of certain aspects of social reality. He sees the degree to which this contradictory operation succeeds as a criterion for judging the quality of artworks.

With the French poststructuralists, the emphasis is less on mimesis as a strategy for developing a critique of society within the domain of art. They too see mimesis as an oppositional agency capable of undermining the dominance of logocentrism. But while in Adorno art is seen as one of the few safe havens still available to mimesis, the French thinkers see it as also regularly operating elsewhere: in texts, in psychoanalysis, in behavioral patterns, in new social movements. Moreover, they are less inclined to speak in terms of a "critique." This difference of perception between Adorno and the poststructuralists has a great deal to do with some more general differences between critical theory and recent French thought.

Adorno's opposition to identity thinking, for instance, is strongly influenced by his sociopolitical position that has its roots in the Marxist tradition; Derrida's deconstruction of metaphysics, on the other hand, came about through a radicalization of a reflection on language. Thus, Adorno puts a strong emphasis on the link between the exchange principle and identity thinking, a relation that Derrida pays little heed to. Adorno's philosophical and aesthetic analyses inevitably lead to conclusions that are sociocritical in content, something that is much less the case with Derrida and other poststructuralists.

Secondly, Adorno, as an exponent of the Frankfurt School, never abandoned his belief in rationality and in the fundamental possibility of ideology critique, despite the numerous modifications he formulates and the note of doubt that can often be heard in his work. For Adorno there is no question that the totality of society forms the horizon of every system of thought, no matter how difficult it may be to grasp the trends and developments that determine it.[106] This sort of claim to rationality and totality is no longer made by the poststructuralists. They confine themselves to suggesting purely local strategies for achieving meaning, rejecting the possibility of having any *fundamental* influence on social reality or of genuinely being able to redirect it in an emancipatory sense. Some of them go as far as to exclude *every* possibility for critique. According to Baudrillard, for instance, the defense mechanisms of the society of the spectacle are so accurate that it can succeed effortlessly in converting every intentional critical reaction into an impulse that supports the system through the game of fashion.[107]

But even when they are rather pessimistic with respect to the possibility of critique, poststructuralists nevertheless repeatedly argue for subversive attitudes and oppositional activities. No longer do these pleas represent an unassailable belief in the project of modernity, but they are symptomatic of a desire to take a stand against the status quo and to break the dominance of the prevailing system. In Lyotard, for instance, this strategy takes on the form of a "rewriting of modernity," with explicit reference to the aims of Adorno, Bloch, and Benjamin.[108] This rewriting, in his view, should take the form of what Freud calls *Durcharbeitung*, a working through or out, a reflective questioning of what is fundamentally concealed. *Durcharbeitung* in psychoanalysis is not just a matter of rationality; it depends rather on having access to memories and associations that should receive an equal amount of attention from the analyst, independent of their logical, ethical, or aesthetic relevance. As I see it, what is involved here is a mimetic operation: rewriting modernity means rethinking it in terms other than just those of objectifying rationality.[109]

From all this one can conclude that mimesis provides one with a key for dealing with reality in *another* way, thus developing margins for critique. Both the work of Adorno and Benjamin and the more recent writings of poststructuralist authors point in this direction. Does it follow that mimesis can also play a critical role in architecture? Can architecture by making use of mimesis—consciously and deliberately or otherwise—develop strategies by which it can present itself as *critical* architecture?

There are undoubtedly arguments for answering this question in the negative. The main objection is that architecture is not an autonomous art form: architecture is always built as the result of a commission from somebody or other; for reasons of social usefulness it must conform to prevailing expectations. Architecture, if it is actually to be built, is almost unavoidably on the side of money and power, thus supporting the status quo.

This argument is valid and can be applied to a very high percentage of what is built. It does not, however, cover architecture entirely. For in analogy with Adorno's argument about the dual character of artworks—that they are both socially determined *and* autonomous—one can argue that architecture as a discipline that has to do with the designing of space does involve an autonomous moment. It is true of course that architecture, more so than literature or the visual arts, is determined by social factors: in the end not only materials and techniques but also context and program are the net result of a series of social determinants. Even so, architecture cannot simply be reduced to a sort of sum total of these factors. Giving form to space cannot be reduced to a simple conformity to heteronomous principles, such as functional or constructional requirements, the psychological needs of the users, or the image a building is intended to convey. There is always an autonomous moment in the design process at which an architect is purely and simply occupied with architecture—with giving form to space.

In the few texts that Adorno wrote about architecture,[110] he does in fact link its critical content with the degree to which it does justice to this autonomous, mimetic moment. He argues, for example, that the matter-of-fact approach of functionalism implies a correct understanding of the social situation, but states that its truth value is primarily dependent on the way that it treats function mimetically. The danger is not inconceivable that this mimetic element will be lost, so that the architecture does not have any critical bite: when *Mimesis an Funktionalität* is reduced to *Funktionalität* pure and simple, every critical distance from the dominant social reality disappears and functional architecture no longer plays anything but an affirmative role.[111]

In functionalism Adorno recognizes the effects of the dialectics of the Enlightenment. That movement, too, was characterized by an intertwining of progressive and regressive moments. By giving reason priority over myth, the Enlightenment aspired toward emancipation and liberation, but this very aspiration reverts to myth when its goal is forgotten and "reason" is reduced to pure instrumental rationality. The same dialectics plays a part in functionalism: inasmuch as its aim was to fulfill genuine "objective" human needs, one can only see it as a progressive moment, one, moreover, that contains a critique of a social situation whose whole effect is to deny these genuine needs; when, however, functionalism is integrated in a social dynamic that employs "functionalism" as an end in itself, with an absence of every reference to any goal beyond it, it represents a regressive position: "The antinomies of *Sachlichkeit* confirm the dialectic of enlightenment: That progress and regression are entwined. The literal is barbaric. Totally objectified, by virtue of its rigorous legality, the artwork becomes a mere fact and is annulled as art. The alternative that opens up in this crisis is: Either to leave art behind or to transform its very concept."[112] The latter alternative—the renunciation of every claim to be art—is precisely the charge that Adorno levels at functionalism in practice. This can clearly be seen in "Functionalism Today," an essay in which he is unsparing in his critique of the renunciation of the autonomous moment. In his view, it is precisely this reduction that is responsible for the dullness and superficiality of so much postwar architecture.

Today it is no longer functionalism that is at stake. Nor is there any longer any dispute over the existence of an "autonomous moment" in architecture. The question remains, however, of whether the critical content of architecture *coincides* with this autonomous moment. It is perhaps necessary to qualify Adorno's claims on this point. The autonomous moment in architecture certainly can be applied critically, but the critical character is by no means inherent in the autonomous moment. In order to genuinely take on the challenge of *critical* architecture, the critical content cannot purely and simply act as a noncommittal commentary that only concerns the packaging of the building while not paying any heed to program or content. As Diane Ghirardo points out, we should not be blind to the fact that the notion of architecture as art and the associating of its critical character with its artistic content has often only served as an ideological mask for the complicity that exists between some highbrow architecture of the postmodern or deconstructivist variety and the vulgar commercial concerns of property developers.[113]

The recognition of an autonomous moment in architecture is therefore a necessary but by no means sufficient requirement for a critical architecture. In every built work of architecture, social interests are also at stake. A critical treatment of social reality therefore inevitably operates at various levels simultaneously and cannot be reduced to the packaging aspects of a building. Questions such as "Who is building and for whom?" "What is its impact on the public domain?" and "Who will profit from this development?" are and will continue to be relevant in this connection. These questions also can be mimetically incorporated in the design, however, giving more weight to its critical aspirations.

Between the Lines

A project in which mimesis is clearly at work is Libeskind's design for the extension of the Berlin Museum with the Jewish Museum (figure 85).[114] The aim of the design is to give form to the broken relation between German and Jewish culture. This relation is anything but unambiguous and it is therefore not simple to represent it in a building. Libeskind's project succeeds in expressing the different aspects of this relation: the mutual ties that persist and proliferate underground, the ineluctable catastrophe of the Holocaust, the cautious hope that a new openness can develop. It is the result of a mimetic process that uses various themes as raw material in order to bring about a work in which the tension between the different parts is increased to the point of climax.

The architect calls this project "Between the Lines." He is referring to two structural lines that are also two lines of thinking: one is a straight line but broken into many fragments; the other is tortuous but continues indefinitely (figure 86). Both lines engage in a dialogue with each other only to separate again. Their mutual relationship delineates the basic structure of the building. This consists of a zigzag volume transected by a number of voids. These voids are five stories high and form an interrupted straight line (figure 87).

Daniel Libeskind, extension of the Berlin Museum with the Jewish Museum, Berlin, 1993–1997, maquette (competition stage).

85

Daniel Libeskind, extension
of the Berlin Museum with
the Jewish Museum, ground-
floor plan.

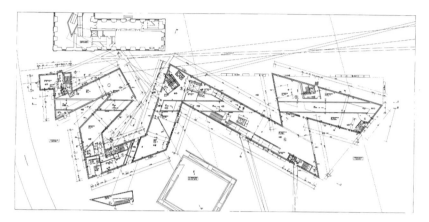

86

Daniel Libeskind, extension of the
Berlin Museum with the Jewish
Museum, sections.

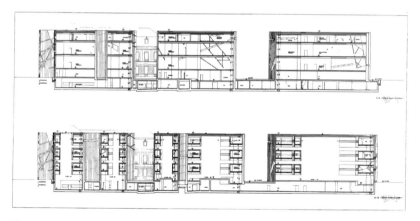

87

Daniel Libeskind, extension
of the Berlin Museum with the
Jewish Museum, view from
the outside.

(Photo: Bitter Bredt.)

88

As visitors follow the zigzag pattern through the museum as dictated by the layout of the building, they are repeatedly confronted by these voids, which are accessible nowhere and which seem to be senseless. The flowing movement of the routing breaks down as a result. The character of the space changes at the places where the voids are spanned: the high spacious galleries turn here into narrow low-ceilinged bridges from which one can glimpse the cold gloomy depths of the voids.

The zigzag-shaped building has no entrance on the outside. It has the appearance of an enigmatic and impenetrable volume (figure 88). Visitors have to enter the building through the old entrance in the main building, which provides a link to the new complex through the basements. To this end an incision has been cut in the main building that is a mirror image of one of the voids in the new complex. This mirror relationship, while it cannot be seen by the unsuspecting visitor, nevertheless forms an active presence, evoking the fatal mutual involvement of German and Jewish culture.

The underground level of the new building contains the areas reserved for the museum's own Jewish collection (figure 89). The whole is organized on three axes. One axis forms the link with the main stair that leads to the exhibition rooms on the upper stories. A second axis is oriented on a freestanding tower-shaped object that, like the incision in the main building, is a "voided void"—echoes, as it were, of the voids that form the straight line that intersects the zigzag-shaped building. While the first void refers to the absence of Jews in Berlin, an absence that is decisive for the identity of the city, this voided void that is white and open to the sky refers to the streams of energy and creative potential that was cut off along with the annihilation of so many people. Finally, there is a third axis in the basement that leads to the "garden of E. T. A. Hoffmann." This consists of a wood of concrete columns at right angles to the sloping ground. A ramp that winds round this square garden gives access to street level.

Despite the fact that its layout is far from self-evident, the new museum is a very effective response to the existing urban situation (figure 90). The slightly protruding facade on the Lindenstrasse accentuates the curve in the street at this point. The front facade of the new extension is extremely narrow here, but it is still clearly

Daniel Libeskind, extension of the
Berlin Museum with the Jewish
Museum, underground plan.

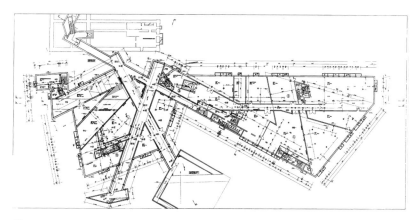

89

Daniel Libeskind, extension
of the Berlin Museum with
the Jewish Museum, site plan
(competition stage).

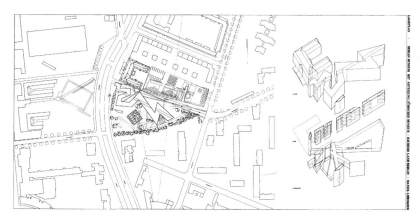

90

Daniel Libeskind, extension of
the Berlin Museum with the
Jewish Museum, Paul Celan Hof.
(Photo: Bitter Bredt.)

91

present. This suggests that the building is subordinate to the old Berlin Museum, a suggestion that is straightaway contradicted once one gets the chance to size up the full scope of the new extension. Between the old building and the zigzag shape of the new one, a narrow alley leading to a courtyard, the Paul Celan Hof, is created that fits in with the Berlin tradition of *Gassen* and *Hinterhöfer* (figure 91). More toward the rear of the building, the high broad volumes forming the last sections of the zigzag are arranged as spatially defining elements for the public gardens situated on both sides of the entire complex. The volumes have an effect that fits in excellently with the rich contrast of architectures in the neighborhood.[115]

According to Libeskind, the design has four basic underlying themes. The first of these came to him when he noted on old maps of the city the addresses of some famous representatives of a rejected culture: Walter Benjamin, Paul Celan, Mies van der Rohe, and others. The network that was created—an invisible matrix of relations printed on the surface of Berlin—took the form of a Star of David (figure 92). A second theme had to do with the music of Arnold Schoenberg and especially his unfinished opera *Moses und Aaron*. The opera deals with the difficult relation between the unimaginable truth that was revealed to Moses and the way that Aaron converted this absolute truth into images that could easily be assimilated. The third theme is the *Gedenkbuch* with the names of the Jews who were deported from Berlin. In its naked materiality, the two volumes of this book, which is as thick as a telephone book, form an extremely compelling testimony to the real impact of the Holocaust—

an endless list of names, dates of birth, and presumed dates and places of death. Finally, there is a fourth theme—Benjamin's *Einbahnstrasse*. Libeskind uses this "urban apocalypse," as he calls the book, as a rhythmic thread through the sixty sections of the trajectory of the museum—the number of texts in *Einbahnstrasse*.

The Star of David that Libeskind states as his starting point for the design is a revealing drawing. It is not only the addresses of the people named in it that give the matrix its form, but also the contours of the Landwehrkanal and the former trajectory of the Wall. The latter figures comprise, as it were, the horizontal supports of the drawing, while the outline of the star is formed by a section cut out of the map of Berlin. By combining this selection of graphic elements a pattern is created that makes the layout of the new building at least plausible, if not totally clear. One recognizes that the history of Berlin is crystallized in the zigzag form of the new extension: the classical pattern of the Friedrichstadt with its rectangular pattern of streets and geometrical squares, the flowing lines of the canal, the broken and shameless line of the Wall—all this is echoed in compressed fashion in the discontinuous shape

Daniel Libeskind, extension
of the Berlin Museum with the
Jewish Museum, site—Star
of David.

Daniel Libeskind, extension of
the Berlin Museum with the
Jewish Museum, names.

93

of the new museum. Unlike a classical site layout plan, what is involved here is not any rational explanation based on the morphotypological qualities of the new building. Instead the aim is to show how different aspects of Berlin as it exists today—both visible and invisible ones—mimetically converge in a new cutting that is grafted onto this organism. This drawing expresses the inner relationship—the *Wahlverwandtschaft*, or elective affinity—between a constellation of existing structural elements and the additional urban figure.

In his text Libeskind suggests that the Moses and Aaron theme has to do with the intertwining of the two lines that gives the building its shape. Schoenberg's opera is incomplete: the second act ends with Moses alone on the stage, expressing his dismay at the breakdown of his relationship with Aaron and consequently with the people of Israel as a whole. Aaron wants to communicate with the people and to lead them to the promised land, whereas Moses is unable to convey what God revealed to him with an image through which he could reach the people. "Oh word, thou word, that I lack!"—these are the final words of the opera. Moses knows the truth, God has revealed it to him, but he is unable to convey the contents of this revelation. His truth does exist, it is unequivocal and consistent, but it cannot be translated; it is incommunicable. The only way he can deal with this truth is through silence, an absence of words, through the void. By contrast, his brother Aaron is associated with the tortuous line of history. Aaron cuts a path for himself around the truth, seeing himself confronted repeatedly with an abyss that he does not dare to enter. The musical content of this unfinished opera has thus to do with the eternal and insoluble conflict between words and music, law and image, revelation and communication. This content is translated mimetically in the architectural form of the building through the interplay of the lines.

The third theme refers to a list of names, names in which history is petrified (figure 93). They are no abstract numbers but individuals who can be traced through their names and their place and date of birth. The paradoxical presence of those who are absent that underlies the *Gedenkbuch* is taken up in the complex interplay of voids and galleries in the building. Here too what is involved is to make visible what is invisible, to make one feel what has been repressed. The Holocaust is a black hole in history, a hole that swallows up all rhetoric of progress, but which is invisible to the naked eye. This invisibility is transformed here into an experience that is incomprehensible and yet ineluctable. The visitor will be subjected physically to the confrontation through a series of spatial experiences that can leave few people unmoved: the entrance via the old building and the underground passages; the sloping basement with its complex axes; the endless stair to the upper floors; the sense of disorientation induced by the zigzag shape; the repeated crossing of the voids. These insistent experiences are reminiscent of the unthinkable events that are interwoven into the identity of our present culture.

Libeskind is not exactly informative with regard to the fourth theme, that of Benjamin's *Einbahnstrasse*. The clues that he gives permit us to draw a connection between the Star of David with its *six* points, Schoenberg's opera that was composed using the *twelve* tone system, and Benjamin's book that consists of *sixty* parts. These different reference points reinforce each other; their effect is to mark out crucial spots in the museum as points where a number of energy lines condense, as it were, in points of convergence that are charged with meaning—the end of the main stair, for instance, or certain points in the basement.

Daniel Libeskind, extension of the Berlin Museum with the Jewish Museum, void and void bridges.
(Photo: Bitter Bredt.)

In a commentary on Libeskind's project, Derrida has drawn attention to the question of whether the materialization of this design does not detract from the multiple, undecidable character that is so typical of Libeskind's earlier drawings and maquettes. A void that is given palpable and visible form in a building is in a certain sense less empty than one's mental picture of a void (figure 94). Derrida points out that Libeskind's void is full of history, of meaning, and of experience and that it is therefore distinct from a completely neutral, purely receptive void, which he designates with the word "chora." Derrida uses this Platonic term to refer to the idea of a nonanthropological, nontheological space that should be understood as a precondition for the existence of any void.[116] The question that Derrida is implicitly raising here is whether Libeskind's building doesn't form a "monument" to the Holocaust—a monument with a clearly defined fixed meaning that may give our memories an excuse for forgetting rather than instigating an unending chain of shifts of meaning.

Libeskind himself rejects this interpretation, and I am inclined to agree with him. Two arguments may be stated here. In the first place, there is the fact that the architectural experience of the building can by no means be called unambiguous: the effect of the light, the abundance of different forms of space, the physical impression created by the sloping floor, and the zigzag trajectory of the building are not subject to a single interpretation. A second consideration is the overdetermined character of the voids. These refer at the same time to the Jews who were eliminated, to the unfathomable truth of the revelation, to the voids that are fundamental to the identity of Berlin—that of the Wall and that of the Holocaust—to the confrontation with the groundlessness of every culture, and to the silence that unspeakably comprises all the rest. This overdetermined character means that the voids escape any simple definition. It is not the end of the story once one realizes that the voids have something to do with the Holocaust. Additional meanings continue to resound, and as long as this process continues, one does not incur any risk of a hasty "monumentalizing" of the Holocaust.

In my eyes this quality of endless resonance is inherent in the mimetic operations on which the design is based. Mimesis raises the question of repressed aspects—those aspects that cannot be contained in a clear-cut logic and which do not lend themselves to a definite meaning. Mimesis creates transitions between different registers and these transitions are rarely unambiguous. To the degree that mimesis "works," a signifying process is generated that has no end. According to Adorno, the mimetic impulse is rooted in a gesture of negativity that does not have any positive goal. It is this negativity that is responsible for the never-ending chain of signifying. Mimesis does not render any positive image of reality, let alone a positive image of what a utopian, ideal reality might be. Rather, it produces negative images, and art is thus the best and most appropriate means to mimetically expose the negative qualities of reality.

This is how Libeskind's design for the extension of the Berlin Museum can be understood. No direct image of utopia is offered us here, but the idea of utopia is preserved because we see clearly how great a distance separates our present reality from a utopian condition of reconciliation. The broken lines of the design testify to a broken reality. They do not succeed in achieving any synthesis because reality does not lend itself to be conceived as healed and complete. Libeskind is therefore correct in claiming that the problem of the Jewish Museum in Berlin should be seen as emblematic of the problem of "culture" as such.

A Tower of Babel

> To stay viable after the opening of the tunnel between England and the continent, the ferry companies operating across the channel propose to make the crossing more exciting. Not only would the boats turn into floating entertainment worlds, but their destinations—the terminals— would shed their utilitarian character and become attractions. The original Babel was a symbol of ambition, chaos, and ultimately failure; this machine proclaims a working Babel that effortlessly swallows, entertains, and processes the travelling masses. The theme reflects Europe's new ambition; the different tribes—the users of the terminal—embarking on a unified future.[117]

This passage in Rem Koolhaas's book *S M L XL*, which introduces the OMA project for a Sea Terminal in Zeebrugge (figure 95), already shows the diversity of elements that are mimetically assimilated in this design: the sea and the land, the poetry of arrivals and departures, an age-old icon of human hubris and divine wrath, a fascination with technology, and an investment in the future (figure 96). The plan was developed in response to a multiple commission for the new outport of Zeebrugge in Belgium. As an opening move in the fierce competition for hegemony in cross-channel links, a consortium of firms and contractors in the port devised the plan of enriching Zeebrugge with a new, striking building that would give weight to its role as a European bridgehead. The multipurpose building was intended to combine facilities for the transport of vehicles and passengers with office accommodation and a conference center. The idea never got beyond the stage of being a successful publicity stunt, but it did produce a number of remarkable plans, among them that of OMA.

Office for Metropolitan Architecture, project for a Sea Terminal in Zeebrugge, 1989. (Photo: Hans Werlemann.)

Office for Metropolitan
Architecture, project for a
Sea Terminal in Zeebrugge,
site plan with inserted
Tower of Babel.

96

The project has the look of an oversized space helmet from an old-fashioned science fiction comic. In this figure—a cross between a sphere and a cone, according to Koolhaas—all the parts of the program are incorporated on the basis of a horizontal stratification with a vertical segmentation superimposed (figure 97). The lower levels are entirely reserved for vehicles: two floors for loading and unloading, another for pedestrian access with two floors of parking in an ascending spiral above it (figure 98). These end up in a floor with facilities for truck drivers. Then comes an open mezzanine level that is two stories high with a public hall that can be reached directly from the access floor by escalator (figure 99). On all sides, one has a view of the sea and the bustle of the docks (figure 100). Above this high-ceilinged hall with its central void is a floor with the facilities that forms the transition to the upper half situated under the glass dome. The segmentation in this upper half has a vertical logic—the space is divided into a trapezium-shaped office building, a hotel that is arranged in a semicircle against the outside wall of the helmet, and exhibition and promotion areas that occupy the intermediate areas. These areas in particular, with their play of sloping levels, voids, and peepholes, offer spectacular views both within the building and outside. The casino and the conference rooms required in the program are situated under the gigantic dome while the office building has a swimming pool on the roof (figure 101). These areas are laid out under the dome in such a way

Office for Metropolitan
Architecture, project for a Sea
Terminal in Zeebrugge, plans.

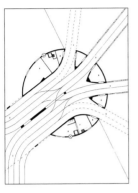

97-1

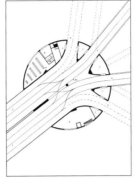

97-2

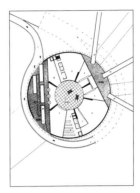

97-3

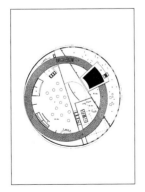

97-4

97-5

97-6

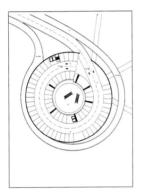

97-7

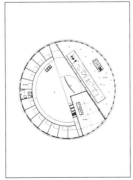

97-8

97-9

Office for Metropolitan
Architecture, project for a Sea
Terminal in Zeebrugge, section.

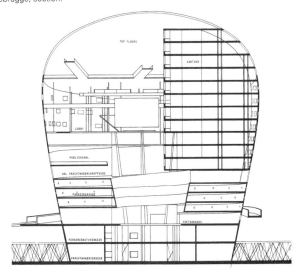

98

Office for Metropolitan
Architecture, project for a Sea
Terminal in Zeebrugge, section.

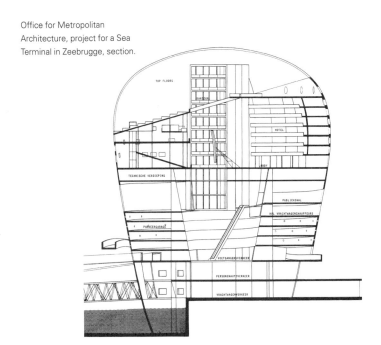

99

Office for Metropolitan
Architecture, project for
a Sea Terminal in Zeebrugge,
sketch of the public hall on
the mezzanine level.

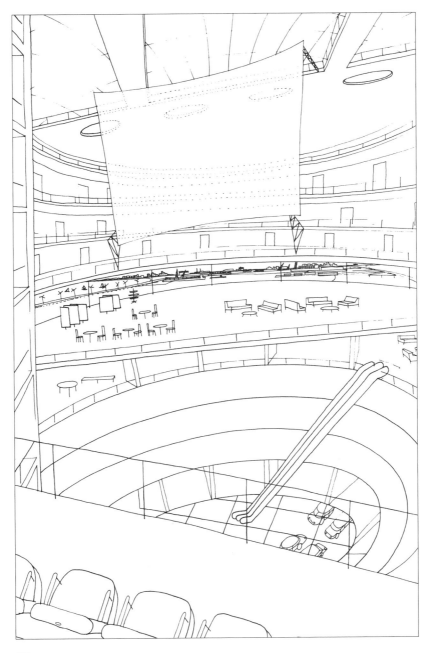

Office for Metropolitan
Architecture, project for a
Sea Terminal in Zeebrugge,
view of the maquette with
its transparent dome.

(Photo: Hans Werlemann.)

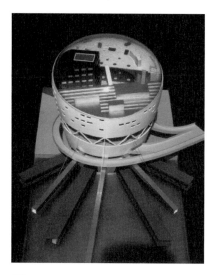

101

that one's gaze is directed toward the endless panoramas of the sea (figure 102), while, on the other side, the central void gives one a view through a glass floor right down to the level where trucks and cars drive on and off and loading and unloading takes place.

The tower of Babel traditionally is a symbol of chaos and the confusion of tongues (figure 103). God, we read in the Bible, punished those people whose arrogance was such that they tried to build a tower that would reach the heavens. He shattered their common language into mutually incomprehensible dialects, so that they were forced to leave their blasphemous project unfinished. OMA turns the tower upside down (see figure 96)—as we can see from the design drawings, the space helmet is a mimetic reinterpretation of the tower in Breughel's version.

Chaos and a confusion of tongues is still the theme, only here the different languages are no longer seen as obstacles to completing the whole. Differences here are incorporated in a machine that functions with great flexibility, organizing and arranging things, providing entertainment, and spewing everything out again. Human hubris is not synonymous here with intolerable insolence and blasphemy, but is transformed into a superior rationality that overcomes tribal infighting by orchestrating the differences in a drama of light, spectacle, and movement.

The building fits in flawlessly with the commission requirements: it is a finely tuned instrument that enables the transition between different systems of transport to take place with the utmost smoothness, so that the inevitable delays are minimized by an overwhelming variety of excitement and diversions. The culture of congestion has presented us with a kaleidoscope in which the public creates itself as theater while at the same time making enthusiastic use of the entertainment on offer. On the other hand, there is also a moment of quiet in the midst of this ballet of movement. The silhouette of the space helmet forms a stable, motionless figure that holds the whole complex fast with the force of a mooring post. The 70-meter-high building forms an indisputable high point in a context that is dominated by a docklands infrastructure and the banal developments along the Belgian coastline. It is a unique landmark with an unmistakable identity seen both from the sea and the land. Its shape, something like that of a pebble that has been scoured by water,[118] fits in perfectly with the eternal interaction of sea and shore.

The project is an embodiment of an ambiguity that can be seen at various levels. It is a sorting machine as befits its function as a traffic confluence point, thus making a contribution to the general trend toward the homogenization of space resulting from the increasing dominance of networks.[119] At the same time, however, it represents a unique locus so that this particular intersection within the network is different from any other, giving character to the nondescript, incoherent area that Zeebrugge is at present. This effect is achieved by the machine's being given a housing. What is involved is a logic of instrumentality and control, but this logic is introduced into a narrative that also contains other elements: the play of light and clouds, the forces of wind and sea, the promises that shimmer with every crossing.

As Fredric Jameson remarks, Koolhaas uses the strategy of the envelope here:[120] it is an amalgam of diversity, programmed or otherwise, packaged in a rigid form that is not motivated by functional considerations. This form offers a structuring context in which specialization and improvisation are given free play. The result is that the congestion is boosted and margins are created within which unexpected possibilities can also come about. In the Zeebrugge Terminal, this means that a whole series of different groups of the public are brought together—from truck drivers to casino visitors, from office workers to conference participants. All of them are included in one and the same context, where they can choose to be confronted with the others or to be left alone. They have the option of the popular allure of the snack bars or the more fashionable surroundings of the hotel lounge. By bringing these differences together within a spatial context that mediates between them, this terminal achieves a sort of "urbanity," a culture of congestion that, without eliminating the differences, can function as a social condenser, thus furthering the desired aim of European integration.

In a rationalized and perfected form the Sea Terminal takes over the motif of Constant's New Babylon project: the provision of large-scale infrastructures where the nomadic

Office for Metropolitan Architecture, project for a Sea Terminal in Zeebrugge, collage.

Pieter Breughel the Elder,
Tower of Babel.
(Collection Museum Boijmans
Van Beuningen, Rotterdam.)

103

inhabitants can drift around in search of adventure and challenging atmospheres. Like Constant's "spatiovores," the space helmet forms an exception within an otherwise uniform network. But while in Constant's work the tension between utopia and reality is mainly to be seen in the graphic elaboration of sketches and paintings, in the OMA project it is given an architectural articulation. The tension is transformed into a caesura between shell and infill. This caesura is the result of the fact that architecture draws on different registers that do not match each other perfectly: the outer form that conforms to a preconceived image of unity and anchoring, the inner volume that itself forms an "outside" for the specialized parts of the program that serve as a pretext for different infrastructures and buildings. This means that form is given to the strange encounter between a high-performance processing of traffic flows and a sublimation of the experience of passage. The project represents a constellation of spectacle and poetry, without, however, any clear distinction being drawn between the one and the other. One cannot distinguish any moment of "authenticity" that would stand out separately from the entertainment value of the whole. In that respect it conforms to what Koolhaas says in *S M L XL* about authenticity, quoting from Habermas: "The authentic work is radically bound to the moment of its emergence: precisely because it consumes itself in actuality; it can bring the steady flow of trivialities to a standstill, break through normality, and satisfy for a moment the immortal longing for beauty—a moment in which the eternal comes into fleeting contact with the actual."[121]

Koolhaas makes further play with the ambiguity that is inherent in this motif of "authenticity." In a bare-faced parody of modernity, he pitches against each other two construction techniques that might possibly be used in the project:

> The first, guided by speed, suggested the establishment of an initial base, then the rapid assembly of prefabricated elements, which would finally be cloaked in a balloon of ferro-concrete foam, sprayed on form-work of chickenwire. In the second scenario, the building became hyper-substantial: it would be built in reinforced concrete by a handful of workers at an enormous expense of time.
>
> In the first case, sudden erection would become spectacle; in the second, almost imperceptible progress, a potential source of suspense: the workers would visibly age during the course of construction; children would become adults as the building remained stubbornly unfinished. More disturbing, the first building would be instant but immaterial; the second, slowly (if ever) completed, but "authentic": opposites ostensibly based on the same plans, sections, architecture.[122]

Here Koolhaas deliberately separates the two moments of spectacle and authenticity so as to point to their inevitable mutual involvement. Modernity unites the contradictory dimensions of the programmatic and the transitory—it refers both to a project that aims to design a future of liberation and emancipation and to an experience of acceleration and melting. The contradiction is driven to an extreme by playing off speed against substance, and artificiality against authenticity. Nevertheless, it is intrinsically the same design that is involved, but materialized in different ways. By making play with this ambiguity, Koolhaas touches on the specific character of the modern that lies precisely in the mutual intertwining of these contradictory dimensions. The extraordinary thing about this project is that all these elements are interlocked in one unique gesture while the hiatus between them nevertheless remains palpable.

The Sea Terminal is an articulation of the deterritorialization that is caused by the networks of transport and communication. This articulation is atectonic: the construction is not congruent with the design, because the helmet is repeatedly drilled and weakened at precisely those spots where it ought to be as strong as possible. It nevertheless succeeds in giving the place a unique resonance. Whereas deterritorialization normally has to do with a homogenization of space and an erasure of differences between places, this particular articulation of a nod in the network is not part of this tendency. This is because *form* is given here to the trend toward formlessness and entropy. What is involved is a mimetic operation in the sense of Lacoue-Labarthe's *typography*: a form (typos) is engraved, grafted, and printed on the very local intersection of the network, and it is precisely this form that permits a caesura to be created, providing for a temporary stoppage in the continual circulation of men and things. In this caesura, in that stoppage, culture is given an opportunity to act in a way that goes beyond mere entertainment and amusement. This caesura means that a margin is provided where something *else* is possible. That is the achievement of mimesis here.

We inhabit the
megalopolis only
to the extent that
we declare it
uninhabitable.
Otherwise we are
just lodged there.

Jean-François Lyotard

Afterword: Dwelling, Mimesis, Culture

"Culture" is no longer an unambiguous coherent entity implying a clearly defined relationship between present, past, and future. Assuming such an entity ever existed—a notion that is inherent in the term "tradition"—modernity introduced the first fissure by breaking with the continuity with the past. "Auschwitz" is the name of the second fissure indicating the broken relation with the future, for "Auschwitz" means the violation of the promise of a new *Heimat* as the goal of modernity.

Already before the Shoah had been accomplished, Benjamin stated that there is no document of civilization that is not at the same time a document of barbarism.[1] This is true not only of the legacy of the past but also of the documents of today. Culture is not innocent and can in no way be innocent as long as it forms part of a social constellation based on injustice and repression. Culture today is therefore marked by tensions that are insoluble.

A reflection on dwelling leads one to the same conclusion. According to Heidegger—the philosopher who never faced up to "Auschwitz"[2]—dwelling stands for a relationship with the fourfold that has become impossible under modern conditions. For Adorno, however, it is clear that Heidegger's treatment of the question of dwelling is symptomatic of what is wrong with his philosophy. Heidegger attempts to reduce the idea of dwelling to an original essence, but this ontological approach disregards the question of concrete dwelling for concrete people and also ignores the banal but very real question of actual housing needs caused by social conditions. An approach like Heidegger's, in Adorno's view, is not capable of giving any impulse for change; rather, it implies an acceptance of historically determined conditions as if they were "eternally human": "No elevation of the concept of Man has any power in the face of his actual degradation into a bundle of functions. The only help lies in changing the conditions which brought the state of affairs to this point—conditions which uninterruptedly reproduce themselves on a larger scale."[3]

Adorno, who despite all his reservations never renounced the project of the Enlightenment, refers here to the dangers of an antimodern mode of thought that all too easily degenerates into a mythical invocation of the gods. For him philosophy always has to do with the struggle for social change in the sense of bringing about emancipation and liberation. Philosophical reflection must never be used to cover up social problems and abuses. Nevertheless, Adorno also is confronted with the problem that the world has become uninhabitable. For him this has everything to do with "Auschwitz." This name resonates with the despair that is provoked by the perversion of Enlightenment's rationality into the efficiency of the gas chambers. This reality is ineluctable and requires that modernity be rewritten.

In order to rewrite modernity, however, it is not sufficient to appeal to humanitarian values. Art, Adorno writes, can only be loyal to humanity through inhumanity toward it.[4] Humanism—the right-mindedness of those who think that all one needs to do to create the future is to appeal to the rationality and good will of everyone—is a totally inadequate foundation for projecting the future. The worn-out appeal to "human values" has proved incapable of averting the worst atrocities. The question should therefore be raised, according to Lyotard, whether the concept of humanism is not in fact the ideal camouflage for the actual inhumanity of the system. Should not another kind of thinking be offered in its place, a mode of thought that does not confine itself to rationality and good will? Lyotard points out that any human is inhabited by the inhuman: in the human person there is always something present of what he was before he developed into a person. Both sorts of inhumanity—the inhumanity of the system and that which inhabits the individual—can hardly be imagined by humanism. Both call for a thought that goes beyond good will, a thought that explores the abysses of culture. Lyotard invokes in this respect a mode of thought that is informed by the slowness of anamnesis and that is not in any hurry to attune everything to a well-ordered system by way of a hermeneutic or dialectic operation.[5]

Such anamnestic thought is tried out in his essay "Domus and the Megalopolis." Lyotard describes the condition of the *domus* as one that has now become impossible: dwelling as a commonplace where a desire to serve and a concern with the community are at work. This domestic community belongs to the past, for the human world has become a megalopolis. "From after the death of Virgil. From after the end of the houses. At the end of the Buddenbrooks." The prevailing system orchestrated by the exchange principle is not the least bit concerned with habit, narrative, or rhythm. Its memory is dominated by the principle of rationality that tramples tradition underfoot. The domus, however, concealed behind this system, does leave some trace of itself. This makes it a *fata morgana* for us, the impossible dwelling. Thought that attempts to resist incorporation by the megalopolis appears as the handwriting of these impossible dwellings: "Baudelaire, Benjamin, Adorno. How to inhabit the megalopolis? By bearing witness to the impossible work, by citing the lost domus. Only the quality of suffering counts as bearing witness. Including, of course, the suffering due to language. We inhabit the megalopolis only to the extent that we declare it uninhabitable. Otherwise we are just lodged there."[6] This impossible notion is for Lyotard what is at stake in thinking, in writing, and in works of art. It also forms, in my opinion, what is at stake in architecture. The Jewish Museum in Berlin is an example of the way in which architecture, "after Auschwitz," can rewrite the meaning of modernity. "Auschwitz" stands for the ultimate uninhabitability of modernity. The impossibility of dwelling, the bankruptcy of modernity's promise of a new *Heimat* is given architectonic form in the cold and gloomy depths of Libeskind's voids. Out of the intertwining of the two lines and the play of space, light, and texture, something else appears: what is involved here is not only despair and mourning; it is also hope for the future that can take shape only through a lucid grasp of the hopelessness of the present. It is here that Libeskind's critical reworking of the legacy of the Enlightenment lies. Rewriting modernity means a face-to-face confrontation with its failures and perversities; an anamnesis of the past is the precondition for taking any step into the future.

Koolhaas is less urgently concerned with reworking the past. Even so, the mimetic strategy of the Sea Terminal provides us with a work that in its "inevitable transformation into a cultural commodity" is witness to "the impossibility of the work," as Lyotard would have it.[7] This project refuses to choose between a banal commercial logic and the aspirations of art. Both are at issue here, both are equally valid. They are inseparably entwined, without being totally fused. It is precisely in the chasm between them that the "margin" exists that forms the tension of the design. In the intertwining of complicity with the system and opposition to the leveling tendencies inherent in it, the project of rewriting modernity is given form.

"To inhabit the megalopolis by declaring it uninhabitable." This is a way of rewriting Benjamin's formula in which he calls for a new sort of dwelling, a dwelling that is appropriate to the "hurried actuality" of the present. In addition to the age-old sense of security and seclusion, dwelling takes on a new level of meaning that has to do with porosity and transparency, with adaptability and flexibility. Seen as a transitive verb, dwelling takes on a more active meaning of making an environment for itself and making oneself at home all over again. "Dwelling" has to do with "enclosing oneself," but in the modern condition this calls for a gesture that is continually renewed. Dwelling means the permanent quest for an ever-new enclosure, because no dwelling can be more than momentary at present: dwelling is continually permeated by its opposite. Dwelling thus understood stands as well for the pastoral image of the *Heimat* where one belongs, and for the transitoriness that in a modern condition inevitably marks this belonging.

The mimetic gesture of "enclosing oneself" is parallel to the quest for identity and self-realization that forms a basic characteristic of modernity. Modernity has to be continually redefined and rewritten in the light of the contradictions and dissonances that are inherent to it. In the same way dwelling is neither simple nor static, but has to be permanently appropriated anew. That means that modernity and dwelling are not to be considered as polar opposites, as is suggested by authors such as Heidegger or Norberg-Schulz. By investigating the multifarious layers and ambivalencies of both these concepts, I hope to have made it clear that modernity and dwelling are interrelated in complex ways. If architecture indeed should see it as its task to come to terms with the experience of modernity and with the desire for dwelling, the first thing to pay attention to is the intricate intertwining that exists between both of these.

It is not without reason that dwelling is the key metaphor that Freud uses in his reflection on the uncanny.[8] According to Freud, the most uncanny experience occurs in the environment that is most familiar to us, for the experience of the uncanny has to do with the intertwining of *heimlich* (what is of the house, but also what is hidden) and *unheimlich* (what is not of the house, what is therefore in a strange way unconcealed yet concealed). Freud makes plausible, in fact, that the uncanny is so frightening because it refers to what is one's "own" but nevertheless must remain hidden. Thus it has to do with that which is repressed. This implies that the figure of repression belongs to dwelling as its other that can neither be completely abandoned nor completely recovered.

Through mimesis and the small shifts and distortions that it generates, architecture is capable of making us feel something of that which is repressed, that which exists beyond the normal and expected. In this way architecture can serve as a guide to this permanent quest for dwelling, not by embodying dwelling in any direct sense—as some Heideggerians might have it[9]—but rather by framing it in modernity. This framing has, more than anything else, to do with the way architecture is offering a context for everyday life. This understanding is for me one of the most significant (if often neglected) contribution of the avant-garde impulse in architecture: that architecture is not just a highbrow discipline that occasionally informs the putting up of prestigious buildings, but that its ambition basically should have to do with the framing of everyday environments.

One thus should accept it as a given that architecture—in its most broadly conceived sense—forms the framework for life. But in accepting this as a starting point, one should also recognize that there can be something more. Providing comfort and convenience for daily life is not architecture's one and only goal—as Loos would have us believe. His judgment that architecture has nothing to do with art should not be taken for granted. The matter is a bit more complicated. Like art and literature, architecture *is* capable of suspending the continuity of the normal and generating a moment of intensity that subverts what is self-evident. Admittedly, what is specific to architecture is its link to everyday life, and this cannot so easily be brought into line with that which causes permanent unease. This, however, is where mimesis comes in. For mimesis makes it possible for a design project to be completely responsive to normal expectations, while at the same time offering something else. Mimesis complicates a transparent relationship between program, context, and form into multiple layers that do not allow for a one-way interpretation and that can conceal something disruptive behind a seemingly perfect fitting of everyday requirements. Thus, mimesis can bring about some experience of what is *unheimlich*, precisely by relying upon things that are proper and convenient.[10]

Mimesis can therefore operate most effectively in projects that are not immediately dissociated from their context and from public expectations, but that contain, as it were, a double entendre, which only gradually affects users and visitors. It is this double entendre, and the contradictions it implies, that make up for the complicated nature of beauty today.

One should indeed admit that the critical impact of an architectural project is not equivalent to its smoothly fitting into the international magazines. The way it interacts with its environment, the way in which it mimetically gives form to a critical dialogue with context and program, is much more determining in this respect. It seems to me, in any case, that Adorno's remark remains valid: "Beauty today can have no other measure except the depth to which a work resolves contradictions. A work must cut through the contradictions and overcome them, not by covering them up, but by pursuing them."[11] Contradictory interpretations and opposing interests play an inevitable role in each architectural realization. The critical import of a design project can only be measured by the level to which it succeeds in mediating these contradictions through the mimetical shaping of the project, without, however, neutralizing their impact by simply neglecting or softening the tensions that exist between them.

Notes

Introduction

1   For my use of the terms *modernity, modernization,* and *modernism,* I rely upon Marshall Berman, *All That Is Solid Melts into Air: The Experience of Modernity* (1982; London: Verso, 1985).

2   I use the term *critical theory* rather loosely. It properly refers to the works of authors from the Frankfurt School, such as Horkheimer, Adorno, Löwenthal, Pollock, or Marcuse. My usage of the term includes related theorists from different backgrounds like Walter Benjamin, Ernst Bloch, or Manfredo Tafuri.

3   The name *Das Neue Frankfurt* stems from the title of the periodical that May published in order to gain public support for his undertakings. It is also adopted to refer to the entirety of the achievements in Frankfurt during May's stay in office.

Architecture Facing Modernity 1

Epigraph: Theo van Doesburg in a letter to J. J. P. Oud, dated December 1918, quoted in Evert van Straaten, ed., *Theo van Doesburg 1883–1931* (The Hague: Staatsuitgeverij, 1983), p. 9: "De mens moet zich telkens weer opnieuw vernietigen om zich weder opnieuw te kunnen opbouwen."

1 This etymological account is based upon the article by H. U. Gumbrecht, "Modern, Modernität, Moderne," in O. Brunner, W. Conze, and R. Kosseleck, eds., *Geschichtliche Grundbegriffe. Historisches Lexikon zur politisch-sozialen Sprache in Deutschland*, vol. 4 (Stuttgart: Klett-Cotta, 1978), pp. 93–131. Although Gumbrecht is primarily focusing on the German language, it is safe to assume that the variety of meanings in English is rather similar, as a look in any dictionary can confirm.

2 Octavio Paz, *The Children of the Mire: Modern Poetry from Romanticism to the Avant-Garde* (Cambridge: Harvard University Press, 1974), p. 23.

3 See Gumbrecht, "Modern, Modernität, Moderne"; Matei Calinescu, *Five Faces of Modernity: Modernism, Avant-Garde, Decadence, Kitsch, Postmodernism* (Durham: Duke University Press, 1987), pp. 23–35; Willem van Reijen, "Postscriptum," in Wayne Hudson and Willem van Reijen, eds., *Modernen versus postmodernen* (Utrecht: HES, 1986), pp. 9–50.

4 Paz, *Children of the Mire*, p. 26.

5 Marshall Berman, *All That Is Solid Melts into Air: The Experience of Modernity* (1982; London: Verso, 1985), p. 16.

6 The term *modernism* normally has a more specialized meaning for each individual discipline. This meaning may also include characteristics of style and a specification of the period. The very broad definition coined by Marshall Berman and used here is particularly interesting because it offers a general framework that can throw new light on specific "modernisms" in particular disciplines.

7 Calinescu, *Five Faces of Modernity*, p. 41.

8 Jürgen Habermas, "Modernity—an Incomplete Project," in Hal Foster, ed., *The Anti-Aesthetic: Essays on Postmodern Culture* (1983; Seattle: Bay Press, 1991), p. 9; translated from "Die Moderne—ein unvollendetes Projekt" (1980), in Habermas, *Kleine politische Schriften I–IV* (Frankfurt: Suhrkamp, 1981), p. 453: "Das Projekt der Moderne, das im 18. Jahrhundert von den Philosophen der Aufklärung formuliert worden ist, besteht nun darin, die objektivierenden Wissenschaften, die universalistischen Grundlagen der Moral und Recht und die autonome Kunst unbeirrt in ihrem jeweiligen Eigensinn zu entwickeln, aber gleichzeitig auch die kognitiven Potentiale, die sich so ansammeln, aus ihren esoterischen Hochformen zu entbinden und für die Praxis, d.h. für eine vernünftige Gestaltung der Lebensverhältnisse zu nützen."

9 English translation as quoted in Calinescu, *Five Faces of Modernity*, p. 48. The French original reads: "La modernité, c'est le transitoire, le fugitif, le contingent, la moitié de l'art, dont l'autre moitié est l'éternel et l'immuable" (Charles Baudelaire, *Oeuvres complètes* [Paris: Seuil, n.d.], p. 553).

10 Jean Baudrillard, "Modernité," in *La modernité ou l'esprit du temps*, Biennale de Paris, Section Architecture, 1982 (Paris: L'Equerre, 1982), p. 28: "un mode de civilisation caractéristique qui s'oppose au mode de la tradition."

11 Ibid., p. 29: "La modernité va susciter à tous les niveaux une esthétique de rupture, de créativité individuelle, d'innovation partout marquée par le phénomène sociologique de l'avant-garde . . . et par la destruction toujours plus poussée des formes traditionelles. . . . En se radicalisant ainsi dans un changement à vue, dans un travelling continuel, la modernité change de sens. Elle perd peu à peu toute valeur substantielle, tout idéologie morale et philosophique de progrès que la sous-tendait au départ, pour devenir une esthétique de changement pour le changement. . . . A la limite, elle rejoint ici purement et simplement la mode, qui est en même temps la fin de la modernité."

12 Bart Verschaffel, "Post-moderniteit," in Verschaffel, *De glans der dingen* (Mechelen: Vlees en Beton, 1989), pp. 43–60; J. F. Lyotard, "Rewriting Modernity," in Lyotard, *The Inhuman: Reflections on Time* (Cambridge: Polity Press, 1991), pp. 24–35 ("Réécrire la modernité,"

in Lyotard, *L'inhumain. Causeries sur le temps* [Paris: Galilée, 1988], pp. 33–44); J. F. Lyotard, "Note on the Meaning of 'Post-,'" in Lyotard, *The Postmodern Explained: Correspondence 1982–1985* (Minneapolis: University of Minnesota Press, 1992), pp. 75–80 ("Note sur les sens de 'post-,'" in Lyotard, *Le postmoderne expliqué aux enfants. Correspondance 1982–1985* [Paris: Galilée, 1986], pp. 117–126).

13   I have taken this distinction from Marshall Berman, who uses it in his discussion of the work of Charles Baudelaire. Berman, *All That Is Solid Melts into Air*, pp. 134–141.

14   Le Corbusier, *Towards a New Architecture* (London: Architectural Press, 1976), p. 82. Translation of *Vers une architecture*, 1923.

15   "Situationists: International Manifesto" (1960), in Ulrich Conrads, ed., *Programs and Manifestoes on 20th Century Architecture* (Cambridge: MIT Press, 1990), p. 172.

16   Berman, *All That Is Solid Melts into Air*, p. 15.

17   Peter L. Berger, Brigitte Berger, and Hansfried Kellner, *The Homeless Mind: Modernization and Consciousness* (New York: Vintage Books, 1974).

18   Ibid., p. 184.

19   Martin Heidegger, "Building, Dwelling, Thinking," in Heidegger, *Poetry, Language, Thought* (New York: Harper and Row, 1971), pp. 143–162; translated from "Bauen Wohnen Denken," in Heidegger, *Vorträge und Aufsätze* (Pfullingen: Neske, 1954), pp. 145–162. The account of the colloquium in Darmstadt was recently republished: *Mensch und Raum. Das Darmstädter Gespräch 1951*, Bauwelt Fundamente 94 (Braunschweig: Vieweg, 1991).

20   Martin Heidegger, "The Origin of the Work of Art," in Heidegger, *Poetry, Language, Thought*, pp. 15–88; for the German text I made use of Martin Heidegger, *Der Ursprung des Kunstwerkes* (1960; Stuttgart: Reclam, 1978).

21   Heidegger, "Building, Dwelling, Thinking," p. 160.

22   Ibid., p. 161; German text: ". . . wie steht es mit dem Wohnen in unserer bedenklichen Zeit? Man spricht allenthalben und mit Grund von der Wohnungsnot. . . . So hart und bitter, so hemmend und bedrohlich der Mangel an Wohnungen bleibt, die *eigentliche Not des Wohnens* bestehlt nicht erst im Fehlen von Wohnungen. . . . Die eigentliche Not des Wohnens beruht darin, dass die Sterblichen das Wesen des Wohnens immer erst wieder suchen, das sie *das Wohnen noch lernen müssen.*" (*Vorträge und Aufsätze*, p. 162.)

23   Martin Heidegger, "Poetically Man Dwells," in Heidegger, *Poetry, Language, Thought*, p. 227; translated from ". . . dichterisch wohnet der Mensch . . . ," in *Vorträge und Aufsätze*, p. 202: "Wohnen *wir* dichterisch? Vermutlich wohnen wir durchaus undichterisch."

24   Ibid., pp. 228, 229; German text: "Das Dichten is das Grundvermögen des menschlichen Wohnens. . . . Ereignet sich das Dichterische, dann wohnet der Mensch menschlich auf dieser Erde, dann ist, wie Hölderlin in seinem letztem Gedicht sagt, 'das Leben des Menschen' ein 'wohnend Leben.'" (*Vorträge und Aufsätze*, pp. 203, 204.)

25   Massimo Cacciari, "Eupalinos or Architecture," *Oppositions*, no. 21 (1980), p. 112.

26   Theodor W. Adorno, *Minima Moralia: Reflections from Damaged Life* (1951; London: Verso, 1991), pp. 38–39; translated from *Minima Moralia. Reflexionen aus dem beschädigten Leben* (1951; Frankfurt: Suhrkamp, 1987), pp. 40–41: "Eigentlich kann man überhaupt nicht mehr wohnen. . . . Das Haus ist vergangen."

27   Ibid.; German text: "es gehört zur Moral, nicht bei sich selber zu Hause zu sein." The sense of the German is more general than the translation would suggest, because "bei sich selber" can also be translated as "with oneself" and not just as "in one's home."

28   Christian Norberg-Schulz, *The Concept of Dwelling* (New York: Electa/Rizzoli, 1985), p. 7.

29   Ibid., p. 30.

30   Ibid., p. 66.

31   Cacciari, "Eupalinos or Architecture," p. 108.

32   Ibid., p. 115.

33   "Contrasting Concepts of Harmony in Architecture," debate between Christopher Alexander and Peter Eisenman, in *Lotus International*, no. 40 (1983), pp. 60–68.

34   Ibid., p. 65.

35   See Christopher Alexander, *The Timeless Way of Building* (New York: Oxford University

Press, 1979). See also Georges Teyssot's introduction to the above-mentioned debate in *Lotus International.*

36 Emmanuel Levinas, "Heidegger, Gagarin and Us" (1961), in Levinas, *Difficult Freedom: Essays on Judaism* (London: Athlone, 1990), pp. 231–241.

Constructing the Modern Movement **2**

Epigraph: Sigfried Giedion, *Space, Time and Architecture: The Growth of a New Tradition* (1941; Cambridge: Harvard University Press, 1980), p. vi.

1 On the meaning of kitsch, see Matei Calinescu, *Five Faces of Modernity: Modernism, Avant-Garde, Decadence, Kitsch, Postmodernism* (Durham: Duke University Press, 1987), pp. 223–262.

2 Adolf Loos, "Heimatkunst," in Loos, *Trotzdem. 1900–1930* (1931; Vienna: Prachner, 1981), pp. 122–133; see also Adolf Behne, "Kunst, Handwerk, Technik," *Die neue Rundschau*, no. 33 (1922), pp. 1021–1037, translated as "Art, Craft, Technology," in Francesco Dal Co, *Figures of Architecture and Thought: German Architecture Culture 1880–1920* [New York: Rizzoli, 1990], pp. 324–338).

3 Clement Greenberg, "Avant-Garde and Kitsch" (1939), in Greenberg, *The Collected Essays and Criticism,* vol. 1: *Perceptions and Judgments 1939–1944* (Chicago: University of Chicago Press, 1986), pp. 5–22.

4 The distinction between avant-garde and modernism is a fairly recent one. Authors such as Adorno, Poggioli, and Weightman used these terms as though they were interchangeable. In recent years, however, a tendency has developed of defining the term avant-garde rather strictly, only using it for the most radical artists who operated collectively. See Jochen Schultesasse, "Foreword: Theory of Modernism versus Theory of the Avant-Garde," in Peter Bürger, *Theory of the Avant-Garde* (Minneapolis: University of Minnesota Press, 1984); translated from *Theorie der Avant-Garde* (Frankfurt: Suhrkamp, 1974), pp. vii–xlvii.

5 Renato Poggioli, *The Theory of the Avant-Garde* (Cambridge: Harvard University Press, 1982); translated from *Teoria dell'arte d'avanguardia* (Bologna: Il Mulino, 1962).

6 Calinescu, *Five Faces of Modernity*, p. 124.

7 Peter Bürger situates his interpretation of the avant-garde in the context of a historical evolution. According to him, the history of art in Western society is characterized by an increasing autonomy of art as an institution and as a system in society as a whole. The summit of this autonomy was attained in the nineteenth century with aestheticism, the tendency that extolled the idea of *l'art pour l'art*. Artists no longer saw themselves as artisans in the service of the rulers or as interpreting some higher ideal, such as religion. Art was now pursued for its own sake; it was answerable only to itself. According to Bürger the avant-garde was a reaction against this notion. The corollary of the fact that art had become an autonomous institution was that it became socially isolated: by retreating into a world of its own—with its own system of values and means of distribution—it had lost any broader relevance and was no longer capable of exercising any influence on social events. The avant-garde wanted to break out of this confinement and to escape from the institutional frame it was trapped in historically.

8 Bürger, *Theory of the Avant-Garde*, p. 49; German text: "Die Avantgardisten intendieren also eine Aufhebung der Kunst—Aufhebung im Hegelschen Sinn des Wortes: Die Kunst soll nich einfach zerstört, sondern in Lebenspraxis überführt werden, wo sie, wenngleich in verwandelter Gestalt, aufbewahrt wäre. . . . Was sie . . . unterscheidet, ist der Versuch von der Kunst aus eine *neue* Lebenspraxis zu organisieren." (*Theorie der Avantgarde*, p. 67.)

9 Miriam Gusevich, "Purity and Transgression: Reflection on the Architectural Avantgarde's Rejection of Kitsch," *Discourse* 10, no. 1 (Fall-Winter 1987–1988), pp. 90–115.

10 The terms used to refer to modern architecture are different in different language areas; these differences also have implications for the concept. The Dutch *Nieuwe Bouwen* and the German *Neues Bauen* explicitly avoid the term "architecture" (which exists in both languages); this suggests a longing for an architecture that is not limited to representative buildings but embraces the whole domain of building and dwelling. This connotation is absent from the French expression *architecture moderne* and from the English "modern architecture." In order to retain the broader concept contained in the German and Dutch expressions I prefer to use the term "New Building."

11 Michael Müller, "Architektur als ästhetische Form oder ästhetische Form als lebenspraktische Architektur?" in Müller, *Architektur und Avantgarde. Ein vergessenes Projekt der Moderne?* (Frankfurt: Suhrkamp, 1984), pp. 33–92.

12 Charles Jencks, *Modern Movements in Architecture* (Harmondsworth: Pelican, 1973); Giorgio Ciucci, "The Invention of the Modern Movement," *Oppositions*, no. 24 (1981), pp. 69–91.

13 K. Michael Hays, *Modernism and the Posthumanist Subject: The Architecture of Hannes Meyer and Ludwig Hilberseimer* (Cambridge: MIT Press, 1992).

14 For a detailed account of Giedion's life and career, see Sokratis Georgiadis, *Sigfried Giedion: An Intellectual Biography* (Edinburgh: Edinburgh University Press, 1994), translated from *Sigfried Giedion, eine intellektuele Biographie* (Zurich: Ammann, 1989).

15 "Sigfried Giedion, eine autobiographische Skizze," in Giedion, *Wege in die Öffentlichkeit, Aufsätze und unveröffentliche Schriften aus den Jahren 1926–1956* (Zurich: Ammann, 1987), p. 9.

16 Manfredo Tafuri, *Theories and History of Architecture* (London: Granada, 1980), pp. 141–170.

17 Sigfried Giedion, *Building in France, Building in Iron, Building in Ferroconcrete*, trans. J. Duncan Berry, with an introduction by Sokratis Georgiadis (Santa Monica: Getty Center for the History of Art and the Humanities, 1995), p. 87; translated from *Bauen in Frankreich, Bauen in Eisen, Bauen in Eisenbeton* (Leipzig: Klinkhardt & Biermann, 1928), p. 3: "Was an der Architektur dieses Zeitraumes unverwelkt bleibt, sind vorab jene seltenen Stellen, an denen die Konstruktion durchbricht.—Die durchaus auf Zeitlichkeit, Dienst, Veränderung, gestellte Konstruktion folgt als einziger Teil im Gebiet des Bauens einer unbeirrbaren Entwicklung. Die Konstruktion hat im 19. Jahrhundert die Rolle des Unterbewusstseins. Nach aussen führt es, auftrumpfend, das alte Pathos weiter; unterirdisch, hinter Fassaden verborgen, bildet sich die Basis unseres ganzen heutigen Seins."

18 Giedion, *Bauen in Frankreich*, pp. 39 ff.; Giedion, *Space, Time and Architecture*, pp. 281 ff.

19 Giedion, *Bauen in Frankreich*, p. 6; Giedion, *Space, Time and Architecture*, pp. 288–289.

20 Giedion, *Building in France*, p. 91; German text: "In den luftumspülten Stiegen des Eiffelturms, besser noch in den Stahlschenkeln eines Pont Transbordeur, stösst man auf das ästhetische Grunderlebnis des heutigen Bauens: Durch das dünne Eissennetz, das in dem Luftraum gespannt bleibt, strömen die Dinge, Schiffe, Meer, Häuser, Maste, Landschaft, Hafen. Verlieren ihre abgegrenzte Gestalt: kreisen im Abwärtsschreiten ineinander, vermischen sich simultan." (*Bauen in Frankreich*, pp. 7–8.)

21 In *Space, Time and Architecture,* where he further elaborates the notion of interpenetration, Giedion includes images as well of the Crystal Palace (fig. 148) and of Delaunay's *Tour Eiffel* of 1909–1910 (fig. 173). For a discussion of the polemics provoked by the Crystal Palace, see Marshall Berman, *All That Is Solid Melts into Air: The Experience of Modernity* (London: Verso, 1985), pp. 235–248.

22 Giedion, *Bauen in Frankreich*, p. 61.

23 Ibid., pp. 94–95.

24 That Giedion gives this spatial *Durchdringung* a really central role is proven by his commentary on a photo of a house by Mallet-Stevens. Here he states that while the architect does make use of the outward characteristics of the New Building (facades without any ornament, flat roofs, cantilevers), he does not succeed in transcending the formal and representative character of the tradition by reaching interpenetration: "The traditional mas-

siveness of the residence is not overcome. The various bodies . . . bump into one another without interpenetration." *Building in France*, p. 192; German text: "Die angestammte Massivität des Hauses ist nicht überwunden. Die verschiedenen Körper . . . stossen aneinander, ohne sich zu durchdringen." (*Bauen in Frankreich*, p. 108.)

25 László Moholy-Nagy, *Von Material bis Architektur* (1929; Berlin: Kupferberg, 1968), p. 236: "aus zwei übereinanderkopierten fotos (negativ) entsteht die illusion räumlicher durch-dringung, wie die nächste generation sie erst—als glasarchitektur—in der wirklichkeit vielleicht erleben wird."

26 For a broad discussion of this topic, see Walter Prigge, "Durchdringung," in Volker Fischer and Rosemarie Höpfner, eds., *Ernst May und Das Neue Frankfurt 1925–1930* (Frankfurt: Deutsches Architektur Museum, 1986), pp. 65–71.

27 Giedion, *Building in France*, p. 90; German text: "Es scheint uns fraglich, ob der be-schränkte Begriff "Architektur" überhaupt bestehen bleiben wird. Wir könnten kaum Auskunft über die Frage geben: Was gehört zur Architektur? Wo beginnt sie, wo endet sie? Die Gebiete durchdringen sich. Die Wände umstehen nicht mehr starr die Strasse. Die Strasse wird in einem Bewegungsstrom umgewandelt. Gleise und Zug bilden mit dem Bahnhof eine einzige Grösse." (*Bauen in Frankreich*, p. 6.)

28 The correspondence on this subject is commented on by Sokratis Georgiadis in the intro-duction to *Building in France*, pp. 49 ff.

29 Georgiadis, *Sigfried Giedion, eine intellektuele Biographie*, p. 57. The idea that *Gestaltung* was of primary importance was not new. In 1925 Adolf Behne published an introduction to modern painting with the title *Vom Kunst zur Gestaltung* (Arbeiterjugend Verlag, Berlin). With Behne, too, the link with a broader social purpose plays a central role, as one can see in the closing sentences of his book (p. 86): "Die alte Kunst trennte, die neue Gestaltung verbindet. Die Grenze des Rahmens wurde gesprengt, die ästhetische Isolation durch-brochen. Der Wille zur Gestaltung nimmt nun alle Kräfte in sich auf. Er verbindet sich mit der Maschine, mit der Technik, nicht um ihnen dienstbar zu werden. Nein, um auch sie als Mittel für sein Ziel zu verwenden: die Ordnung unserer Welt als ein Gemeinschaft aller in Freiheit Arbeitenden." ("The old art separated; the new design connects. The boundaries of the domain were dissolved, the aesthetic isolation was disrupted. The will to design now strives to contain all forces. It is being linked with the machine, with technology, but not in order to serve them. No, its aim is rather to make use of them as instruments to at-tain its goal: the ordering of our world as a community of all those who work in freedom.")

30 Giedion certainly has reservations with respect to the applicability of the new ideas on housing. He states for instance: "One would not wish to carry over into housing this ab-solute experience that no previous age has known. Yet it remains embryonic in each de-sign of the new architecture: there is only a great, indivisible space in which relations and interpenetrations, rather than boundaries, reign." *Building in France*, pp. 91–93; German text: "Man wird diese absolute Erlebnis, das keine Zeit vorher gekannt hat, nicht auf Häuser übertragen wollen. Keimhaft aber liegt in jeder Gestaltung des neuen Bauens: Es gibt nur einen grossen, unteilbaren Raum, in dem Beziehungen und Durchdringungen herrschen, an Stelle von Abgrenzungen." (*Bauen in Frankreich*, p. 8.)

31 Sigfried Giedion, *Befreites Wohnen* (1929; Frankfurt: Syndikat, 1985), p. 8: "Das Haus ist ein Gebrauchswert. Es soll in absehbare Zeit abgeschrieben und amortisiert werden."

32 Giedion, *Befreites Wohnen*, p. 8: "Wir brauchen heute ein Haus, das sich in seiner ganzen Struktur im Gleichklang mit einem durch Sport, Gymnastik, sinngemässe Lebensweise be-freiten Körpergefühl befindet: leicht, lichtdurchlassend, beweglich. Es ist nur eine selbst-verständliche Folge, dass dieses geöffnete Haus auch eine Widerspiegelung des heutigen seelischen Zustandes bedeutet: Es gibt keine isolierten Angelegenheiten mehr. Die Dinge durchdringen sich."

33 Antonio Sant'Elia and Filippo Tommaso Marinetti, "Futurist Architecture" (1914), in Ulrich Conrads, ed., *Programs and Manifestoes on 20th Century Architecture* (Cambridge: MIT Press, 1990), pp. 34–38.

34 Giedion, *Building in France*, p. 92; German text: "Die verschiedenen Niveaudifferenzen der

Verkehrswege, das nur durch Notwendigkeit bestimmte Nebeneinander der Objeckte, enthält doch—gleichsam unbewusst und im Rohstoff—Möglickeiten, wie wir später unsere
Städte offen und ohne Zwang starren Niveaubeibehaltung gestalten werden." (*Bauen in Frankreich*, p. 8.)

35　Bürger outlines the character of the avant-garde work of art as relying upon the principle of "montage." In traditional aesthetics, he argues, a work of art is regarded as constituting an organic unity: the whole and the parts should be linked with each other in a self-evident relationship based on principles of balance and harmony. The avant-garde work on the other hand is nonorganic: it does have a unity, but this unity does not come about in a self-evident way. The avant-garde work contains discrepancies and dissonances because it is constructed on the basis of a montage of fragments: elements that are separated out from a contextual totality and are combined in a new relationship. Archetypal examples of this are the cubist paintings of Picasso and Braque, and John Heartfield's photomontages. In literature one can refer to texts such as *Le paysan de Paris* by Louis Aragon and André Breton's *Nadja*.

36　Giedion, *Space, Time and Architecture*, p. vi. I am quoting from the ninth impression (1980) of the fifth edition (1967). There were a number of revised editions of the book; on each occasion it was enlarged and more recent material was added. The structure of the book, however, and its line of argument essentially remained the same. For purposes of comparison I have also made use of the Dutch translation: *Ruimte, tijd en bouwkunst* (Amsterdam: Wereldbibliotheek, 1954). The latter is based on the first edition.

37　Giedion is not the first, nor was he the only person to be interested in relationships of this sort. For a detailed study of the subject see Linda Dalrymple-Henderson, *The Fourth Dimension and Non-Euclidean Geometry in Modern Art* (Princeton: Princeton University Press, 1983).

38　Giedion, *Space, Time and Architecture*, p. 14.

39　Ibid., p. 13.

40　Ibid., pp. 495–496. This most famous of Giedion's analogies has been heavily attacked by later critics. Colin Rowe and Robert Slutzky, for example, develop a critique of Giedion's claim that the space-time concept is operative within both architecture and painting, by analyzing the different "modes" of transparency that are at stake in the Bauhaus and in *L'Arlésienne*. See Colin Rowe and Robert Slutzky, "Transparency: Literal and Phenomenal," in Colin Rowe, *The Mathematics of the Ideal Villa and Other Essays* (Cambridge: MIT Press, 1976), pp. 159–183.

41　The text on Mies forms part of the additions made in 1954 for the third edition of *Space, Time and Architecture;* that on Aalto was added in 1949 in the second edition; that on Utzon constituted the bulk of the revisions for the fifth edition published in 1967.

42　Giedion, *Space, Time and Architecture*, pp. 496–497.

43　Ibid., p. 880.

44　Giedion, *Building in France*, pp. 190–191: "For the first time in history, not the upper class, but the lower class is a factor in the creation of a style." German text: "Zum erstenmal in der Geschichte wirkt nicht die Schicht mit den grössten Ansprüchen, sondern die Schicht mit den geringsten Ansprüchen als stilbildender Faktor." (*Bauen in Frankreich*, p. 107.)

45　The phrase "the tradition of the new" was coined by Harold Rosenberg to describe modern art. See Calinescu, *Five Faces of Modernity*, p. 225.

46　Giedion, *Space, Time and Architecture*, pp. xxxii–xxxiii.

47　A good summary of these arguments, which Giedion often returned to in his later work, can be found in Sigfried Giedion, *Walter Gropius: Work and Teamwork* (New York: Reinhold, 1954), p. 36: "The cause is, again, that grievous split between thinking and feeling which affects all levels of society and which must never be underestimated. One highly developed method of thinking (science) is valued in every quarter. Quite another attitude is taken up in regard to the realm of feeling (art). The art of the 'ruling taste' as we have termed it has now become part of the dream world of the masses and their representatives. Here it lives on and gives rise to nostalgic images with which they oppose impotently, arrogantly and with loathing, all expressions of truly creative art whose roots reach back through the ages."

48 Giedion himself gave a remarkable sketch of the development of modern architecture in an article of 1934, "Leben und Bauen," reprinted in Giedion, *Wege in die Öffentlichkeit*, pp. 118–121. Here he describes the initiatives that can be considered "avant-garde" as mere phases in a development that the modern movement has in the meantime surpassed. According to this article, the New Building began out of a concern with the question of housing and with the new technological possibilities of the age (Frank Lloyd Wright and Tony Garnier). The second phase was distinguished by the emergence of a formal vocabulary, partly influenced by developments within the visual arts: Le Corbusier, Gropius, and Oud succeeded in giving the new ideas a formal shape. During the third phase, when the social dimension of architecture was the prime object of attention, the "aesthetic problem" was put on ice. The names of Mart Stam and Hans Schmidt are associated with this phase. CIAM succeeded in bringing about a confrontation between the second and the third phases that resulted in a new process of maturation. This was the pretext for the fourth phase that is supposed to have been reached in 1934 when questions of city planning were the order of the day. Based as it is on a dialectic link between different concepts and stressing the notion of a reconciliation between the disparate tendencies in the modern movement, this view of things is typical of Giedion's pastoral and programmatic approach.

49 Giedion, *Space, Time and Architecture*, pp. 11–17, 875–881. See also Giedion, "Art Means Reality," in Gyorgy Kepes, *Language of Vision* (Chicago: Theobald, 1944), pp. 6–7.

50 Giedion, *Building in France*, p. 87; German text: "Wir werden in einen Lebensprozess getrieben, der nicht teilbar ist. Wir sehen das Leben immer mehr als ein bewegliches, aber unteilbares Ganzes. . . . Die Gebiete durchdringen sich, befruchten sich, indem sie sich durchdringen. . . . Wir werten die Gebiete gar nicht untereinander, sie sind uns gleichberechtigte Ausflüsse eines obersten Impulses: LEBEN! Das Leben als Gesamtkomplex zu erfassen, keine Trennungen zuzulassen, gehört zu den wichtigsten Bemühungen der Zeit." (*Bauen in Frankreich*, p. 3.)

51 Giedion, *Space, Time and Architecture*, p. 880.

52 On the basis of information provided by May himself (*Das Neue Frankfurt* 1/1930) the usual estimate is 15,000. It is possible, however, that this figure was not wholly accurate. See D. W. Dreysse, *May-Siedlungen. Architekturführer durch acht Siedlungen des neuen Frankfurts 1926–1930* (Frankfurt: Fricks, 1987), p. 5.

53 The subtitle of the magazine changed through the years: *Monatsschrift für die Fragen der Grosstadtgestaltung* (1926–1927), *Monatsschrift für die Probleme moderner Gestaltung* (1928–1929), and *Internationale Monatsschrift für die Probleme kultureller Neugestaltung* (1930–1931).

54 Ernst May, "Das Neue Frankfurt" (*Das Neue Frankfurt* 1/1926–27), in Heinz Hirdina, ed., *Neues Bauen, Neues Gestalten. Das neue Frankfurt/die neue stadt. Eine Zeitschrift zwischen 1926 und 1933* (Berlin: Elefanten Press, 1984), pp. 62–70; see also Christian Mohr and Michael Müller, *Funktionalität und Moderne. Das neue Frankfurt und seine Bauten 1925–1933* (Cologne: Rudolf Müller Verlag, 1984), pp. 14–15.

55 Hirdina, ed., *Neues Bauen, Neues Gestalten*, pp. 62–64: "Wie drängen Erkenntnisse heutiger Gestaltung gleichsam nach homogener Zusammenfassung! . . . schon strömen aus hunderten und tausenden von Quellen, Bächlein und Bäche zusammen, um einst einen neuen, in breitem Bette sicher dahinfliessenden Strom geschlossener Kultur zu bilden. Überall stossen wir auf das Bestreben zur Ausmerzung des Schwächlichen, Imitatorischen, Scheinhaften, Unwahren, überall bemerken wir zielbewussten Kampf um Kräftigung, kühne Neugestaltung, Materialgerechtheit und Wahrheit."

56 Ibid., pp. 68–70: "Menschlicher Wille allein wird nie eine Entwicklung heraufbeschwören. Zielbewusste Massnahmen können ihr aber diese Weg ebnen, ihr Tempo beschleunigen. Die . . . Monatzeitschrift '*Das Neue Frankfurt*' verfolgt dieses Ziel. Ausgehend von der städtebaulichen Gestaltung der Grosstadtorganismus, basierend auf seinen wirtschaftlichen Grundlagen, wird sie ihr Arbeitsgebiet aufdehnen auf alle Gebiete, die für die Formung einer neuen, geschlossenen Grosstadtkultur von Bedeutung sind."

57 See Mohr and Müller, *Funktionalität und Moderne*, pp. 163–204.

58 See Ernst May, "Mechanisierung der Wohnungsbau" (*Das Neue Frankfurt* 2/1926–27), in Hirdina, ed., *Neues Bauen, Neues Gestalten*, pp. 105–112; Grethe Lihotzky, "Rationalisierung in Haushalt" (*Das Neue Frankfurt* 5/1926–27), in ibid., pp. 179–183; Mart Stam, "Das Mass, das richtige Mass, das Minimummass" (*Das Neue Frankfurt* 2/1929), in ibid., pp. 215–216; Ernst May, "Die Wohnung für das Existenzminimum" (1929), in Martin Steinmann, ed., *CIAM. Dokumente 1928–1939* (Basel: Birkhäuser, 1979), pp. 6–12; Ferdinand Kramer, "Die Wohnung für das Existenzminimum," *Die Form*, 24 (1929), in F. Schwarz and F. Gloor, *"Die Form." Stimme des Deutschen Werkbundes 1925–1934* (Gütersloh: Bertelsmann, 1969), pp. 148–151.

59 Franz Schuster (*Das Neue Frankfurt* 5/1926–27), in Hirdina, ed., *Neues Bauen, Neues Gestalten*, p. 174: "Angesichts der Errungenschaften des XX. Jahrhunderts, die uns täglich umgeben, die unser Leben ganz neu geformt haben und unser Denken und Tun neu bestimmten, wird es breiten Kreise klar, dass auch das Haus in seinem Aufbau und seiner Konstruktion dieselbe Wandlung durchmachen muss wie etwa die Postkutsche zur Eisenbahn, Auto und Luftschiff, der Spiegeltelegraf zur Radio, die alte Handwerkstatt zur Fabrik und das ganze Arbeits- und Wirtschaftsleben vergangener Zeiten zu dem unseres Jahrhunderts."

60 Marcel Breuer, "metallmöbel und moderne räumlichkeit" (*Das Neue Frankfurt* 1/1928), in Hirdina, ed., *Neues Bauen, Neues Gestalten*, p. 210: "da die aussenwelt heute mit den intensivsten und verschiedensten ausdrücken auf uns wirkt, verändern wir unsere lebensformen in rascherer folge, als in früheren zeiten. es ist nur selbstverständlich dass auch unsere umgebung entsprechende veränderungen unterliegen muss. wir kommen also zu einrichtungen, zu räumen, zu bauten, welche in möglichst allen ihren teilen veränderlich, beweglich und verschieden kombinierbar sind."

61 Typical of this perception of a "new culture" are these remarks on the architecture of Römerstadt by Count Kessler, a German diplomat who was sympathetic to the modern movement in art and architecture: "Another expression of this new feeling for life is the new architecture and the new domestic way of living. . . . This architecture is simply an expression of the same vitality which impels youngsters to practise sport and nudity. . . . This German architecture cannot be understood unless it is visualized as part of an entirely new *Weltanschauung*." In C. Kessler, ed., *The Diaries of a Cosmopolitan: Count Harry Kessler 1918–37* (London, 1971), p. 390, quoted in Nicholas Bullock, "Housing in Frankfurt 1925 to 1931 and the 'neue Wohnkultur,'" *Architectural Review* 163, no. 976 (June 1978), p. 335.

62 Stam, "Das Mass, das richtige Mass, das Minimum-Mass," in Hirdina, ed., *Neues Bauen, Neues Gestalten*, pp. 215–216: "Die richtigen Masse sind diejenigen, die unseren Ansprüchen genügen, die ohne jede repräsentative Absicht den Bedürfnissen entsprechen, die nicht mehr scheinen wollen als sie sind. Die richtigen Masse sind die Masse, die mit einem Minimum an Aufwand genügen. Jedes Mehr wäre Ballast . . . So ist der Kampf der modernen Architektur ein Kampf gegen die Repräsentation, gegen das Übermass und für das Menschenmass."

63 See Giulio Carlo Argan, *Gropius und das Bauhaus* (1962; Braunschweig: Vieweg, 1983), pp. 54–55. Argan, however, pushes this argument to an extreme, treating Walter Gropius's development of an *Existenzminimum* housing exclusively in aesthetic terms. That results in a somewhat distorted picture that is certainly not accurate in the case of *Das Neue Frankfurt*.

64 *Das Neue Frankfurt*, 1/1928 and 11/1929.

65 Joseph Gantner, "Die Situation" (*Das Neue Frankfurt* 6/1931), in Hirdina, ed., *Neues Bauen, Neues Gestalten*, pp. 79–81.

66 Ernst May, "Die Wohnung für das Existenzminimum" (1929), in Steinmann, ed., *CIAM*, p. 6: "Wir befragen im Geiste das Heer des Entrechteten, die sehnsüchtig einer menschen-

würdigen Unterkunft harren. Wären sie damit einverstanden, dass eine geringe Zahl von ihnen grosse Wohnungen bekommt, während die Masse dafür Jahre und Jahrzehnte lang ihre Elend zu tragen verurteilt wird, oder nähmen sie lieber mit einer kleinen Wohnung vorlieb, die trotz räumlicher Beschränkung den Anforderungen genügt, die wir an eine neuzeitliche Wohnung zu stellen haben, wenn dafür in kurzer Zeit das Übel der Wohnungsnot ausgerottet werden kann?"

67 See Giorgio Grassi, "Das Neue Frankfurt et l'architecture du Nouveau Francfort," in Grassi, *L'architecture comme métier et autres écrits* (Liège: Mardaga, 1983), pp. 89–124.

68 See Ernst May, "Stadsuitbreiding met satellieten," in Henk Engel and Endry van Velzen, eds., *Architectuur van de stadsrand. Frankfurt am Main 1925–1930* (Delft: Technische Universiteit Delft, 1987), pp. 23–31.

69 The program of the *Siedlungen* was by no means confined to housing projects; amenities such as creches, schools, neighborhood centers, shops, and laundries were also planned. Shortage of money, however, prevented the building of many of these amenities.

70 During his short time in office (1925–1930), May concentrated primarily on the problem of housing. It was, however, his intention once the worst housing shortage had been alleviated also to deal programmatically with the infrastructure. Building the *Siedlungen* on the outskirts of the city was partially defended with the argument that good road and rail links with the center would soon be provided.

71 Manfredo Tafuri, "Sozialpolitik and the City in Weimar Germany," in Tafuri, *The Sphere and the Labyrinth* (Cambridge: MIT Press, 1987), pp. 197–233.

72 See Grassi, "Das Neue Frankfurt et l'architecture du Nouveau Francfort"; and Gerhard Fehl, "The Niddatal Project: The Unfinished Satellite Town on the Outskirts of Frankfurt," *Built Environment* 9, no. 3/4 (1983), pp. 185–197.

73 May had worked for some time in Unwin's office, which gave him firsthand experience of his ideas and concrete production.

74 The original intention was to build a road linking the Hadrianstrasse with the city center. (See Dreysse, *May-Siedlungen*, p. 14.) This never happened, however, and the present character of the *Siedlung* of Römerstadt is largely determined by the expressway that cuts it in two at right angles to the Hadrianstrasse.

75 This little building has turned out to be a meeting place for the residents of this *Siedlung*, even though it was not designed for this purpose either functionally or in terms of its site. See Dreysse, *May-Siedlungen*, p. 21.

76 See J. Castex, J. C. Depaule, and P. Panerai, *De rationele stad. Van bouwblok tot wooneenheid* (Nijmegen: SUN, 1984), pp. 147–174; G. Uhlig, "Sozialräumliche Konzeption der Frankfurter Siedlungen," in V. Fischer and Rosemarie Höpfner, eds., *Ernst May und das Neue Frankfurt 1925–1930* (Frankfurt: Deutsches Architektur Museum, 1986).

77 With future developments in mind, the floor plans of the low-rise flats were designed to include the possibility of making a single family flat out of two small flats on top of each other. At the end of the 1980s this transformation was in full swing. See Dreysse, *May-Siedlungen*, p. 21.

78 Sixty years later there is in fact no longer any question of "monotony"—the alterations, large and small, that the residents have introduced and the overgrowing of gardens and lawns make for a scene with plenty of variety. In Westhausen a range of lively community activities has sprung up and very few of the residents seek rehousing. Dreysse also informs us that Westhausen was a working-class estate (the rents were low enough here for it to qualify as such!) that was among the most socialist of the *Siedlungen*, continuing to be a center of resistance during the Nazi era. See Dreysse, *May-Siedlungen*, p. 20.

79 Ernst May: "Wir bemühen uns, ruhige, klare Strassenräume zu gestalten, die einzelne Fassade der Gesamtwirkung des Strassenzuges einzuordnen." *Das Neue Frankfurt*, 5/1926–27; rpt. in Hirdina, ed., *Neues Bauen, Neues Gestalten*, p. 123. ("We aimed to achieve a calm and clear design of the street areas by subordinating the individual facades to the effect of the whole.")

80 W. Boesiger and H. Girsberger, eds., *Le Corbusier 1910–1965* (Zurich: Editions d'architecture, 1967), pp. 44–46.

81 See Christian Mohr, "Das Neue Frankfurt und die Farbe," *Bauwelt*, no. 28 (July 25, 1986), pp. 1059–1061.

82 See Uhlig, "Sozialräumliche Konzeption." See also Ruth Diehl's conclusion that in terms of art history May's achievements in Frankfurt should be judged as "second rank International Style architecture." Diehl, "Die Tätigkeit Ernst Mays in Frankfurt am Main in den Jahren 1925–1930 unter besonderer Berücksichtigung der Siedlungbaus" (dissertation, Goethe-Universität, Frankfurt, 1976), p. 119.

83 Giedion rarely talks in any detail about May's work in Frankfurt. *Befreites Wohnen* contains a number of photos of May's achievements in Frankfurt, but in *Space, Time and Architecture* he devotes no more than one paragraph to the topic (p. 481).

84 Pessac is discussed at length in Giedion, *Bauen in Frankreich*, pp. 86–92.

85 Mentioned in Joseph Gantner, "Bericht über den II. Internationalen Kongress für Neues Bauen, Frankfurt-M., bis 26. Oktober 1929," in Hirdina, ed., *Neues Bauen, Neues Gestalten*, pp. 90–93.

86 Hirdina, ed., *Neues Bauen, Neues Gestalten*, p. 70: "Wenn auch die Formung der Stadt Frankfurt am Main der Hauptgegenstand unserer Betrachtung sein wird, so soll das nicht gleichbedeutend sind mit der Beschränkung des Mitarbeiterkreises auf unsere Stadt. Wir beabsichtigen vielmehr, führende Köpfe aus allen Teilen unseres Landes wie des Auslandes zu Worte kommen zu lassen, deren Denken und Handeln verwandten Zielen zustrebt. Sie werden unser Schaffen anregen und ergänzen."

87 *Das Neue Frankfurt* 1/1926–27, in Mohr and Müller, *Funktionalität und Moderne*, p. 15: "Wir wollen stolz sein auf die Traditionen unserer herrlichen Stadt am Main, auf ihr Aufblühen durch schwere und frohe Tage. Wir lehnen es aber ab, diese Traditionen dadurch zu ehren, dass wir ihre Schöpfungen kopieren. Wir wollen im Gegenteil uns dadurch ihrer würdig zeigen, dass wir mit festen Füssen in der heutigen Welt stehen und aus den lebendigen Lebensbedingungen unserer Zeit heraus entschlossen Neues gestalten."

88 See Michael Müller's commentary on Bürger's *Theory of the Avant-Garde*: "Architektur als ästhetische Form oder Form als lebenspraktische Architektur?" in Müller, *Architektur und Avantgarde*, pp. 33–92.

89 This terminology is borrowed from the work of Georg Simmel, who describes the experience of modernity as that of a growing discrepancy between the "objective spirit"—the totality of the objective knowledge and skills that are available in the various fields of culture from language and law via the technology of production to the arts and sciences—and the "subjective" personal development of the individual who becomes increasingly incapable of assimilating what this rising "objective" culture has to offer. Simmel, "The Metropolis and Mental Life" (1903), in Richard Sennett, ed., *Classic Essays on the Culture of Cities* (Englewood Cliffs: Prentice Hall, 1969), pp. 47–60. This essay is discussed in the introduction to chapter 3, below.

90 In their standard work on *Das Neue Frankfurt*, Müller and Mohr formulate this basic intention thus: "The essential point of this idea of establishing a new culture is the hope that the classless convergence of cultural and material reality that it had achieved would in the course of time bring the subjective and objective sides of life closer together. Not only would this call for what Simmel called an 'immense organization of things and powers' to carry it out; it would also require people with their cultural needs and requirements experiencing themselves as mass. If the former 'type of metropolitan individualism' becomes capable everywhere—whether at home or practicing sports, in the office or caught in the traffic of the modern city—of embracing this clearly designed homogeneity, then it will also be able to reconcile itself with the objective side of life." *Funktionalität und Moderne*, p. 189: "Das Kernstück dieser Kulturgestaltung ist die Hoffnung, dass die von ihr zustande gebrachte klassenlose Gleichzeitigkeit der kulturellen und materiellen Wirklichkeit mit der Zeit die subjektive Seite des Lebens an die objektive Seite des Lebens heranführen könnte. Diese wäre dann nicht mehr nur von den 'ungeheuren Organisationen von Dingen und Mächten' erfüllt, wie Simmel es noch beschrieben hatte, sondern in gleicher Weise von den sich als Masse erfahrenden Menschen und deren kulturellen Bedürfnisse und

Forderungen. Gelänge es dem vormaligen 'Typus der grossstädtischen Individualität', in diese überall—ob zuhause, beim Sport, in den Büros, in dem Bewegungsfluss der Stadt und ihren Bildern—sichtbar gestaltete Homogenität einzugehen, so sollte er sich mit der objektiven Seite des Lebens versöhnen können."

91 See May, "Die Wohnung für das Existenzminimum" (1929), in Mohr and Müller, *Funktionalität und Moderne*, pp. 147–148.

92 See, for instance, Karin Wilhelm, "Von der Phantastik zur Phantasie. Ketzerische Gedanken zur 'Funktionalistischen' Architektur," in Jürgen Kleindienst, ed., *Wem gehört die Welt? Kunst und Gesellschaft in der Weimarer Republik* (Berlin: Neue Gesellschaft für Bildende Kunst, 1977), pp. 72–86; L. Murard and P. Zylberman, "Ästhetik des Taylorismus. Die rationale Wohnung in Deutschland (1924–1933)," in *Paris-Berlin 1900–1933* (Munich: Prestel, 1979), pp. 384–391.

93 J. Rodríguez-Lores and G. Uhlig, "Einleitende Bemerkungen zur Problematik der Zeitschrift Das Neue Frankfurt," in Rodríguez-Lores and Uhlig, eds., *Reprint aus: Das Neue Frankfurt / die neue stadt (1926–1934)* (Aachen: Lehrstuhl für Planungstheorie der RWTH Aachen, 1977), pp. xi–xliv.

Reflections in a Mirror **3**

Epigraph: Walter Benjamin, "Erfahrung und Armut," in Benjamin, *Illuminationen. Ausgewälte Schriften* (Frankfurt: Suhrkamp, 1977), p. 293: "Ganzliche Illusionslosigkeit über das Zeitalter und dennoch ein rückhaltloses Bekenntnis zu ihm . . .".

1 Hermann Bahr, "The Modern" (1890), in Francesco Dal Co, *Figures of Architecture and Thought: German Architectural Culture 1880–1920* (New York: Rizzoli, 1990), p. 288; translated from "Die Moderne," in Bahr, *Zur Überwindung des Naturalismus. Theoretische Schriften 1887–1904* (Stuttgart: Kohlhammer, 1968), p. 35: "Es geht eine wilde Pein durch diese Zeit und der Schmerz is nicht mehr erträglich. Der Schrei nach dem Heiland ist gemein und Gekreuzigte sind überall. Ist es das grosse Sterben, das über die Welt gekommen? . . . Dass aus dem Leide das Heil kommen wird und die Gnade aus der Verzweiflung, dass es tagen wird nach dieser entsetzlichen Finsternis und dass die Kunst einkehren wird bei den Menschen—an dieser Auferstehung, glorreich und selig, das ist der Glaube der Moderne."

2 Ibid., pp. 290–291; German text: "der Einzug des auswärtigen Lebens in den innern Geist, das ist die neue Kunst. . . . Wir haben kein anderen Gesetz als die Wahrheit, wie jeder sie empfindet. . . . Dieses wird die neue Kunst sein, welches wir so schaffen. Und es wird die neue Religion sein. Denn Kunst, Wissenschaft und Religion sind dasselbe." (*Zur Überwindung des Naturalismus*, pp. 37–38.)

3 Bahr, *Secession* (Vienna, 1900), pp. 33 ff., quoted in E. F. Sekler, *Josef Hoffmann* (Vienna: Residenz, 1982), p. 33: "Über dem Thore wäre ein Vers aufgeschrieben: der Vers meines Wesens, und das, was dieser Vers in Worten ist, dasselbe müssten alle Farben und Linien sein, und jeder Stuhl, jede Tapete, jede Lampe wären immer wieder derselbe Vers. In einem solchen Haus würde ich überall meine Seele wie in einem Spiegel sehen."

4 Georg Simmel, "The Metropolis and Mental Life" (1903), in Richard Sennett, ed., *Classic Essays on the Culture of Cities* (Engelwood Cliffs: Prentice Hall, 1969), p. 48; translated from Georg Simmel, "Die Grossstadt und das Geistesleben," in Simmel, *Brücke und Tür. Essays* (Stuttgart: K. F. Koehler, 1957), p. 228: "So schafft der Typus des Grossstädters—der natürlich von tausend individuellen Modifikationen umspielt ist—sich ein Schutzorgan gegen die Entwurzelung, mit der die Strömungen und Discrepanzen seines äusseren Milieus ihn bedrohen: statt mit dem Gemüte reagiert er auf diese im wesentlichen mit dem Verstande."

5 At the end of this essay Simmel refers to one of his own books, *Philosophie des Geldes*, which first appeared in 1900.

6   Simmel, "The Metropolis and Mental Life," p. 49; German text: "Denn das Geld fragt nur nach dem, was ihnen allen gemeinsam ist, nach dem Tauschwert, der alle Qualität und Eigenart auf die Frage nach dem blossen wieviel nivelliert. Alle Gemütsbeziehungen zwischen Personen gründen sich auf deren Individualität, während die verstandesmässigen mit den Menschen wie mit Zahlen rechnen." (*Brücke und Tür*, p. 229.)

7   For the cultural context of turn-of-the-century Vienna in which Loos operated, see Allan Janik and Stephen Toulmin, *Wittgenstein's Vienna* (New York: Simon and Schuster, 1973); Carl Schorske, *Fin-de-siècle Vienna: Politics and Culture* (London: Weidenfeld and Nicholson, 1979); Jean Clair, ed., *Vienne 1880–1938. L'apocalypse joyeuse* (Paris: Centre Pompidou, 1986); Bart Verschaffel, "Het Grote Sterven," in Verschaffel, *De glans der dingen* (Mechelen: Vlees en Beton, 1989), pp. 25–42.

8   See the essay "Die überflüssigen," in Adolf Loos, *Trotzdem. 1900–1930* (1931; Vienna: Prachner, 1982), pp. 71–73.

9   Adolf Loos, *Spoken into the Void: Collected Essays 1897–1900* (Cambridge: MIT Press, 1982), p. 49; translated from *Ins Leere gesprochen. 1897–1900* (1921; Vienna: Prachner, 1981), p. 107: "Die hebung des wasserverbrauches ist eine der dringendsten kulturaufgaben." It was Loos's habit to write the German languange in a way that was grammatically incorrect: he refused to give a capital first letter to nouns. Not all editors of his work, however, let him have his way in this. I follow the usage of the source from which I am quoting.

10 In 1903 Loos published two issues of a magazine of his own: *Das Andere. Ein blatt zur Einführung abendländischer Kultur in Österreich.*

11 See, for instance, the articles by J. J. P. Oud, B. Taut, and G. A. Platz in B. Rukschcio, ed., *Für Adolf Loos* (Vienna: Löcker, 1985); A. Roth, *Begegnungen mit Pionieren* (Stuttgart: Birkhäuser, 1973).

12 The article was first published in 1913, in French. Ozenfant and Le Corbusier reprinted it in *L'Esprit Nouveau* in 1921. Ferdinand Kramer managed to get it published in a German paper, *Die Frankfurter Zeitung*, on the eve of the CIAM congress in Frankfurt in 1929. See Christian Mohr and Michael Müller, *Funktionalität und Moderne. Das neue Frankfurt und seine Bauten 1925–1933* (Cologne: Rudolf Müller, 1984), p. 63.

13 Adolf Loos, "The Poor Little Rich Man," in Loos, *Spoken into the Void*, p. 127; translated from "Von einem armen, reichen manne," in Loos, *Ins Leere gesprochen*, p. 203: "Er fühlte: Jetzt heisst es lernen, mit seinem eigenen Leichnam herumzugehen. Jawohl! Er ist fertig! Er ist komplett!"

14 Loos, *Spoken into the Void*, pp. 23–24; German text: "Ich bin gott sei dank noch in keiner stilvollen wohnung aufgewachsen. Damals kennte man das noch nicht. Jetzt ist es leider auch in meine familie anders geworden. Aber damals! Hier der tisch, ein ganz verrücktes krauses möbel, ein ausziehtisch, mit einer fürchterlichen schlosserarbeit. Aber unser tisch, unser tisch! Wisst ihr, was das heisst? Wisst ihr, welche herrlichen Stunden wir da erlebt haben? ... Jedes möbel, jedes ding, jeder gegenstand erzählt eine geschichte, die geschichte der familie. Die wohnung war nie fertig, sie entwickelt sich mit uns un wir in ihr." (*Ins Leere gesprochen*, pp. 76–77.)

15 Adolf Loos, "Vernacular Art," in Yehuda Safran and Wilfried Wang, eds., *The Architecture of Adolf Loos: An Arts Council Exhibition* (London, 1987), pp. 110–113; translated from Loos, *Trotzdem*, p. 129: "Das haus sei nach aussen verschwiegen, im inneren offenbare es seinen ganzen reichtum."

16 Loos, *Spoken into the Void*, p. 67; German text: "Dieses gesetz lautet also: Die möglichkeit, das bekleidete material mit der bekleidung verwechseln zu können, soll auf alle fälle ausgeschlossen sein." (*Ins Leere gesprochen,* p. 142.)

17 Adolf Loos, *Die Potemkinsche Stadt* (Vienna: Prachner, 1983), p. 206: "Der moderne intelligente mensch muss für die menschen eine maske haben. Diese maske ist die bestimmte, allen menschen gemeinsame form der kleider. Individuelle kleider haben nur geistig beschränkte. Diese haben das bedürfnis, in alle welt hinauszuschreien, was sie sind und wie sie eigentlich sind." ("One who is modern and intelligent must have a mask

for people. This mask takes a form which is very specific and common to all: choice of dress. Only mentally disabled people dress in an individual way because they have a need to cry out to the world who they are and how they are.")

18 Adolf Loos, "Architecture," in Safran and Wang, eds., *The Architecture of Adolf Loos*, p. 104; translated from Loos, *Trotzdem*, p. 91: "jene ausgeglichenheit des inneren und äusseren menschen, die allein ein vernünftiges denken und handeln verbürgt."

19 Adolf Loos, "Cultural Degeneration," in Safran and Wang, eds., *The Architecture of Adolf Loos*, pp. 98–99; translated from Loos, *Trotzdem*, p. 75.

20 Loos, *Trotzdem*, p. 75: "Den stil unserer zeit haben wir ja. Wir haben ihn überall dort, wo der künstler, also das mitglied jenes bundes bisher seine nase noch nicht hineingesteckt hat." My translation.

21 Adolf Loos, "Ornament and Crime," in Safran and Wang, eds., *The Architecture of Adolf Loos*, p. 100; translated from *Trotzdem*, p. 79: "Evolution der kultur ist gleichbedeutend mit dem entfernen des ornaments aus den gebrauchgegenstande."

22 Loos, *Trotzdem*, p. 86.

23 Ibid., pp. 23, 56.

24 Loos, *Die Potemkinsche Stadt*, p. 213: "Was ich vom Architekten will, ist nur eines: dass er in seinem Bau Anstand zeige." On the issue of propriety, see also Miriam Gusevich, "Decoration and Decorum: Adolf Loos's Critique of Kitsch," *New German Critique*, no. 43 (Winter 1988), pp. 97–124.

25 Loos, *Trotzdem*, p. 99.

26 See the essay on this subject in Loos, *Trotzdem*, pp. 122–130. English translation: "Vernacular Art," in Safran and Wang, eds., *The Architecture of Adolf Loos*, pp. 110–113.

27 Loos, "Architecture," p. 108. German text: "Das haus hat allen zu gefallen. Zum unterschiede vom kunstwerk, das niemandem zu gefallen hat. Das kunstwerk ist eine privatangelegenheit des künstlers. Das haus ist es nicht. Das kunstwerk wird in die welt gesetzt, ohne dass ein bedürfnis dafür vorhanden wäre. Das haus deckt ein bedürfnis. Das kunstwerk ist niemandem verantwortlich, das haus einem jeden. Das kunstwerk will die menschen aus ihrer bequemlichkeit reissen. Das haus hat der bequemlichkeit zu dienen. Das kunstwerk ist revolutionär, das haus konservativ. Das kunstwerk weist der menschheit neue wege und denkt an die zukunft. Das haus denkt an der gegenwart. Der mensch liebt alles, was seiner bequemlichkeit dient. Er hasst alles, was ihn aus seiner gewonnen und gesicherten position reissen will und belästigt. Und so liebt er das haus und hasst die kunst. *So hätte also das haus nichts mit kunst zu tun und wäre die architektur nicht unter die kunste einzureihen? Es ist so.* Nur ein ganz kleiner teil der architektur gehört der kunst an: das grabmal und das denkmal. Alles andere, was einem zweck dient, ist aus dem reiche der kunst auszuschliessen." (*Trotzdem*, p. 101.)

28 Karl Kraus's famous aphorism is quoted in Safran and Wang, eds., *The Architecture of Adolf Loos*, p. 42: "Adolf Loos and I, he literally and I linguistically, have done nothing more than to demonstrate that there is a difference between an urn and a chamber-pot, and that only in this difference does culture find its elbow-room. However, the others, the positive ones, are grouped into those who use the urn as a chamber pot, and the others who use the chamber-pot as an urn." The German original can be found in Rukschcio, ed., *Für Adolf Loos*, p. 27: "Adolf Loos und ich, er wörtlich, ich sprachlich, haben nichts weiter getan als gezeigt, dass zwischen einer Urne und einem Nachttopf ein Unterschied ist und dass in diesem Unterschied erst die Kultur Spielraum hat. Die andern aber, die Positiven, teilen sich in solche, die den Urne als Nachttopf, und die den Nachttopf als Urne gebrauchen."

29 For a detailed discussion of Loos's work see Benedetto Gravagnuolo, *Adolf Loos: Theory and Works* (Milan: Idea Books, 1982); B. Rukschcio and R. Schachel, *Adolf Loos. Leben und Werk* (Salzburg: Residenz, 1982).

30 Francesco Dal Co, "Notities over de fenomenologie van de grens in de architectuur," in *Oase*, no. 16 (1987), pp. 24–30. See also the chapters on Loos in Massimo Cacciari, *Architecture and Nihilism: On the Philosophy of Modern Architecture*, trans. Stephen Sartarelli (New Haven: Yale University Press, 1993).

31   Loos, *Trotzdem*, pp. 214–215.

32   Arnold Schoenberg in Rukschcio, ed., *Für Adolf Loos*, pp. 59–60: "Wenn ich einem Bau-
     werk von Adolf Loos gegenüberstehe . . . sehe ich . . . unzusammengesetzte, unmittel-
     bare, *dreidimensionale* Konzeption, der volkommen zu folgen vielleicht nur vermag, wer
     gleichartig begabt ist. Hier ist im Raum gedacht, erfunden, komponiert, gestaltet . . . un-
     mittelbar, so als ob alle Körper durchsichtig wären; so, wie das geistige Auge den Raum in
     allen seinen Teilen und gleichzeitig als Ganzes vor sich hat."

33   Beatriz Colomina, "The Split Wall: Domestic Voyeurism," in Colomina, ed., *Sexuality and
     Space* (New York: Princeton Architectural Press, 1992), p. 85.

34   Ibid., p. 74.

35   Ibid, p. 86.

36   For a lengthy and detailed analysis see Johan van de Beek, "Adolf Loos' Patronen
     stadswoonhuizen," in Max Risselada, ed., *Raumplan versus plan libre* (Delft: Delft Univer-
     sity Press, 1987), pp. 25–45. English edition: Max Risselada, ed., *Raumplan versus plan li-
     bre: Adolf Loos and Le Corbusier* (New York: Rizzoli, 1988).

37   Loos, *Die Potemkinsche Stadt*, p. 122: "Um beim Haus auf dem Michaelerplatz Geschäfts-
     haus und Wohnhaus zu trennen, wurde die Ausbildung der Fassade differenziert. Mit den
     beiden Hauptpfeilern und den schmäleren Stützen wollte ich den Rythmus betonen, ohne
     den es keine Architektur gibt. Die Nichtübereinstimmung der Achsen unterstützt die Tren-
     nung. Um dem Bauwerk die schwere Monumentalität zu nehmen und um zu zeigen dass
     ein Schneider, wenn auch ein vornehmer, sein Geschäft darin afgeschlagen hat, gab ich
     den Fenstern die Form englischer Bow-windows, die durch die kleine Scheibenteilung die
     intime Wirkung im Innern verbürgen."

38   Cacciari, *Architecture and Nihilism*, pp. 179 ff.

39   Loos, *Trotzdem*, p. 43.

40   Theodor W. Adorno, "A l'écart de tous les courants," in Adorno, *Über Walter Benjamin*
     (Frankfurt: Suhrkamp, 1970), pp. 96–99.

41   Benjamin gained his Ph.D. in Bern in 1919. To have the right to teach at a German univer-
     sity, one had to have an additional degree of *Habilitation*.

42   The Institut für Sozialforschung (Institute for Social Research) was set up by Horkheimer
     and Adorno and also included Herbert Marcuse. During the Nazi era it moved to Geneva
     and then to New York. After the war it was housed once more in Frankfurt. For a detailed
     study of the history of this institute, see Martin Jay, *The Dialectical Imagination: A History
     of the Frankfurt School and the Institute of Social Research, 1923–1950* (Boston: Little,
     Brown, 1973), and Rolf Wiggershaus, *The Frankfurt School: Its History, Theories and Po-
     litical Significance* (Cambridge: Polity Press, 1995).

43   Among the writings to which Benjamin owed his reputation of being a radical left-wing au-
     thor are "Der Autor als Produzent" ("The Author as Producer"), in Benjamin, *Reflections:
     Essays, Aphorisms, Autobiographical Writings* (1978; New York: Schocken, 1986), and
     "Das Kunstwerk in Zeitalter seiner technischen Reproduzierbarkeit" ("The Work of Art in
     the Age of Mechanical Reproduction"), in *Illuminations: Essays and Reflections* (1968;
     New York: Schocken, 1969).

44   See Reinhard Markner and Thomas Weber, eds., *Literatur über Walter Benjamin. Kom-
     mentierte Bibliographie 1983–1992* (Hamburg: Argument, 1993).

45   Lieven de Cauter, *De dwerg in de schaakautomaat. Benjamins verborgen leer* (Nijmegen:
     SUN, in press).

46   See Michael Müller, *Architektur und Avant-garde. Ein vergessenes Projekt der Moderne?*
     (1984; Frankfurt: Athenäum, 1987), in particular the essay "Architektur für das 'schlechte
     Neue,'" pp. 93–148. The work of Benjamin is definitely an important reference point for
     the authors of the Venice School (Tafuri, Dal Co, Cacciari). See also K. Michael Hays, *Mod-
     ernism and the Posthumanist Subject: The Architecture of Hannes Meyer and Ludwig
     Hilberseimer* (Cambridge: MIT Press, 1992), and Beatriz Colomina, *Privacy and Publicity:
     Modern Architecture as Mass Media* (Cambridge: MIT Press, 1994).

47   Three essays by Benjamin are relevant here: "Über Sprache überhaupt und über die

Sprache der Menschen," an early essay of 1916 translated as "On Language as Such and on the Language of Man" in *Reflections*, pp. 314–332, and two short, later essays, that are essentially variations of the same text: "Lehre vom Ähnlichen" and "Über das mimetische Vermogen," of which only the latter one, "On the Mimetic Faculty," has been translated (in *Reflections*, pp. 333–336).

48   The term *unsinnliche Ähnlichkeit* has been translated in various ways: Susan Buck-Morss uses the term "non-representational correspondence" in *The Origin of Negative Dialectics* (Brighton: Harvester, 1978), p. 88; Edmund Jephcott, the translator of *Reflections*, opts for "nonsensuous similarity."

49   Cyrille Offermans, *Nacht als trauma. Essays over het werk van Theodor W. Adorno, Walter Benjamin, Herbert Marcuse and Jürgen Habermas* (Amsterdam: De Bezige Bij, 1982), p. 109: "Een tekst is voor Benjamin (en voor Adorno) een soort semantisch krachtveld: er vindt in de woorden een uitwisseling plaats van semantische energie. Bewust taalgebruik . . . komt neer op het construeren van zo'n krachtveld. . . . Naarmate een tekst nu bewuster geconstrueerd is, en de woorden dus beter gemotiveerd zijn, neemt het arbitraire karakter van de woorden -hun abstracte en toevallige relatie tot de dingen—af. De ervaring van die dingen wordt in de tekst als het ware tastbaar, ofschoon geen enkel *afzonderlijk* woord voor die presentie verantwoordelijk kan gesteld worden."

50   "Die Ähnlichkeit [ist] das Organon der Erfahrung": Walter Benjamin, *Das Passagenwerk*, 2 vols. (Frankfurt: Suhrkamp, 1983), p. 1038.

51   For an excellent discussion of this topic, see John McCole, *Walter Benjamin and the Antinomies of Tradition* (Ithaca: Cornell University Press, 1993), pp. 2 ff.

52   Walter Benjamin, "On Some Motifs in Baudelaire," in *Illuminations*, p. 157; translated from Benjamin, *Illuminationen*, p. 186: "In der Tat ist die Erfahrung eine Sache der Tradition im kollektiven wie im privaten Leben. Sie bildet sich weniger aus einzelnen in der Erinnerung streng fixierten Gegebenheiten denn aus gehäuften, oft nicht bewussten Daten, die im Gedächtnis zusammenfliessen."

53   Benjamin is referring here to the famous passage from Proust's *A la recherche du temps perdu*, in which the author tells how suddenly the taste and smell of a madeleine cake triggered an involuntary memory of the smells and atmosphere of Combray, the city in which he lived part of his youth, but of which he had very few conscious memories.

54   Walter Benjamin, *Gesammelte Schriften*, 12 vols. (Frankfurt: Suhrkamp, 1980), vol. 3, p. 198.

55   Benjamin, *Illuminations*, p. 221; German text: "was im Zeitalter der technischen Reproduzierbarkeit des Kunstwerks verkümmert, das ist sein Aura. Der Vorgang ist symptomatisch; seine Bedeutung weisst über den Bereich der Kunst hinaus. Die Reproduktionstechnik, so liesse sich allgemein formulieren, löst das Reproduzierte aus dem Bereich der Tradition ab. Indem sie die Reproduktion verfielfältigt, setzt sie an die Stelle seines einmaligen Vorkommens sein massenweises." (*Illuminationen*, p. 141.)

56   Ibid., p. 222; German text: "einmalige Erscheinung einer Ferne, so nah sie sein mag" (*Illuminationen*, p. 142.)

57   This is the case, for instance, with the essay "Der Erzähler" ("The Storyteller," in *Illuminations*, pp. 83–110), and with the essay on Baudelaire.

58   Benjamin, "Erfahrung und Armut," p. 293: "Ganzliche Illusionslosigkeit über das Zeitalter und dennoch ein rückhaltloses Bekenntnis zu ihm ist ihr Kennzeichen."

59   Walter Benjamin, "Theses on the Philosophy of History," in *Illuminations*, pp. 257–258; translated from *Illuminationen*, p. 255: "Es gibt ein Bild von Klee, das Angelus Novus heisst. Ein Engel is darauf dargestellt, der aussieht, als wäre er im Begriff, sich von etwas zu entfernen, worauf er starrt. Seine Augen sind augerissen, sein Mund steht offen und seine Flügel sind ausgespannt. Der Engel der Geschichte muss so aussehen. Er hat das Antlitz der Vergangenheit zugewendet. Wo eine Kette von Begebenheiten vor *uns* erscheint, da sieht *er* eine einzige Katastrophe, die unablässig Trümmer auf Trümmer häuft und sie ihm vor die Füsse schleudert. Er möchte wohl verweilen, die Toten wecken und das Zerschlagene zusammenfugen. Aber ein Sturm weht vom Paradiese her, der sich in seinen Flügeln verfangen hat und so stark ist, dass der Engel sie nicht mehr schliessen kann. Dieser Sturm treibt ihn unaufhaltsam in der Zukunft, der er den Rücken kehrt, während der Trümmerhaufen vor ihm zum Himmel wächst. Das, was wir den Fortschritt nennen, ist *dieser* Sturm."

60   Ibid., p. 257; German text: "die Geschichte gegen den Strich zu bürsten" (*Illuminationen*, p. 254).

61   Ibid., pp. 262–263; German text: "Wo das Denken in einer von Spannungen gesättigten Konstellation plötzlich einhält, da erteilt es derselben einen Chock, durch den es sich als Monade kristallisiert. Der historischen Materialist geht an einen geschichtlichen Gegenstand einzig und allein da heran, wo er ihm als Monade entgegentritt. In dieser Struktur erkennt er das Zeichen einer messianischen Stillstellung des Geschehens, anders gesagt, einer revolutionären Chance im Kampfe für die unterdrückte Vergangenheit. Er nimmt sie wahr, um eine bestimmte Epoche aus dem homogenen Verlauf der Geschichte herauszusprengen." (*Illuminationen*, p. 260.)

      The term "monad" that Benjamin uses refers to the philosophy of Leibniz (1646–1716), for whom the cosmos consisted of an infinite quantity of points of energy that he called monads, each of which reflects and contains the whole cosmos in itself; these monads have no openings, and consequently no direct relationship with each other. For Benjamin it was the first point that mattered: the monad is a fragment in which the whole cosmos is contained.

62   Ibid., p. 264; German text: "Den Juden wurde die Zukunft aber darum doch nicht zur homogenen und leeren Zeit. Denn in ihr war jede Sekunde die kleine Pforte, durch die der Messias treten konnte." (*Illuminationen*, p. 261.)

63   De Cauter, *De dwerg in de schaakautomaat*.

64   Benjamin, *Das Passagenwerk*, p. 1002.

65   Richard Sieburth, "Benjamin the Scrivener," in Gary Smith, ed., *Benjamin: Philosophy, History, Aesthetics* (Chicago: University of Chicago Press, 1989), pp. 13–37.

66   Benjamin, *Das Passagenwerk*, p. 1006.

67   Ibid., pp. 1051–1052: "Strassen sind die Wohnung des Kollektivs. Das Kollektivum ist ein ewig waches, ewig bewegtes Wesen, das zwischen Häuserwänden soviel erlebt, erfährt, erkennt und ersinnt wie Individuen im Schutze ihrer vier Wände. Diesem Kollektivum sind die glänzenden emaillierten Firmenschilder so gut und besser ein Wandschmuck wie im Salon dem Bürger ein Ölgemälde, Mauern mit der "Défense d'Afficher" sind sein Schreibpult, Zeitungskioske seine Bibliotheken, Briefkästen seine Bronzen, Bänke sein Schlafzimmermobiliar und die Café-Terrasse der Erker, von dem er auf sein Hauswesen heruntersieht. Wo am Gitter Asphaltarbeiter den Rock hängen haben, da ist das Vestibül, und die Torfahrt, die aus der Flucht von Höfen ins Freie leitet, der lange Korridor, der den Bürger schreckt, ihnen der Zugang in die Kammern der Stadt. Von denen war die Passage der Salon. Mehr als an jeder andern Stelle gibt die Strasse sich in ihr als das möblierte, ausgewohnte Interieur der Massen zu erkennen."

68   Walter Benjamin, "Paris, Capital of the Nineteenth Century," in *Reflections*, p. 151.

69   Benjamin, *Das Passagenwerk*, p. 1045.

70   Benjamin, *Reflections*, p. 153.

71   Ibid., p. 148; German text: "In dem Traum, in dem jeder Epoche die ihr folgende in Bildern vor Augen tritt, erscheint die letztere vermählt mit Elementen der Urgeschichte, das heisst einer klassenlose Gesellschaft." (*Das Passagenwerk*, p. 47.)

72   "Die rauschhafte Durchdringung van Strasse und Wohnung, die sich im Paris des 19ten Jahrhundert vollzieht—und zumal in der Erfahrung des Flaneurs—hat prophetischen Wert. Denn diese Durchdringung lässt die neue Baukunst nüchterne Wirklichkeit werden." Benjamin, *Das Passagenwerk*, p. 534.

73   Rolf Tiedemann, "Einleitung des Herausgebers," in Benjamin, *Das Passagenwerk*, pp. 9–41. English translation: Rolf Tiedemann, "Dialectics at a Standstill: Approaches to the *Passagenwerk*," in Gary Smith, ed., *On Walter Benjamin* (Cambridge: MIT Press, 1988), pp. 260–291.

74 Benjamin, *Gesammelte Schriften,* vol. 1, p. 1049: "Der Automobilist, der mit seinen Gedanken 'ganz wo anders' z.B. bei seinem schadhaften Motor ist, wird sich an die moderne Form der Garage besser gewöhnen, als der Kunsthistoriker, der sich vor ihr anstrengt, nur ihren Stil zu ergründen."

75 Benjamin, *Illuminations*, p. 240; German text: "Die Aufgaben, welche in geschichtlichen Wendezeiten dem menschlichen Wahrnehmungsapparat gestellt werden, sind auf dem Wege der blossen Optik, also der Kontemplation, gar nicht zu lösen. Sie werden allmählich nach Anleitung der taktilen Rezeption, durch Gewöhnung, bewähltigt." (*Illuminationen*, pp. 166–167.)

76 Benjamin, *Das Passagenwerk*, p. 292.

77 Walter Benjamin, *Die Ursprung des deutschen Trauerspiels* (1928; Frankfurt: Suhrkamp, 1990); translated as *The Origin of German Tragic Drama* (London: NLB, 1977). See McCole, *Walter Benjamin*, p. 115.

78 See Asja Lacis's reminiscences, quoted in Susan Buck-Morss, *The Dialectics of Seeing: Walter Benjamin and the Arcades Project* (Cambridge: MIT Press, 1990), p. 15.

79 Benjamin, *Die Ursprung des deutschen Trauerspiels*, p. 139. See also commentary in McCole, *Walter Benjamin*, p. 131.

80 Benjamin, *Die Ursprung des deutschen Trauerspiels*, p. 164.

81 McCole, *Walter Benjamin*, p. 138.

82 Rainer Nägele, *Theater, Theory, Speculation: Walter Benjamin and the Scenes of Modernity* (Baltimore: Johns Hopkins University Press, 1991), p. 93.

83 Ibid., p. 92.

84 Benjamin, *Reflections*, p. 302; German text: "Einige überliefern die Dinge, indem sie unantastbar machen und konservieren, andere die Situationene, indem sie sie handlich machen und liquidieren. Diese nennt man die Destruktieven." (*Illuminationen*, p. 290.) For an interesting comment on this essay by Benjamin, see Irving Wohlfarth, "No-man's-land: On Walter Benjamin 'Destructive Character,'" in Andrew Benjamin and Peter Osborne, eds., *Walter Benjamin's Philosophy: Destruction and Experience* (London: Routledge, 1994), pp. 155–182.

85 Benjamin, *Reflections*, p. 272; German text: "Wenn die menschliche Arbeit nur aus der Zerstörung besteht, dann ist es wirklich menschliche natürliche, edle Arbeit" (*Illuminationen*, p. 383); the quotation is from Adolf Loos, *Trotzdem*, p. 184.

86 Benjamin, *Reflections*, pp. 272–273; German text: "Der Durchschnittseuropäer hat sein Leben mit der Technik nicht zu vereinen vermocht, weil er am Fetisch schöpferischen Daseins festhielt. Man muss schon Loos im Kampf mit dem Drache 'Ornament' verfolgt, muss das stellare Esperanto Scheerbartscher Geschöpfe vernommen oder Klees 'Neuen Engel', welcher die Menschen lieber befreite, indem er ihnen nähme, als beglückte, indem er ihnen gäbe, gesichtet haben, um eine Humanität zu fassen, die sich an der Zerstörung bewährt." (*Illuminationen*, p. 384.)

87 Ibid., p. 271; German text: "Erst der Verzweifelnde entdeckte im Zitat die Kraft: nicht zu bewahren, sondern zu reinigen, aus dem Zusammenhang zu reissen, zu zerstören; die einzige, in der noch Hoffnung liegt, dass einiges aus diesem Zeitraum überdauert—weil man es nämlich aus ihm herausschlug." (*Illuminationen*, p. 382.)

88 McCole, *Walter Benjamin*, p. 171.

89 Benjamin, *Reflections*, p. 303; German text: "Der destruktive Charakter ist der Feind des Etui-Menschen. Der Etui-Mensch sucht seine Bequemlichkeit, und das Gehäuse ist ihr Inbegriff. Das innere des Gehäuses ist die mit Samt ausgeschlagene Spur, die er in die Welt gedrückt hat. Der destruktive Charakter verwischt sogar die Spuren der Zerstörung." (*Illuminationen*, p. 290.)

90 Benjamin, *Das Passagenwerk*, pp. 291–292: "Die Urform allen Wohnens ist das Dasein nicht im Haus sondern im Gehäuse. Dieses trägt den Abdruck seines Bewohners. Wohnung wird im extremsten Falle zum Gehäuse. Das neunzehnten Jahrhundert war wie kein ander wohnsüchtig. Es begriff die Wohnung als Futteral des Menschen und bettete ihn mit all seinem Zubehör so tief in sie ein, dass man ans Innere eines Zirkelkastens denken

könnte, wo das Instrument mit allen Ersatzteilen in tiefe, meistens violette Sammethöhlen gebettet, daliegt."

91 Ibid., p. 53; translated in *Reflections*, p. 155.

92 Benjamin, *Reflections*, p. 154; German text: "Die Erschütterung des Interieurs vollzieht sich um die Jahrhundertwende im Jugendstil. Allerdings scheint er, seiner Ideologie nach, die Vollendung des Interieurs mit sich zu bringen. Die Verklärung der einsamen Seele erscheint als sein Ziel. Der Individualismus ist seine Theorie. Bei Van de Velde erscheint das Haus als Ausdruck der Persönlichkeit. Dat Ornament ist diesem Hause was de Gemälde die Signatur." (*Das Passagenwerk*, p. 52.)

93 Benjamin, *Das Passagenwerk*, p. 684.

94 Ibid., p. 298.

95 Ibid., p. 282.

96 Ibid., pp. 681, 695.

97 Benjamin, *Reflections*, p. 155; German text: "der Versuch des Individuums, auf Grund seiner Innerlichkeit mit der Technik es aufzunehmen, führt zu seinem Untergang" (*Das Passagenwerk*, p. 53).

98 Benjamin, *Gesammelte Schriften*, vol. 3, p. 310.

99 Benjamin, *Das Passagenwerk*, p. 292: "Das zwanzigste Jahrhundert machte mit seiner Porosität, Transparenz, seinem Freilicht- und Freiluftwesen dem Wohnen im alten Sinne ein ende. . . . Der Jugendstil erschütterte das Gehäusewesen aufs tiefste. Heut ist es abgestorben und das Wohnen hat sich vermindert: für die Lebendem durch Hotelzimmer, für die Toten durch Krematorien."

100 Benjamin, *Gesammelte Schriften*, vol. 8, pp. 196–197: "Denn in der Signatur dieser Zeitwende steht, dass dem Wohnen im alten Sinne, dem die Geborgenheit an erster Stelle stand, die Stunde geschlagen hat. Giedion, Mendelsohn, Corbusier machen dem Aufenthaltsort vom Menschen vor allem zum Durchgangsraum aller erdenklichen Kräfte und Wellen von Licht und Luft. Was kommt, steht im Zeichen der Transparenz: Nicht nur der Räume, sondern, wenn wir den Russen glauben, die jetzt die Abschaffung des Sonntags zugunsten von beweglichen Feierschichten vorhaben, sogar die Wochen."

101 Walter Benjamin, "Surrealism," in *Reflections*, p. 180; translated from *Gesammelte Schriften*, vol. 2, p. 298: "Im Glashaus zu leben ist eine revolutionäre Tugend par excellence. Auch das ist ein Rausch, ist ein moralischer Exhibitionismus, den wir sehr nötig haben. Die Diskretion in Sachane eigener Existenz ist aus einer aristokratischen Tugend mehr und mehr zu einer Angelegenheit arrivierter Kleinbürger geworden."

102 Benjamin, *Illuminationen*, p. 294: "in verschiebbaren beweglichen Glashäusern wie Loos und Le Corbusier sie inzwischen aufführten. Glas ist nich umsonst ein so hartes und glattes Material, an dem sich nichts festsetzt. Auch ein kaltes und nüchternes. Die Dinge aus Glas haben keine 'Aura'. Das Glas ist überhaupt der Feind der Geheimnisses. Es ist auch der Feind des Besitzes." A closer look at the architecture of Adolf Loos shows that as far as the "adjustable flexible glass houses" were concerned, Benjamin linked Loos and Le Corbusier somewhat too easily. Loos rarely used glass for its transparency, being inclined rather to highlight its potential for reflection. See the discussion earlier in this chapter.

103 See Benjamin, *Illuminationen*, p. 360; *Reflections*, p. 247: "Indeed to secure private life against morality and concepts in a society that perpetrates the political radioscopy of sexuality and family, of economic and physical existence, in a society that is in the process of building houses with glass walls, and patios extending far into the drawing rooms that are no longer drawing rooms—such a watchword would be the most reactionary of all. . . ."

104 In a review of 1929 he refers explicitly to this book, describing it as a "ganz ungewöhnlichen Werk." Benjamin, *Gesammelte Schriften*, vol. 8, p. 170. In the *Passagenwerk* there are a large number of quotations and references to it.

105 Adolf Behne, *Neues Wohnen—Neues Bauen* (Leipzig: Prometheus-Bücher, 1927); Le Corbusier, *Urbanisme* (Paris: G. Crès, 1925).

106 See Hays, *Modernism and the Posthumanist Subject*.

107 See Benjamin, *Berliner Kindheit um 1900* (Frankfurt: Suhrkamp, 1970).

108 Ernst Bloch, *The Principle of Hope*, trans. Neville Plaice, Stephen Plaice, and Paul Knight (Oxford: Basil Blackwell, 1986), p. 6; translated from *Das Prinzip Hoffnung* (Frankfurt: Suhrkamp, 1959), p. 4: "besonders ausgedehnt ist in diesem Buch der Versuch gemacht, an die Hoffnung, als eine Weltstelle, die bewohnt ist wie das beste Kulturland und unerforscht wie die Antarktis, Philosophie zu bringen."

109 Ibid., p. 9; German text: "die noch ungewordene, noch ungelungene Heimat, wie sie im dialektisch-materialistischen Kampf des Neuen mit dem Alten sich herausbildet, heraufbildet" (*Das Prinzip Hoffnung*, p. 8).

110 Ibid., p. 1376: "There arises in the world something which shines into the childhood of all and in which no one has yet been: homeland." German text: "so entsteht in der Welt etwas, das allen in die Kindheit scheint und worin noch niemand war: Heimat" (*Das Prinzip Hoffnung*, p. 1628).

111 Ibid., p. 15; German text: "Utopisches auf die Thomas Morus-Weise zu beschränken oder auch nur schlechthin zu orientieren, das wäre, als wollte man die Elektrizität auf den Bernstein reduzieren, von dem sie ihren griechischen Namen hat und an dem sie zuerst bemerkt worden ist." (*Das Prinzip Hoffnung*, p. 14.)

112 See "Something's Missing: A Discussion between Ernst Bloch and Theodor W. Adorno on the Contradictions of Utopian Longing," in Ernst Bloch, *The Utopian Function of Art and Literature: Selected Essays*, trans. Jack Zipes and Frank Mecklenburg (Cambridge: MIT Press, 1988), pp. 1–17.

113 Wayne Hudson, *The Marxist Philosophy of Ernst Bloch* (London: Macmillan, 1982).

114 Ernst Bloch, *Erbschaft dieser Zeit*, foreword to the first edition (Zurich: Oprecht & Helbling, 1935), pp. 15–20.

115 Bloch, *The Principle of Hope*, p. 744; German text: "ein Produktionversuch menschlicher Heimat" (*Das Prinzip Hoffnung*, p. 870).

116 Ibid., p. 745; German text: "Das Umschliessende gibt Heimat oder berührt sie: sämtliche grossen Bauwerke waren sui generis in die Utopie, die Antizipation eines menschadäquaten Raums hineingebaut. . . . Die bessere Welt, welche der grosse Baustil ausprägt und antizipierend abbildet, besteht so ganz unmythisch, als reale Aufgabe vivis ex lapidibus, aus den Steinen des Lebens." (*Das Prinzip Hoffnung*, p. 872.)

117 Ibid., pp. 714–721.

118 This passage, from the 1923 edition, is included in Bloch, *The Utopian Function of Art and Literature*, p. 79; German text: "Sie verstand es, die Maschine, alles so leblos und untermenschlich in einzelnen zu machen, wie es unsere, neuen Viertal im ganzen sind. Ihr eigentliches Ziel ist das Badezimmer und Klosett, die fragelosesten und originalsten Leistungen dieser Zeit. . . . Jetzt aber regiert die Abwaschbarkeit, irgendwie fliesst überall das Wasser von den Wanden herab." *Geist der Utopie*, revised version from the 1923 2d ed. (Frankfurt: Suhrkamp, 1985), p. 21.

119 Bloch, *The Utopian Function of Art and Literature*, p. 78; German text: "Zuerst zwar sieht uns fast alles hohl entgegen. Wie könnte das freilich anders sein, und woher sollte das lebendige, schön geartete Gerät kommen, nachdem niemand mehr das dauernde Wohnen kennt, sein Haus warm und stark zu machen?" (*Geist der Utopie*, p. 20.)

120 Bloch, *The Principle of Hope*, p. 733, quoted from his own work. German text: "eine Geburtszange muss glatt sein, eine Zuckerzange mitnichten" (*Geist der Utopie*, p. 23).

121 Bloch, *The Utopian Function of Art and Literature*, pp. 85–86; German text: "So lebt noch dieses Dritte zwischen Stuhl und Statue, wohl gar über der Statue: ein 'Kunstgewerbe' höherer Ordnung, in dem sich, statt des behaglichen, gleichsam abgestandenen, aus Ruheständen zusammengesetzten, rein luxuriösen Gebrauchsteppichs, ein echter, ein hinüberweisender Teppich der reinen abstrakten Form ausstreckt." (*Geist der Utopie*, p. 29.)

122 See also Rainer Traub and Harald Wieser, eds., *Gespräche mit Ernst Bloch* (Frankfurt: Suhrkamp, 1977), p. 35.

123 Bloch, *Erbschaft dieser Zeit*, expanded edition (Frankfurt: Suhrkamp, 1985), p. 220: "Selbst-

verständlich ist kommunistische Sachlichkeit nicht nur die spätkapitalistische minus Ausbeutung; vielmehr: fällt die Ausbeutung weg . . . so erhalten die kalkweissen Mietsblöcke, worin heute Arbeitstiere minderer Grösse hausen, Farbe und ganz andere Geometrie, nämlich von einem wirklichen Kollektiv."

124 There are two English translations of this essay. In addition to the version in *The Principle of Hope* that I quote from here, a more recent one is included in *The Utopian Function of Art and Literature*.

125 Bloch, *The Principle of Hope*, p. 733; German text: "Heute sehen die Häuser vielerorts wie reisefertig drein. Obwohl sie schmucklos sind oder eben deshalb, drückt sich in ihnen Abschied aus. Im Innern sind sie hell und kahl wie Krankenzimmer, in äusseren wirken sie wie Schachteln auf bewegbaren Stangen, aber auch wie Schiffe." (*Das Prinzip Hoffnung*, p. 858.)

126 Ibid., p. 734; German text: "Das breite Fenster voll lauter Aussenwelt braucht ein Draussen voll anziehender Fremdlinge, nicht voll Nazis; die Glastüre bis zum Boden setzt wirklich Sonnenschein voraus, der hereinblickt und eindringt, keine Gestapo." (*Das Prinzip Hoffnung*, p. 859.)

127 Ibid., p. 734; German text: "Die Entinnerlichung wurde Hohlheit, die südliche Lust zur Aussenwelt wurde, beim gegenwärtigen Anblick der kapitalistischen Aussenwelt, kein Glück." (*Das Prinzip Hoffnung*, p. 859.)

128 Ibid., p. 736; German text: "Auch die Stadtplanung dieser unentwegten Funktionalisten ist privat, abstrakt; vor lauter 'être humain' werden die wirklichen Menschen in diesen Häusern und Städten zu genormten Termiten oder, innerhalb einer 'Wohnmaschine' zu Fremkörpern, noch allzu organischen; so abgehoben ist das alles von wirklichen Menschen, von Heim, Behagen, Heimat." (*Das Prinzip Hoffnung*, p. 861.)

129 Ibid., 737; German text: "Eben weil diese [die Baukunst] weit mehr als die anderen bildenden Künste eine soziale Schöpfung ist und bleibt, kann sie im spätkapitalistischen Hohlraum überhaupt nicht blühen. Erst die Anfänge einer anderen Gesellschaft ermöglichen wieder echten Architektur, eine aus eigenem Kunstwollen konstruktiv und ornamental zugleich durchdrungene." (*Das Prinzip Hoffnung*, p. 862.)

130 Ernst Bloch, "Bildung, Ingenieursform, Ornament," *Werk und Zeit*, no. 11/12 (1965), p. 2: "Unbeschadet der Frage, ob der gesellschaftliche Habitus, der den faulen Zauber der Gründerzeit gesetzt halte, selber so viel ehrlicher geworden sei. Ob die ornamentfreie Ehrlichkeit aus reiner Zweckform nicht selber die Form eines Feigenblatts annehmen könnte, um eine nicht ganz so grosse Ehrlichkeit der sonstige Verhältnisse zu verdecken."

131 Ibid., p. 3: "'Graf dieser Mortimer starb auch sehr gelegen', heisst es in Maria Stuart, dergleichen gilt auch, mutatis mutandis, für den gar noch bejubelten Ornamenttod, für eine auch noch synthetisch hergestellte Phantasielosigkeit."

132 Ibid., p. 3: "eine Architektur, die Flügel brauchte, und eine Malerei-Plastik, der öfter eher Blei in die Sohlen zu giessen wäre."

133 Dennis Sharp, *Modern Architecture and Expressionism* (New York: George Braziller, 1966); Wolfgang Pehnt, *Expressionist Architecture* (London: Thames and Hudson, 1979); Iain Boyd Whyte, ed., *The Crystal Chain Letters* (Cambridge: MIT Press, 1985).

134 See the interview "Erbschaft aus Dekandenz?" in Taub and Wieser, eds., *Gespräche mit Ernst Bloch*, pp. 28–40.

135 See Ernst Bloch, "Discussing Expressionism" (1938), in Ernst Bloch et al., *Aesthetics and Politics* (London: Verso, 1980), pp. 16–27.

136 Bloch, "Discussing Expressionism," p. 23.

137 Bloch, *Erbschaft dieser Zeit*, p. 221: "In der technische und kulturellen Montage jedoch wird der Zusammenhang der alten Oberfläche zerfällt, ein neuer gebildet. Er kann als neuer gebildet werden, weil der alte Zusammenhang sich immer mehr als scheinhafter, brüchiger, als einer der Oberfläche enthüllt. Lenkte die Sachlichkeit mit glänzendem Anstrich ab, so macht manche Montage das Durcheinander dahinter reizvoll oder kühn verschlungen. . . . Insofern zeigt die Montage weniger Fassade und mehr Hintergrund der Zeit als die Sachlichkeit."

138 Ibid., p. 228: "Diese Art hat alles Negative der Leere, doch sie hat auch, mittelbar, als

möglich Positives: dass die Trümmer in einen anderen Raum schafft—wider den gewohnten Zusammenhang. Montage im Spätbürgertum ist der Hohlraum seiner Welt, erfüllt mit Funken und Überschneidungen einer 'Erscheinungsgeschichte', die nicht die rechte ist, doch gegebenfalls ein Mischort der rechten. Eine Form auch, sich der altem Kultur zu vergewissern: erblickt aus Fahrt und Betroffenheit, nicht mehr aus Bildung."

139 Alexander Schwab, born in 1887, was a communist writer and journalist. In 1930 he published *Das Buch vom Bauen*, in which he analyzes all aspects of architecture and dwelling. In 1933 he was arrested by the Nazis "as an enemy of the state." He died in 1943, still in prison. *Das Buch vom Bauen* was reprinted in 1973 (Düsseldorf: Bertelsmann) with a foreword by Diethart Kerbs.

140 Ernst Bloch, *Spuren* (1930; Frankfurt: Suhrkamp, 1985), p. 163: "Ein höchst heiteres Kreisen ging fühlbar zwischen Drinnen und Draussen, Schein und Tiefe, Kraft und Oberfläche. 'Hören sie', sagte da mein Freund, 'wie gut das Haus in Gang is'. Und man hörte die Ruhe, das richtig Eingehängte, wie es läuft, die wohlbekannte Kameradschaft mit den Dingen, die jeder Gesunde fühlt, die Lebensluft um sie her und die taohafte Welt."

141 See also Taub and Wieser, eds., *Gespräche mit Ernst Bloch*, p. 206.

142 See *Architectural Design Profile 59* (supplement to *Architectural Design* 55, no. 5/6 [1985]), realized by guest editor Luciano Semerani, special issue entirely on the Istituto Universitario di Architettura. For a survey of the activities in Tafuri's own department, see Paolo Morachiello, "The Department of Architectural History: A Detailed Description," in ibid., pp. 70–71.

143 See the illuminating introduction by Patrizia Lombardo, "Introduction: The Philosophy of the City," in Cacciari, *Architecture and Nihilism,* pp. ix–lviii.

144 Dal Co, *Figures of Architecture and Thought,* p. 9.

145 Manfredo Tafuri, *Architecture and Utopia: Design and Capitalist Development,* trans. Barbara Luigia La Penta (Cambridge: MIT Press, 1976), p. vii; translated from *Progetto e utopia. Architettura e sviluppo capitalistico* (Bari: Laterza, 1973).

146 Ibid., pp. 86, 88.

147 Ibid., p. 88.

148 Ibid., pp. 84–86: "all the historical avant-garde movements arose and succeeded each other according to the typical law of industrial production, the essence of which is the continual technical revolution."

149 Ibid., p. 89.

150 Ibid., pp. 55–56.

151 Ibid., p. 56.

152 Ibid., p. 93.

153 Ibid., p. 95.

154 Ibid.

155 Ibid. Tafuri is referring to the congress of constructivists and dadaists held in Weimar in 1922. Among those who attended were Theo and Nelly van Doesburg, Kurt Schwitters, Tristan Tzara, Hans Arp, László and Lucia Moholy-Nagy, El Lissitzky, Hans Richter, Hannah Höch, Cornelis van Eesteren, Karel Maes, Alfréd Kemény, Werner Gräff, Alexa and Peter Röhl, and Max and Lotte Buchartz. One distinguished example of the "merging" of Dada and De Stijl is of course Theo van Doesburg, who wrote Dadaist poems under the pseudonym of I. K. Bonset.

156 Ibid., p. 96.

157 Ibid., p. 98.

158 Ibid., p. 100.

159 Ibid.

160 Ibid., p. 107.

161 Ibid., p. 119. The opposition between "town" and "large city" refers to the notions of *Gemeinschaft* (community) and *Gesellschaft* (society), derived from Ferdinand Tönnies, a conservative German sociologist (1855–1936), whose book *Gemeinschaft und Gesellschaft* dates from 1887.

162 Ibid., p. 124.

163 Ibid., p. 88.

164 Massimo Cacciari, "The Dialectics of the Negative and the Metropolis," in Cacciari, *Architecture and Nihilism,* pp. 1–96. See also Massimo Cacciari, "Notes sur la dialectique du négatif à l'époque de la metropole (essai sur Georg Simmel)," *VH 101,* no. 9 (Autumn 1972), pp. 58–72. Benjamin's study on Baudelaire can be found in "On Some Motifs in Baudelaire," in Benjamin, *Illuminations,* pp. 155–201.

165 Cacciari, *Architecture and Nihilism,* p. 13. See also Lombardo's introduction, p. xxv.

166 Cacciari, *Architecture and Nihilism,* p. 13.

167 With Simmel what is involved is a certain coincidence rather than any causal link between the process of rationalization in personal realtions and the increasing dominance of the commodity system.

168 Cacciari, *Architecture and Nihilism,* p. 12.

169 Ibid., p. 19.

170 Letter from Benjamin to Scholem, June 12, 1938, in Gershom Scholem, ed., *Walter Benjamin/Gershom Scholem, Briefwechsel* (Frankfurt: Suhrkampf, 1985), pp. 266–273.

171 Cacciari, *Architecture and Nihilism,* p. 64.

172 Tomás Llorens, "Manfredo Tafuri: Neo-Avant-Garde and History," *Architectural Design* 51, no. 6/7 (1981), p. 88.

173 Dal Co, *Figures of Architecture and Thought,* p. 19.

174 Ibid., p. 35.

175 For a discussion of this text, see chapter 1 above.

176 Dal Co, *Figures of Architecture and Thought,* p. 42.

177 Manfredo Tafuri, *Theories and History of Architecture*, trans. Giorgio Verrecchia (London: Granada, 1980), p. 141; translated from *Teorie e storia dell'architettura* (Bari: Laterza, 1968).

178 In particular, Tafuri raises a number of objections to Giedion's interpretations of the plans of Sixtus V for sixteenth-century Rome. Tafuri, *Theories and History of Architecture,* pp. 151–152; see Sigfried Giedion, *Space, Time and Architecture: The Growth of a New Tradition* (1941; Cambridge: Harvard University Press, 1980), pp. 75–106.

179 Tafuri, *Theories and History of Architecture,* p. 151.

180 Ibid., p. 172.

181 Ibid., p. 229.

182 Tafuri, moreover, does not go into the question of whether this form of criticism also has an ideological content. See Llorens, "Manfredo Tafuri: Neo-Avant-Garde and History," p. 85.

183 Tafuri, *Architecture and Utopia,* p. ix.

184 Frederic Jameson, "Architecture and the Critique of Ideology," in Joan Ockman, ed., *Architecture, Criticism, Ideology* (Princeton: Princeton Architectural Press, 1985), p. 65.

185 Jameson sees a reason here for including Tafuri's work under the same heading as that of Adorno and Barthes. I disagree with him, at least as far as Tafuri's affinity with Adorno is concerned. Like Patrizia Lombardo, I think that Benjamin's writings shed much more light on Tafuri than do those of Adorno. Not only is there textual evidence for this (Tafuri refers much more to Benjamin than to Adorno); it is also something that Tafuri has stated in interviews, such as the one with Françoise Véry, published in *Architecture—Mouvement—Continuité* in 1976 and quoted in Hélène Lipstadt and Harvey Mendelsohn, "Philosophy, History and Autobiography: Manfredo Tafuri and the 'Unsurpassed Lesson' of Le Corbusier," *Assemblage,* no. 22 (December 1993), pp. 58–103. Moreover, the subliminal influence of Cacciari on Tafuri is indisputable, and Jameson seems somewhat too hasty in treating Cacciari's "negative thought" as though it were comparable with Adorno's "negative dialectics." Cacciari explicitly acknowledges that he adheres to a "Marxism without dialectics," and this makes his stance fundamentally different from that of Adorno. Furthermore, Cacciari considers that negative thought will continue to be functional within the future development of capitalism, while Adorno, as I intend to show in the following chapter, continued to cherish a hope—even if a slender one—that his negative dialectics would

keep a minimal escape route open. In *Aesthetic Theory,* too, Adorno continues to adhere to the possibility of art being able to exercise a critique of the increasing one-dimensionality of the system; in this respect as well, his ideas are different from those of Tafuri.

186 Carla Keyvanian, "Manfredo Tafuri's Notion of History and Its Methodological Sources" (master's thesis, MIT, Cambridge, Mass., 1992).

187 Manfredo Tafuri and Francesco Dal Co, *Modern Architecture,* trans. Robert Erich Wolf (New York: Abrams, 1979), p. 7; translated from *Architettura contemporanea* (Milan: Electa, 1976).

188 Llorens, "Manfredo Tafuri: Neo-Avant-Garde and History," p. 90.

189 Benjamin, "Theses on the Philosophy of History."

190 Manfredo Tafuri, "The Historical Project," in Tafuri, *The Sphere and the Labyrinth: Avant-Gardes and Architecture from Piranesi to the 1970s,* trans. Pellegrino D'Acierno and Robert Connolly (Cambridge: MIT Press, 1987), pp. 1–21; translated from *La sfera e il labirinto. Avanguardie e architettura da Piranesi agli anni '70* (Turin: Einaudi, 1980).

191 For an interesting comment on Tafuri's position see Joan Ockman, "Postscript: Critical History and the Labors of Sisyphus," in Ockman, ed., *Architecture, Criticism, Ideology,* pp. 182–189.

192 Tafuri, "The Historical Project," p. 16.

193 Ibid., p. 9.

Architecture as Critique of Modernity 4

Epigraph: Theodor W. Adorno, "Functionalism Today," *Oppositions,* no. 17 (1979), p. 41; translated from "Funktionalismus heute" (1965), in Adorno, *Gesammelte Schriften,* vol. 10, pt. 1 (Frankfurt: Suhrkamp, 1977), p. 395: "Schönheit heute hat kein anderes Mass als die Tiefe, in der die Gebilde die Widersprüche austragen, die sie durchfuhren und die sie bewältigen einzig, indem sie ihnen folgen, nicht indem sie sie verdecken."

1 Max Bill, "Education and Design," in Joan Ockman, ed., *Architecture Culture 1943–1968* (New York: Rizzoli, 1993), pp. 159–162.

2 Max Bill, ed., *Robert Maillart* (Erlenbach and Zurich: Verlag für Architektur, 1949).

3 Cobra (an acronym for Copenhagen-Brussels-Amsterdam) was founded in 1948 by Asger Jorn, Christian Dotremont, and Constant. The movement originated in dissatisfaction with the approach of the surrealists who dominated the avant-garde art world at the time. The members of Cobra considered that the surrealists attached too much importance to psychic automatism (the technique involving the quasi-automatic production of impulses from the subconscious). Cobra, on the contrary, stood for a belief in experimental and spontaneous works of art. Only these would give one access to genuine needs and sensual desires. Typical of the artistic and literary products of the Cobra group is an unrestrained freedom and a rejection of all accepted norms. There is a fascination in their work with motifs from children's drawings, myths, and folk art. The paintings of the Cobra artists teem with a motley collection of animals, symbolic themes, and carnival figures. For Jorn and Constant, this preoccupation had to do with their desire for a social revolution. Both of them in their Cobra period defended the thesis that the creativity of the artist should be linked to the struggle to achieve social freedom. The fact that this "political" attitude was not shared by all the members of Cobra was one reason why the group disintegrated after a few years. For the history of the Cobra movement, see Willemijn Stokvis, *Cobra: An International Movement in Art after the Second World War* (New York: Rizzoli, 1988).

4 Asger Jorn, "Notes on the Formation of an Imaginist Bauhaus," in Ken Knabb, ed., *Situationist International Anthology* (Berkeley: Bureau of Public Secrets, 1981), pp. 16–17.

5 On Constant's oeuvre, see Jean-Clarence Lambert, *Constant. Les trois espaces* (Paris: Cercle d'Art, 1992).

6 For the history of the Situationist International, see Elisabeth Sussmann, ed., *On the Pas-*

sage of a Few People through a Rather Brief Moment in Time: The Situationist International 1957–1972 (Cambridge: MIT Press, 1991); Sadie Plant, The Most Radical Gesture: The Situationist International in a Postmodern Age (London: Routledge, 1992); R. J. Sanders, Beweging tegen de schijn. De situationisten, een avant-garde (Amsterdam: Huis aan de Drie Grachten, 1989). Also see Simon Sadler, The Situationist City (Cambridge: MIT Press, 1998); Libero Andreotti and Xavier Costa, eds., Situationists: Art, Politics, Urbanism (Barcelona: ACTAR, 1996).

7   Constant in an interview with Fanny Kelk, in Elsevier, July 6, 1974, pp. 54–55.

8   Gilles Ivain, "Formulay for a New Urbanism," in Knabb, ed., Situationist International Anthology, p. 2; translated from "Formulaire pour un urbanisme nouveau," in Internationale Situationniste, no. 1 (June 1958), pp. 15–20: "Le complexe architectural sera modifiable. Son aspect changera en partie ou totalement suivant la volonté de ses habitants. . . . L'entrée de la notion de relativité dans l'esprit moderne permet de soupçonner le côté EXPERIMENTALE de la prochaine civilisation. . . . Sur les bases de cette civilisation mobile, l'architecture sera—au moins à ses débuts—un moyen d'expérimenter les mille façons de modifier la vie, en vue d'une synthèse qui ne peut être que légendaire."

9   Guy Debord, "Théorie de la dérive," in Internationale Situationniste, no. 2 (December 1958), pp. 19–23; English translation in Knabb, ed., Situationist International Anthology, pp. 50–54.

10 See Constant and Guy Debord, "Declaration of Amsterdam," in Ulrich Conrads, ed., Programs and Manifestoes on 20th Century Architecture (Cambridge: MIT Press, 1990), pp. 161–162; translated from "La déclaration d'Amsterdam," Internationale Situationniste, no. 2 (December 1958), pp. 31–32. "L'urbanisme unitaire se définit dans l'activité complexe et permanente qui consciemment recrée l'environment de l'homme selon les conceptions les plus évoluées dans tous les domaines."

11 Ibid.

12 Constant, "New Babylon na tien jaren" (lecture at the Technical University of Delft, May 23, 1980): "La création d'ambiances favorables à ce développement est la tâche immédiate des créateurs d'aujourd'hui."

13 Constant, "Une autre ville pour une autre vie," Internationale Situationniste, no. 3 (December 1959), pp. 37–40, translated as Constant, "A Different City for a Different Life," October, no. 79 (Winter 1997), pp. 109–112; Constant, "Description de la zone jaune," Internationale Situationniste, no. 4 (June 1960), pp. 23–26.

14 See the report of Constant's expulsion in Internationale Situationniste, no. 5 (December 1960), p. 10; see also Constant, "New Babylon na tien jaren."

15 See "Critique de l'urbanisme," Internationale Situationniste, no. 6 (August 1961), pp. 5–11, translated as Editorial Notes, "Critique of Urbanism," October, no. 79 (Winter 1997), pp. 113–119.

16 The artists of the German section of the Situationist International, the SPUR group, formed an exception to this rule. They produced a "SPUR building," for instance, in 1963, which can also be seen as foreshadowing the future world of play. See Wolfgang Dressen, Dieter Kunzelmann, and Eckard Stepmann, eds., Nilpferd des höllischen Urwalds—Spuren in eine unbekannte Stadt—Situationisten, Gruppe SPUR, Kommune I, catalogue of an exhibition at the Werkbund-Archiv, Berlin (Giessen: Anabas, 1991).

17 Attila Kotanyi and Raoul Vaneigem, "Programme élémentaire du bureau d'urbanisme unitaire," Internationale Situationniste, no. 6 (August 1961), pp. 16–19: "La participation devenue impossible est compensée sous forme de spectacle. Le spectacle se manifeste dans l'habitat et le déplacement (standing du logement et des véhicules personnels). Car, en fait, on n'habite pas un quartier d'une ville, mais le pouvoir. On habite quelque part dans la hiérarchie." English translation adapted from Knabb, ed., Situationist International Anthology, pp. 65–67.

18 Ibid.: "L'urbanisme unitaire est le contraire d'une activité spécialisée; et reconnaître un domaine urbanistique séparé, c'est déjà reconnaître tout le mensonge urbanistique et le mensonge dans toute la vie."

19 Ibid.: "Nous avons inventé l'architecture et l'urbanisme qui ne peuvent pas se réaliser sans la révolution de la vie quotidienne; c'est-à-dire l'appropriation du conditionnement par tous les hommes, son enrichissement indéfini, son accomplissement."

20 Vaneigem's report for the Situationist International congress in Göteborg, Sweden, August 28–30, 1961, quoted in Stewart Home, *The Assault on Culture: Utopian Currents from Lettrisme to Class War* (Stirling: A.K. Press, 1991), p. 38.

21 *Internationale Situationniste*, no. 9 (August 1964), p. 25: "Nous sommes des artistes par cela seulement que nous ne sommes plus des artistes; nous venons réaliser l'art." English translation adapted from Knabb, ed., *Situationist International Anthology*, p. 139.

22 Guy Debord, *Society of the Spectacle* (Detroit: Black & Red, 1983), p. 2; translated from *La société du spectacle* (1967; Paris: Lebovici, 1989), p. 9: "Toute la vie des sociétés dans lesquelles règnent les conditions modernes de production s'annonce comme une immense accumulation de *spectacles*. Tout ce qui était directement vécu s'est éloigné dans une représentation."

23 Henri Lefebvre, *Critique de la via quotidienne*, 2d ed. (Pairs: L'Arche, 1958).

24 Raoul Vaneigem, *The Revolution of Everyday Life* (London: Aldgate, 1983), p. 183; translated from *Traité de savoir-vivre à l'usage des jeunes générations* (Paris: Gallimard, 1967), p. 245: "La société nouvelle, telle qu'elle s'élabore confusément dans la clandistinité, tend à se définir pratiquement comme une transparence de rapports humains favorisant la participation réelle de tous à la réalisation de chacun.—La passion de la création, la passion de l'amour, et la passion du jeu sont à la vie ce que le besoin de se nourrir et le besoin de se protéger sont à la survie."

25 See Virginie Mamadouh, *De stad in eigen hand. Provo's, kabouters en krakers als stedelijke sociale beweging* (Amsterdam: Sua, 1992).

26 Alexander Tzonis and Liane Lefaivre, "In de naam van het volk / In the Name of the People," *Forum*, no. 3 (1976), pp. 3–33.

27 Constant, "New Babylon, een schets voor een kultuur," in J. L. Locher, ed., *New Babylon*, exhibition catalogue (The Hague: Gemeentemuseum, 1974), p. 60.

28 "Il s'agit d'arriver à l'inconnu par le dérèglement de tous les sens." Rimbaud as quoted by Constant, ibid., p. 57.

29 Constant, "Opkomst en ondergang van de avant-garde," in Constant, *Opstand van de homo ludens. Een bundel voordrachten en artikelen* (Bussum: Paul Brand, 1969), pp. 11–48.

30 Constant, "Over normen in de cultuur," in *Opstand van de homo ludens*, pp. 111–141.

31 Constant, *Opstand van de homo ludens*, p. 73.

32 Henri Lefebvre, *Writings on Cities* (Oxford: Blackwell, 1996), p. 158: "The *right to the city* cannot be conceived of as a simple visiting right or as a return to traditional cities. It can only be formulated as a transformed and renewed *right to urban life*. It does not matter whether the urban fabric encloses the countryside and what survives of peasant life, as long as the 'urban,' place of encounter, priority of use value, inscription in space of a time promoted to the rank of a supreme resource among all resources, finds its morphological base and its practico-material realization." Translated from Lefebvre, *Le droit à la ville* (Paris: Anthropos, 1968), p. 132: "Le droit à la ville ne peut se concevoir comme un simple droit de visite ou de retour vers les villes traditionelles. Il ne peut se formuler comme droit à la vie urbaine, transformée, renouvelée. Que la tissue urbaine enserre la campagne et ce qui survit de vie paysanne, peu importe, pourvu que 'l'urbain', lieu de rencontre, priorité de la valeur d'usage, inscription dans l'espace d'un temps promu au rang de bien suprème parmi les biens, trouve sa base morphologique, sa réalisation pratico-sensible."

For Lefebvre's own memories about his collaboration with the situationists (which are not completely reliable as to factual data about Constant and New Babylon), see a 1983 interview with Kristin Ross, recently published as "Lefebvre on the Situationists: An Interview," *October*, no. 79 (Winter 1997), pp. 69–84.

33 Mamadouh, *De stad in eigen hand*, pp. 72–73.

34 Constant, "Description de la zone jaune."

35 Autodialoog, in the 1974 Hague catalogue *New Babylon*, pp. 71–72.

36 See "New Babylon na tien jaren," p. 3: "Het bleek dat mijn maquettes meer verwarring te-weeg brachten dan begrip kweekten voor mijn streven een wereld te verbeelden die zo hartgrondig verschilde van de wereld waarin we leven of de werelden waarvan we enige historische kennis hebben. Tenslotte greep ik weer naar penseel en palet als het meest doelmatige middel om het onbekende zichtbaar te maken." ("Apparently my maquettes have sown confusion, rather than furthering any understanding of my efforts to imagine a world that differs so profoundly from the world in which we live or from any world of which we have any historical knowledge. Finally I resorted once more to brush and palette as the most appropriate means of rendering visible the unknown.")

37 See Jeroen Onstenk, "In het labyrint. Utopie en verlangen in het werk van Constant," *Krisis*, no. 15 (1984), pp. 4–21.

38 Debord, *Society of the Spectacle*, p. 178.

39 Bart Verschaffel, "'Architektuur is (als) een gebaar'. Over het 'echte' als architecturaal criterium," in Hilde Heynen, ed., *Wonen tussen gemeenplaats en poëzie. Opstellen over stad en architectuur* (Rotterdam: 010 Publishers, 1993), pp. 67–80.

40 Theodor W. Adorno, *Aesthetic Theory*, trans. Robert Hullot-Kentor (Minneapolis: University of Minnesota Press, 1997), p. 32; translated from Adorno, *Ästhetische Theorie* (1970; Frankfurt: Suhrkamp, 1973), p. 55: "Zentral unter den gegenwärtigen Antinomien ist, dass Kunst Utopie sein muss und will und zwar desto entschiedener, je mehr der reale Funktionszusammenhang Utopie verbaut; dass sie aber, um nicht Utopie an Schein und Trost zu verraten, nicht Utopie sein darf."

41 I refer to Frederic Jameson's argument about the topicality of Adorno's work for present theory, which I fully agree with. See Jameson, *Late Marxism: Adorno, or, The Persistence of the Dialectic* (London: Verso, 1990), especially pp. 227–261: "Adorno in the Postmodern."

42 Martin Jay, *Adorno* (London: Fontana Paperbacks, 1984), pp. 11–23.

43 Because he emigrated at an early stage in the Nazi period, the personal consequences of the Holocaust for Adorno were relatively limited compared to the experiences of those who had to face the concentration camps. The most decisive factor for him was that the literally unthinkable really had occurred: this was why the question had to be posed as to whether philosophy was still possible "after Auschwitz." See Theodor W. Adorno, *Negative Dialectics* (New York: Continuum, 1983), pp. 361–365.

44 This correspondence is perhaps not entirely a coincidence, seeing that during the 1930s Benjamin was in contact with the circle around Bataille and Klossowski, whose work is well known to Derrida.

45 Adorno was profoundly influenced by Walter Benjamin. This influence was particularly powerful with regard to his ideas about language and his analysis of the concept of "mimesis," as we shall see later in this chapter. For a detailed study of the relation between the two thinkers, see Susan Buck-Morss, *The Origins of Negative Dialectics* (Brighton: Harvester, 1978).

46 Buck-Morss, *The Origins of Negative Dialectics*, p. 58.

47 See, for instance, Theodor W. Adorno, *Notes to Literature*, 2 vols. (New York: Columbia University Press, 1991, 1992).

48 See Adorno, *Negative Dialectics*, p. xx: "It [negative dialectics] attempts by means of logical consistency to substitute for the unity principle, and for the paramountcy of the supra-ordinated concept, the idea of what would be outside of such unity." Translated from Theodor W. Adorno, *Negative Dialektik* (1966; Frankfurt: Suhrkamp, 1970), p. 8: "Mit konsequenzlogischen Mitteln trachtet sie [die Negative Dialektik], anstelle des Einheitsprinzip und des Allherrschaft der übergeordneten Begriffs die Idee dessen zu rücken, was ausserhalb des Banns solcher Einheit wäre."

49 Adorno, *Negative Dialectics*, p. 161 (translation modified); German text: "Was ist, ist mehr als es ist. Dies Mehr wird ihm nicht oktroyiert, sondern bleibt, als das aus ihm Verdrängte, ihm immanent. Insofern wäre das Nicht-identische die eigene Identität der Sache, gegen ihre Identifikationen." (*Negative Dialektik*, p. 162.)

50 Ibid., p. 163; German text: "Was am Nichtidentischen nicht in seinem Begriff sich definieren lässt, übersteigt sein Einzeldasein, in das es erst in der Polarität zum Begriff, auf diesen hinstarrend, sich zusammenzieht." (*Negative Dialektik,* p. 163.)

51 Ibid., p. 162; German text: "Sie [die Sprache] bietet kein blosses Zeichensystem für Erkenntnisfunktionen. Wo sie wesentlich als Sprache auftritt, Darstellung wird, definiert sie nicht ihre Begriffe. Ihre Objektivität verschafft sie ihnen durch das Verhältnis, in das sie die Begriffe, zentriert om eine Sache, setzt. Damit dient sie der Intention des Begriffs, das Gemeinte ganz auszudrücken. Konstellationen allein repräsentieren, von aussen, was der Begriff im Innern weggeschnitten hat, das Mehr, das er sein will so sehr, wie es nicht sein kann." (*Negative Dialektik,* p. 162.)

52 Theodor W. Adorno, introduction to Adorno et al., *The Positivist Dispute in German Sociology* (London: Heinemann, 1976), p. 52; translated from "Einleitung zum Positivismusstreit in der deutschen Soziologie," in Adorno, *Gesammelte Schriften,* vol. 8 (Frankfurt: Suhrkamp, 1972), p. 337: "Die Wittgensteinsche Formulierung dichtet ihren Horizont dagegen ab, das vermittelt, komplex, in Konstellationen auszusprechen, was klar, unmittelbar sich nicht aussprechen lässt."

53 Adorno, *Negative Dialectics,* p. 146; German text: "Das Tauschprinzip, die Reduktion menschlicher Arbeit auf den abstrakten Allgemeinbegriff der durchschnittlichen Arbeitszeit, ist urverwandt mit dem Identifikationsprinzip. Am Tausch hat es sein gesellschaftliche Modell, und es wäre nicht ohne es; durch ihn werden nichtidentische Einzelwesen und Leistungen kommensurabel, identisch. Die Ausbreitung der Prinzip verhält die ganze Welt zum Identischen, zum Totalität." (*Negative Dialektik,* p. 147.)

54 Theodor W. Adorno, "The Essay as Form," in Adorno, *Notes to Literature,* vol. 1, pp. 3–23.

55 It is precisely this quality in Adorno's prose that is not respected in several English translations of his work. Unlike their German originals, both the first (1984) translation of *Aesthetic Theory* and *Negative Dialectics* are, for instance, split up into short paragraphs. For an interesting discussion of this and related topics, see Robert Hullot-Kentor, "Translator's Introduction," in Adorno, *Aesthetic Theory,* pp. xi–xxi.

56 Max Horkheimer and Theodor W. Adorno, *Dialectic of Enlightenment* (New York: Herder and Herder, 1972), p. xi; translated from *Dialektik der Aufklärung. Philosophische Fragmente,* ed. G. Schmid Noerr (1947; Frankfurt: Fischer, 1987), p. 16: "Was wir uns vorgesetzt hatten, war tatsächlich nicht weniger als die Erkenntnis, warum die Menschheit anstatt in einer wahrhaft menschlichen Zustand einzutreten, in eine neue Art von Barbarei versinkt."

57 Horkheimer and Adorno illustrate this figure through an interesting interpretation of the Odysseus myth.

58 It is this reading that colors, for instance, Jürgen Habermas's interpretation. See "The Entwinement of Myth and Enlightenment: Horkheimer and Adorno," in Habermas, *The Philosophical Discourse of Modernity: Twelve Lectures* (Cambridge: Polity Press, 1987), pp. 106–130.

59 Horkheimer and Adorno, *Dialectic of Enlightenment,* p. 135; German text: "Ernste Kunst hat jenen sich verweigert, denen Not und Druck des Daseins den Ernst zum Hohn macht und die froh sein müssen, wenn sie die Zeit, die sie nicht am Triebrad stehen, dazu benutzen können, sich treiben zu lassen. Leichte Kunst hat die autonome als Schatten begleitet. Sie ist das gesellschaftlich schlechte Gewissen der ernsten. . . . Die Spaltung selbst ist die Wahrheit: sie spricht zumindest die Negativität der Kultur aus, zu der die Sphären sich addieren. Der Gegensatz lässt am wenigsten sich versöhnen, indem man die leichte in die ernste aufnimmt oder umgekehrt. Das aber versucht die Kulturindustrie." (*Dialektik der Aufklärung,* p. 160.)

60 Ibid., p. xiii; German text: "Wir hegen keinen Zweifel—und darin liegt unsere petitio principii—, dass die Freiheit in der Gesellschaft vom aufklärenden Denken unabtrennbar ist. Jedoch glauben wir, genauso deutlich erkannt zu haben, dass der Begriff eben dieses Denkens, nicht weniger als die konkreten historischen Formen, die Institutionen der Gesellschaft in die es verflochten ist, schon der Keim zu jenem Rückschritt enthält, der heute überall sich ereignet." (*Dialektik der Aufklärung,* p. 18.)

61 Jean-François Lyotard, *The Postmodern Explained: Correspondence 1982–1985* (Minneapolis: University of Minnesota Press, 1992), p. 65; translated from *Le postmoderne expliqué aux enfants. Correspondance 1982–1985* (Paris: Galilée, 1986), p. 103.

62 Adorno, *Minima Moralia: Reflections from Damaged Life* (London: Verso, 1991), p. 236; translated from *Minima Moralia. Reflexionen aus dem beschädigten Leben* (Frankfurt: Suhrkamp, 1987), p. 318: "Das Neue, um seiner selbst willen gesucht, gewissermassen im Laboratorium hergestellt, zum begrifflichen Schema verhärtet, wird im jähen Erscheinen zur zwangshaften Rückkehr des Alten."

63 Ibid., pp. 233, 238; German text: "Im Kultus des Neuen und damit in der Idee der Moderne wird dagegen rebelliert, dass es nichts Neues mehr gebe . . . das Neue ist die heimliche Figur aller Ungeborenen." (*Minima Moralia*, p. 316.)

64 For a detailed analysis of the concept of mimesis in Adorno's work, see Josef Früchtl, *Mimesis. Konstellation eines Zentralbegriffs bei Adorno* (Würzburg: Königshausn & Neumann, 1986).

65 Horkheimer and Adorno, *Dialectic of Enlightenment*, pp. 17–18; German text: "Als Zeichen kommt das Wort an die Wissenschaft; als Ton, als Bild, als eigentliches Wort wird es unter die verschiedenen Künste aufgeteilt, ohne dass es sich durch deren Addition, durch Synästhesie oder Gesamtkunst je wiederherstellen liesse. Als Zeichen soll Sprache zur Kalkulation resignieren, um Natur zu erkennen, den Anspruch ablegen, ihr ähnlich zu sein. Als Bild soll sie zum Abbild resignieren, um ganz Natur zu sein, den Anspruch ablegen, sie zu erkennen." (*Dialektik der Aufklärung*, p. 40.)

66 Ibid., p. 18; German text: "Die Trennung von Zeichen und Bild ist unabwendbar. Wird sie jedoch ahnungslos selbstzufrieden nochmals hypostasiert, so treibt jedes der beiden isolierten Prinzipien zur Zerstörung der Wahrheit hin." (*Dialektik der Aufklärung*, p. 40.)

67 Adorno, *Aesthetic Theory*, p. 54; *Ästhetische Theorie*, pp. 86–87.

68 Ibid., pp. 54–55; *Ästhetische Theorie*, p. 87.

69 Ibid., p. 227; *Ästhetische Theorie*, pp. 336–337.

70 Adorno, *The Jargon of Authenticity* (Evanston: Northwestern University Press, 1973), p. 107; translated from *Jargon der Eigentlichkeit. Zur deutschen Ideologie* (Frankfurt: Suhrkamp, 1964), p. 91: "am Tausch geschulten Denken."

71 Adorno, *Aesthetic Theory*, p. 104: "The mimesis of artworks is their resemblance to themselves." German text: "Die Mimesis der Kunstwerke ist Ähnlichkeit mit sich selbst" (*Ästhetische Theorie*, p. 159).

72 Ibid., p. 34; *Ästhetische Theorie*, p. 57.

73 Ibid.

74 Michael Cahn, "Subversive Mimesis: T. W. Adorno and the Modern Impasse of Critique," in Mihai Spariosu, ed., *Mimesis in Contemporary Theory*, vol. 1 (Philadelphia: J. Benjamins, 1984), p. 49.

75 Adorno, *Aesthetic Theory*, p. 133; German text: "Ohne Beimischung des Giftstoffs, virtuell die Negation des Lebendigen, wäre der Einspruch der Kunst gegen die zivilisatorische Unterdrückung, tröstlich-hilflos." (*Ästhetische Theorie*, p. 201.)

76 Ibid., p. 133; German text: "so zediert sich darin . . . die Mimesis der Kunst an ihr Widerspiel. Genötigt wird Kunst dazu durch die soziale Realität. Während sie der Gesellschaft opponiert, vermag sie doch keinen ihr jenseitigen Standpunkt zu beziehen; Opposition gelingt ihr einzig durch Identifikation mit dem, wogegen sie aufbegehrt." (*Ästhetische Theorie*, p. 201.)

77 Ibid., p. 289; German text: "Die Opposition der Kunstwerke gegen die Herrschaft ist Mimesis an diese. Sie müssen dem herrschaflichen Verhalten sich angleichen, um etwas von der Welt der Herrschaft qualitativ Verschiedenes zu produzieren." (*Ästhetische Theorie*, p. 430.)

78 Ibid., p. 105; German text: "Noch indem Kunst das verborgene Wesen, das sie zur Erscheinung verhält, als Unwesen verklagt, ist mit solcher Negation als deren Mass ein nicht gegenwärtiges Wesen, das der Möglichkeit, mitgesetzt; Sinn inhäriert noch die Leugnung des Sinns." (*Ästhetische Theorie*, p. 161.)

79   This point of view is related to the Jewish tradition of the ban on images. See Gertrud Koch, "Mimesis und Bilderverbot in Adornos Ästhetik. Ästhetische Dauer als Revolte gegen den Tod," *Babylon. Beiträge zur jüdischen Gegenwart*, no. 6 (October 1989), pp. 36–45.

80   Adorno, in the discussion between Bloch and Adorno in Ernst Bloch, *The Utopian Function of Art and Literature: Selected Essays* (Cambridge: MIT Press, 1987), p. 12.

81   Adorno, *Aesthetic Theory*, p. 154: "Works of the highest level of form that are meaningless or alien to meaning are therefore more than simply meaningless because they gain their content [*Gehalt*] through the negation of meaning." German text: "Die sinnlosen oder sinnfremden Werke des obersten Formniveaus sind darum mehr als bloss sinnlos, weil ihnen Gehalt in der Negation des Sinns zuwächst." (*Ästhetische Theorie*, p. 231.)

82   *Aesthetic Theory*, p. 21; German text: "Moderne ist Kunst durch Mimesis ans Verhärtete und Entfremdete; dadurch, nicht durch Verleugnung des Stummen wird sie beredt; dass sie kein Harmloses mehr duldet, entspringt darin." (*Ästhetische Theorie*, p. 39.)

83   *Aesthetic Theory*, p. 321; German text: "In bestimmter Negation rezipiert sie 'die Kunst' die membra disiecta der Empirie, in der sie ihre Stätte hat, und versammelt sie durch ihre Transformation zu dem Wesen, welches das Unwesen ist." (*Ästhetische Theorie*, p. 475.)

84   Adorno, "Über den Fetischcharakter in der Musik," in Adorno, *Gesammelte Schriften*, vol. 14 (Frankfurt: Suhrkamp, 1973), pp. 18–19: "Die Verführungskraft des Reizes überlebt dort bloss, wo die Kräfte der Versagung am Stärksten sind: in der Dissonanz, die dem Trug der bestehenden Harmonie den Glauben verweigert. . . . Schlug ehedem Askese den ästhetischen Anspruch reaktionär nieder, so ist sie heute zum Siegel der avancierten Kunst geworden: . . . Kunst verzeichnet negativ eben jene Glücksmöglichkeit, welcher die bloss partielle positive Vorwegnahme des Glücks heute verderblich entgegensteht."

85   Adorno, *Aesthetic Theory*, p. 12; *Ästhetische Theorie*, p. 26.

86   Ibid., p. 110; *Ästhetische Theorie*, p. 168.

87   Theodor W. Adorno, "Commitment," in Adorno, *Notes to Literature*, vol. 2, p. 89.

88   Ibid., p. 93

89   Ibid.

90   The discussion between Benjamin and Adorno is documented in Ernst Bloch et al., *Aesthetics and Politics* (London: Verso, 1977), pp. 100–141.

91   Ibid., p. 122; translated from Theodor W. Adorno, *Über Walter Benjamin* (Frankfurt: Suhrkamp, 1970), p. 128: "das l'art pour l'art [ist] der Rettung bedürftig."

92   Bloch et al., *Aesthetics and Politics*, p. 123; German text: "Beide tragen die Wundmale des Kapitalismus, beide enthalten Elemente der Veränderung . . . beide sind die auseinandergerissenen Hälften der ganzen Freiheit, die doch aus ihnen nicht sich zusammenaddieren lässt." (Adorno, *Über Walter Benjamin*, p. 129.)

93   See also Peter Osborne, "Adorno and the Metaphysics of Modernism: The Problem of a 'Postmodern' Art," in Andrew Benjamin, ed., *The Problems of Modernity: Adorno and Benjamin* (London: Routledge, 1991), pp. 23–48.

94   See also Lambert Zuidervaart, *Adorno's Aesthetic Theory: The Redemption of Illusion* (Cambridge: MIT Press, 1991), pp. 225–236.

95   Miriam Hansen, "Mass Culture as Hieroglyphic Writing: Adorno, Derrida, Kracauer," *New German Critique*, no. 56 (Spring-Summer 1992), pp. 43–75.

96   Peter Bürger, "Adorno's Anti-Avant-Gardism," *Telos*, no. 86 (Winter 1990–1991), pp. 49–60.

97   Martin Heidegger, "The Origin of the Work of Art," in Heidegger, *Poetry, Language, Thought* (New York: Harper and Row, 1975), p. 41; translated from *Der Ursprung des Kunstwerkes* (1960; Stuttgart: Reclam, 1978), pp. 40–41: "Wir fragen jetzt die Wahrheitsfrage im Blick auf das Werk. Damit wir jedoch mit dem, was in der Frage steht, vertrauter werden, ist es nötig, das Geschehnis der Wahrheit im Werk sichtbar zu machen. Für diesen Versuch sei mit Absicht ein werk gewählt, das nicht zur darstellenden Kunst gerechnet wird. Ein Bauwerk, ein Griechischer Tempel, bildet nichts ab."

98   Philippe Lacoue-Labarthe, *L'imitation des Modernes (Typographies 2)* (Paris: Galilée, 1986), p. 10.

99 Philippe Lacoue-Labarthe, "Typographie," in Sylviane Agacinski et al., *Mimesis. Désarticulations* (Paris: Flammarion, 1975), pp. 165–270; English translation: "Typography," in Lacoue-Labarthe, *Typography: Mimesis, Philosophy, Politics* (Cambridge: Harvard University Press, 1989), pp. 43–138.

100 Lacoue-Labarthe, "Typography," p. 95; French text: "Cela reste fragile. Et de fait, si toute l'opération consiste à surenchir sur la mimesis pour la maîtriser, s'il s'agit de *contourner* la mimesis, mais avec ses propres moyens (sans quoi, bien entendu, ce serait nul et non-avenu), comment serait-il possible d'avoir la moindre chance de réussir, puisque la mimesis est précisément l'absence de moyens appropriés—et que c'est même ce qu'il s'agit de *montrer*? Comment (s')approprier l'impropre? Comment (s')approprier l'impropre sans aggraver encore l'impropre?" ("Typographie," p. 224.)

101 Lacoue-Labarthe, *L'imitation des Modernes*, p. 191.

102 Jacques Derrida, "White Mythology: Metaphor in the Text of Philosophy," in Derrida, *Margins of Philosophy* (Chicago: University of Chicago Press, 1982), p. 253; translated from "La mythologie blanche. La métaphore dans le texte philosophique," in Derrida, *Marges de la philosophie* (Paris: Minuit, 1972), p. 302: "C'est une métaphore de la métaphore; expropriation, être-hors-de-chez-soi, mais encore dans une demeure, hors de chez soi mais dans un chez-soi où l'on se retrouve, se reconnaît, se rassemble ou se ressemble, hors de soi en soi."

103 Mark Wigley, *The Architecture of Deconstruction: Derrida's Haunt* (Cambridge: MIT Press, 1993), p. 104.

104 Jacques Lacan, "Le stade du miroir comme formateur de la fonction du Je," in Lacan, *Ecrits 1* (Paris: Seuil, 1966), pp. 89–97.

105 Lacoue-Labarthe, "Typography," pp. 126–129; "Typographie," pp. 257–260.

106 Frederic Jameson, *Late Marxism: Adorno, or, the Persistence of the Dialectic* (London: Verso, 1990), pp. 242–245.

107 See Jean Baudrillard, *The Ecstasy of Communication* (New York: Semiotext(e), 1988); Jean Baudrillard, *Fatal Strategies* (New York: Semiotext(e), 1990).

108 Jean-François Lyotard, "Rewriting Modernity," in Lyotard, *The Inhuman: Reflections on Time* (Cambridge: Polity Press, 1988), pp. 24–35; translated from "Réécrire la modernité," in Lyotard, *L'inhumain. Causeries sur le temps* (Paris: Galilée, 1988), pp. 33–44.

109 Lyotard himself does not use the term "mimesis" in this sense. In *Heidegger and "the Jews"* (Minneapolis: University of Minnesota Press, 1990) he uses the term to refer to the "Greek" element in Heidegger's thought, while associating *Durcharbeitung* with Jewish thought that is based on a constantly renewed activity of interpretation.

110 There is only one essay that is explicitly concerned with architecture. It is a lecture that Adorno gave in 1965 at a meeting of the Werkbund on the subject of *Bildung durch Gestalt*: "Funktionalismus heute," *Gesammelte Schriften*, vol. 10, pt. 1, pp. 375–395; translated as "Functionalism Today," *Oppositions*, no. 17 (1979), pp. 31–41. There is also the passage in the *Ästhetische Theorie* about the dialectics of functionalism (pp. 96–97; *Aesthetic Theory*, pp. 60–61), in addition to some more passing references.

111 I once clarified the difference between *Funktionalität* and *Mimesis an Funktionalität* with reference to Hannes Meyer's design for the Petersschule in Basel. See Hilde Heynen, "Architecture between Modernity and Dwelling: Reflections on Adorno's *Aesthetic Theory*," *Assemblage*, no. 17 (1992), pp. 78–91.

112 Adorno, *Aesthetic Theory*, p. 61; German text: "Die Antinomien der Sachlichkeit bezeugen jenes Stück Dialektik der Aufklärung, in dem Fortschritt und Regression ineinander sind. Das Barbarische ist das Buchstäbliche. Ganzlich versachlicht wird das Kunstwerk, kraft seiner puren Gesetzmässigkeit, zum blossen Faktum und damit als Kunst abgeschafft. Die Alternative, die in der Krisis sich öffnet, ist die, entweder aus der Kunst herauszufallen oder deren eigenen Begriff zu verändern." (*Ästhetische Theorie*, p. 97.)

113 Diane Ghirardo, introduction to Ghirardo, ed., *Out of Site: A Social Criticism of Architecture* (Seattle: Bay Press, 1991), pp. 9–17.

114 Daniel Libeskind, *Erweiterung des Berlin Museums mit Abteilung Jüdisches Museum*, ed. Kristin Feireiss (Berlin: Ernst & Sohn, 1992).

115 Bernhard Schneider, "Daniel Libeskinds Architektur im Stadtraum," in Alois Martin Müller, ed., *Daniel Libeskind. Radix—Matrix* (Munich: Prestel, 1994), pp. 128–135.

116 "Jacques Derrida zu 'Between the Lines,'" in ibid., pp. 115–117.

117 Office for Metropolitan Architecture, *S M L XL* (Rotterdam: 010 Publishers, 1995), p. 581.

118 Geert Bekaert, "Lessen in architectuur," in Bekaert, ed., *Sea Trade Center Zeebrugge* (Antwerp: Standaard Uitgeverij, 1990), p. 21.

119 For a lucid analysis of the impact of networks on dwelling and the city, see Bart Verschaffel, "De kring en het netwerk," in Verschaffel, *Figuren / Essays* (Leuven: Van Halewijck, 1995), pp. 105–120.

120 Fredric Jameson, interview with Michael Speaks in *Assemblage*, no. 17 (1992), pp. 30–37.

121 Jürgen Habermas, "Modernity's Consciousness of Time," in Habermas, *The Philosophical Discourse of Modernity* (Cambridge: MIT Press, 1990); quoted in Office for Metropolitan Architecture, *S M L XL*, p. xxviii.

122 Office for Metropolitan Architecture, *S M L XL*, p. 601. At an earlier stage when there was still a possibility of the project being implemented, the story of construction techniques was quite different. In 1990 there were two different possibilities for the dome: a classical one based on a steel and glass construction and a more revolutionary, pneumatic structure with a thin skin consisting of a transparent fiber-reinforced coating that would keep its concave shape due to a slight pressure generated inside the building. See Bekaert, ed., *Sea Trade Center Zeebrugge*, p. 32.

Afterword: Dwelling, Mimesis, Culture

Epigraph: Jean-François Lyotard, "Domus and the Megalopolis," in Lyotard, *The Inhuman: Reflections on Time* (Cambridge: Polity Press, 1988), p. 200; translated from "Domus et la mégalopole," in *L'inhumain. Causeries sur le temps* (Paris: Galilée, 1988), p. 212: "On n'habite la mégapole qu'autant qu'on la désigne inhabitable. Sinon, on y est seulement domicilié."

1 Walter Benjamin, "Theses on the Philosophy of History" (1940), in Benjamin, *Illuminations* (New York: Schocken, 1968), p. 256; translated from "Über den Begriff der Geschichte," in Benjamin, *Illuminationen* (Frankfurt: Surhrkamp, 1977), p. 254: "Es ist niemals ein Dokument der Kultur, ohne zugleich ein solches der Barbarei zu sein."

2 Heidegger never questioned his support of the Nazi regime—he was a member of the party from 1933 to 1945 and rector of the University of Freiburg in 1933–1934. Despite repeated pressure from many people—Karl Löwith, Paul Celan, and Herbert Marcuse to name but a few—he refused ever to condemn the Holocaust publicly. For a clearly written survey of the issue, see Richard Wolin, ed., *The Heidegger Controversy: A Critical Reader* (Cambridge: MIT Press, 1993). The cat was really set among the pigeons with the publication in France of Victor Farias, *Heidegger et le nazisme* (Paris: Verdier, Lagrasse, 1987), translated as *Heidegger and Nazism* (Philadelphia: Temple University Press, 1989).

3 Theodor W. Adorno, *The Jargon of Authenticity* (Evanston: Northwestern University Press, 1973), p. 68; translated from *Jargon der Eigentlichkeit* (Frankfurt: Suhrkamp, 1964), p. 59: "Keine Erhöhung des Begriffs vom Menschen vermöchte etwas gegen seine tatsächliche Erniedrigung zum Funktionsbündel, sondern bloss die Änderung der Bedingungen, die es dahin brachten und die unablässig erweitert sich reproduzieren."

4 Theodor W. Adorno, *Aesthetic Theory*, trans. Robert Hullot-Kentor (Minneapolis: University of Minnesota Press, 1997), p. 197; translated from Adorno, *Ästhetische Theorie* (1970; Frankfurt: Suhrkamp, 1973), p. 293.

5 Jean-François Lyotard, "Introduction: About the Human," in Lyotard, *The Inhuman* ("Avant-propos: de l'humain," in *L'inhumain*).

6 Lyotard, "Domus and the Megalopolis," p. 200; French text: "Baudelaire, Benjamin, Adorno. Comment habiter la mégapole? En témoignant de l'oeuvre impossible, en alléguant la *domus* perdue. Seule la qualité de la souffrance vaut témoignage. Y compris,

bien sûr, la souffrance due à la langue. On n'habite la mégapole qu'autant qu'on la désigne inhabitable. Sinon, on y est seulement domicilié." (*L'inhumain*, p. 212.)

7   Lyotard, ibid., in an explicit reference to Adorno.

8   Sigmund Freud, "The Uncanny" (1919), in Freud, *Art and Literature,* The Pelican Freud Library, vol. 14 (Harmondsworth: Penguin, 1985), pp. 335–376; translated from "Das unheimliche," in Freud, *Gesammelte Werke*, vol. 12 (Frankfurt: Fischer, 1947), pp. 229–268. See also Anthony Vidler, introduction to *The Architectural Uncanny: Essays in the Modern Unhomely* (Cambridge: MIT Press, 1992), pp. 3–14.

9   Christian Norberg-Schulz, *The Concept of Dwelling* (New York: Electa/Rizzoli, 1985).

10   Loos might be right insofar as that it is not correct for architecture to deliberately posit the *unheimliche* as its theme. I am afraid that an architecture explicitly set up to generate uncanny effects often overshoots its mark. For everyday life tends to neutralize any such effect by declaring it the result of a would-be "originality" of the architect and thus ignoring its possibly disturbing influence. Such a gesture relegates such intended "deconstructive" architecture to a reservation of recognized art and deprives it of any genuine social impact. This could, for instance, be the fate of Libeskind's museum, if it were not for the congruency that exists between its program and its form. Since it is a museum, one might expect that everyday reflexes would weaken and that visitors would be open toward new and unknown experiences.

11   Theodor W. Adorno, "Functionalism Today," *Oppositions*, no. 17 (1979), p. 41; translated from "Funktionalismus heute," in Adorno, *Gesammelte Schriften*, vol. 10, pt. 1 (Frankfurt: Suhrkamp, 1977), p. 395: "Schönheit heute hat kein anderes Mass als die Tiefe in der die Gebilde die Widersprüche austragen, die sie durchfuhren und die sie bewältigen einzig, in dem sie ihnen folgen, nicht, indem sie sie verdecken."

Index